PRINCESS MARGARET

Helen Cathcart

SAPERE
BOOKS

PRINCESS MARGARET

Published by Sapere Books.
20 Windermere Drive, Leeds, England, LS17 7UZ,
United Kingdom

saperebooks.com

ISBN: 978-1-80055-349-1.

TABLE OF CONTENTS

1: THE SURPRISE PRINCESS

A month now since the Duchess of York announced her 'retirement', yet the Yorks were at Covent Garden with the King and Queen to see *Die Fledermaus*. To judge pre-natal influences, this child will be musical, artistic, imaginative...

Family correspondence, May 1930

I

In the early spring of 1930 the Ceremonial Secretary of the Home Office found it difficult not to tell his wife the enticing news that the young Duchess of York was expecting another baby. The birth of a future possible heir to the British throne seemed to him a matter of great moment and, travelling between Whitehall and his home near Sloane Square, Mr Harry Boyd hugged the gratifying thought that he was among the few to be entrusted with the secret outside the Royal Family. He was indeed the only man in the Ministry with experience of how these affairs should be handled. When the request had arrived from Buckingham Palace that the Secretary of State for Home Affairs should hold himself in readiness to attend the Duchess of York at any hour between August 6th and 12th next, Mr Boyd had personally taken the letter to his chief along the corridor. As it happened, Mr J. R. Clynes had been in office less than a year with Ramsay MacDonald's second Labour government. Harry Boyd explained that it was traditionally incumbent upon the Home Secretary to be technically present at the royal birth, and Mr Clynes replied in his quiet shy way, 'I know nothing of these things. I shall leave them to you as far as possible.'

On April 16th the news was made public. The *Court Circular* appeared with the announcement, 'The Duchess of York has cancelled her forthcoming engagements and she is not undertaking any further functions during the summer,' and Mr Boyd felt free at last to recount everything to his lady. Having no children of their own, the Boyds liked to involve themselves in the family events of others and now here they were, or rather Harry was, at the heart of a royal domestic occasion of the happiest consequence.

The new baby might prove to be King George V's first grandson in the male line of succession and, in view of the preponderance of boys in both the Windsor and Strathmore families, public and private opinion evidently regarded this as a certainty. Ada Boyd glowed on seeing the Duke and Duchess of York with the King and Queen one Saturday night at *Die Fledermaus* at Covent Garden, and the audience rose to give the Duchess a warm ovation, as if in fervent greeting to a prince. Circumspect as he was, Harry Boyd felt his stock rising among his friends on the fact that he had similarly been present four years earlier at the birth of Princess Elizabeth. 'It simply means a lot of waiting about,' he said, with more prescience than he knew.

The Duchess had chosen then to have her first baby at the London home of her parents, 17 Bruton Street. The Home Secretary in Mr Baldwin's government on that occasion had been Sir William Joynson-Hicks and, at Mr Boyd's insistence, they had arrived in the rain at Bruton Street shortly after breakfast, and had remained to lunch and dinner as the day wore on. 'If there have to be gentlemen waiting outside my bedroom door,' the little Duchess had said, with a glint of mischief, 'I hope it's someone we know.' So the story goes, with the undoubted grain of truth that Mr Boyd gained his ceremonial appointment not many months before Princess Elizabeth was born and was a kinsman by marriage of the Duchess of York's eldest brother, both having found brides in the Osborne family. At all events, Mr Boyd realized, Lady Strathmore had pleasantly made him feel at home 'as one of the family'. The anxious vigil with the young Duke of York had lasted into the small hours until, at 2.40 a.m., Princess Elizabeth uttered her overdue first cry, and the doctors, the yawning Minister of the Crown and the sleepy civil servant could presently go home to bed.

For a few carefree weeks in 1930, Mr Boyd imagined that the young mother would decide to await her second child at 145 Piccadilly, the Yorks' official London residence, and very appropriate, too, he considered, if a future king should be born in a mansion overlooking Buckingham Palace. Then on a warm evening in May the Duke and Duchess dined with the King and Queen — George V and Queen Mary — and Mr Boyd gathered a topic of their conversation a few days later when he learned that the Duchess was proposing to have her baby at her parents' Scottish home, Glamis Castle. 'But this will never do,' he told Mr Clynes in high consternation. 'The difficulty of the arrangements — so far away! What will people think?'

When a Home Office colleague suggested that he and the Home Secretary could take hotel rooms in Perth, the meticulous Mr Boyd was patently horrified. 'Supposing the birth should occur in the early hours of the morning and the Home Secretary could not get to Glamis?' The Palace recommended that he should talk it over with Lady Airlie, Queen Mary's close friend, who lived eight miles from Glamis at Airlie Castle and was then in London. In her intended memoirs Lady Airlie wrote of the 'small anxious-looking man' who confronted her, agitated lest the seclusion of Glamis should give the people the impression that everything was going to be conducted in 'an irregular hole and corner way', as he put it. 'If this child's birth is not properly witnessed, its legal right might be questioned. It has happened before in history.' And to Lady Airlie's utter astonishment he produced a book with passages marked in red ink on the birth of the son of James II and Mary of Modena and the supposed substitution of a changeling son as heir to the throne, alleged to have been smuggled into the bedchamber in a warming pan. 'We must not risk anything of that sort,' said Mr Boyd, in all solemnity.

An obvious solution was for the Home Secretary to stay at Glamis Castle itself, that vast ancestral pile where in more ample days beds had once been made up for eighty-eight guests. On this prospect Mr Boyd met a curious silence, impregnable and loftily distant as its ancient slate turrets. With hindsight, one considers that the young husband concerned, the Duke of York, had doubted the legal necessity of the Home Secretary's presence ever since that day-and-night vigil for Princess Elizabeth. 'I always wanted him to come up when he was sent for, which would have been so much simpler,' he privately wrote from Glamis.

Convinced in his own mind that his elder brother, the Prince of Wales, would one day marry and settle down, perhaps in a year or two after becoming King, he felt it would be time enough then for the cradle protocol. But who could indeed foretell the misty future? (It was not until the following year — in May, 1931 — that the Prince first met Mrs Simpson and so began treading the path of fate that led to the Abdication.) While his father reigned, the Duke of York could not question the constitutional need for observing the old custom of attendance. But in due course, as King George VI, he learned that in reality no law or statutory requirement existed to give it substance, and before the birth of Prince Charles in 1948 he was to abolish the archaic practice merely by announcing that he felt it 'unnecessary to continue further'.

Impelled by Mr Boyd's fervour, however, Mr Clynes accepted an invitation to stay at Airlie Castle and he left London on August 4th, the thirtieth birthday of the expectant mother. Whatever his illusions about the Scottish aristocracy — and as a former cotton-mill piecer he may have held many — he was enraptured by the homely quality of Lady Airlie's hospitality and wrote with gusto of the Scottish teas with fresh-baked scones, the game pies and freshly caught trout. Airlie Castle is in fact the smallest occupied castle in Scotland, little more than 'one room and a corridor thick', and in those days there were only two spare rooms for visitors. Mr Clynes' detective had to be lodged in a nearby cottage and, when Mr Boyd gazed up doubtfully at the single wire rigged up between Airlie and Glamis for telephone calls, accommodation also had to be found in the neighbourhood for an army dispatch rider with a motorbike to stand by day and night. Yet the homely Mr Clynes delighted in everything: the oil lamps lit at dusk, the kettles of hot water, the family atmosphere. At a luncheon party at Glamis the Duchess of York apologized charmingly for having brought him so far: 'We are so sorry you missed my birthday party, but now you are keeping us all in birthday mood.'

The mood nevertheless grew strained as the days went by, still without the awaited infant prince putting in an appearance. No one seems to have contemplated any prospect except that the baby would be a boy, a future male heir third in line to the Throne. 'The estate had to be put almost in a state of siege,' Mr Clynes noted, 'and some of the sensation-mongering tourists were roughly treated by dour tenantry.' Mr Boyd meantime fretted and fussed. On the 10th he met Sir Henry Simpson, the royal accoucheur, and sat up all night on being assured that the child would certainly be born on the 11th. The word spread and, on the summit of Hunter's Hill overlooking Glamis, the brushwood was piled high for the beacon fires to greet a Scottish-born prince. On the 14th, Lady Airlie recorded, 'Mr Boyd was in a panic and reminded the Home Secretary so severely of his duty when he was on the point of going out for a drive that we returned to the house to sit making conversation.' Yet still nothing happened.

On the 21st, the Ceremonial Secretary was 'wild-eyed and haggard' after sitting up all night, leaping to his feet when the Duke of York's comptroller telephoned from Glamis only to report that there was still no news. It rained all day and in the evening a fantastic sunset began to break against the clearing sky … when the telephone rang again. 'What? In an hour! You haven't given us much time,' Lady Airlie heard Mr Boyd's anguished cry.

When they set off pell-mell in the car, Mr Clynes was so moved by the pageantry of the crimson clouds that he launched into poetry. 'Look at that sunset! "In such a night Troilus, methinks, mounted the Trojan walls…"' The roads were wet, and their local police driver wary of skidding, but to Mr Boyd's lasting satisfaction they were still in time. The tower clock had just struck nine and on the other side of the castle, in a bedroom overlooking the private garden, the baby was delivered twenty-two minutes later. 'A doctor came down to me and asked me to go to an ante-room,' wrote the Home Secretary, 'where the Duke of York, the child's grandmother, another doctor, nurses and a few privileged persons were waiting.' The little scene occurred in fact in the tapestry or music room, more recently used as a billiard room, where he was shown not the expected infant prince but 'a baby girl who might one day be a queen'. And with impressions tinged more with romance than with realism he added, 'She was lying perfectly still and evidently content, in a cot, her wide-open eyes looking with apparent interest at the strange new world.'

II

The expected boy was a girl, a six-pound-eleven-ounce princess, and apparently the only person not taken aback was Mr Boyd. He had an alternative telegram ready to send to the Lord Mayor of London and to the long list of fifty-six Governors-General and Governors of the Dominions and Crown Colonies. He had only to amend his draft of the first bulletin, 'Yesterday evening at 22 minutes after nine o'clock Her Royal Highness the Duchess of York was safely delivered of a Princess at Glamis Castle. His Royal Highness the Duke of York and the Countess of Strathmore and Kinghorne were present. Mr Secretary Clynes was also present,' to which the doctors, Scotsmen all three, gleefully added the phrase, 'Her Royal Highness and the Infant Princess are doing fine.'

South of the border, the homely Scottish phrase was primly amended to 'are doing perfectly well'. Next morning the bells of St Paul's pealed over Fleet Street, although in those more leisurely days the news had missed the earliest editions. Said *The Times*, 'There will be some natural disappointment that the baby is a girl and not a boy, but she is nevertheless sure of a loving welcome.' A royal salute of forty-one guns boomed from the Tower of London, echoed by the guns of the Royal Horse Artillery in Hyde Park where, as *The Times* meticulously recorded, 'the men in the crowd doffed their hats and the onlookers cheered heartily for the Princess and her mother.'

As the 'wireless news' went out, Mayfair grew suddenly 'festive with flags on its shops and clubs'. The bells of Westminster Abbey — and indeed of Dundee and elsewhere — pealed in greeting. In the county town of Forfar, eight miles from Glamis, the great 300-year-old Bell of Forfar rang at breakfast-time, and at noon the burgh council drank the unnamed royal baby's health as 'the youngest Forfarian', whereupon the oldest Forfarian, the ninety-year-old town clerk, equally proposed the toast, 'the Princess Elizabeth'. Meanwhile, at Glamis, that young lady, aged four and four months, had been taken to see 'baby sister' and, of her own accord, had responded sweetly by collecting together all her choicest toys in a petticoat and heaping them around the baby's cot. That night Elizabeth is supposed to have been lifted to a castle window to see the flames of the beacon burning in her sister's honour, but in reality the torches were not applied to the brushwood until 9.45 p.m. and one doubts whether a four-year-old would have been taken from her bed merely to see the twinkle of a fire two miles distant. Throughout the evening, on the other hand, cars and coaches were bringing lively crowds from as far away as Edinburgh and Aberdeen. At sunset the Glamis pipe band in its Strathmore tartan piped the celebrating throngs along the muddy tracks to the top of Hunter's Hill, where two barrels of beer were broached for the estate workers, the foresters and ploughmen, by the factor, Mr Ralston. The bagpipes played 'Highland Lassie' and 'The Duke of York's Welcome'; the torches were the selfsame ones used to light a similar beacon for the Duke and Duchess's wedding seven years earlier, and all the young folk of the district danced and sang around the flames.

Next day, a bulletin announced the satisfactory progress of mother and child, and at the weekend the doctors were still reassuring the anxious that the Duchess of York had enjoyed 'another excellent night's sleep'. More to the point was an amendment to Lilibet's (Princess Elizabeth's) favourite family game of Three Bears, in which her father was the Big Bear, her mother the Rather Big Bear and herself the Little Bear. 'Now we can play Four Bears,' she announced. 'The baby will be the Very Little Bear.' And into the month of September indeed the new baby had no other title, save for the cooing endearments of her innumerable aunts and uncles.

Intent on a son, the young parents had deliberately neglected to consider what they should call a girl, lest it should tempt the fates. 'I think that Ann of York sounds pretty,' the Duchess wrote to Queen Mary, when her daughter was six days old. 'Lots of people have suggested Margaret, but it has no family links really on either side.' Charles, the name of her maternal grandfather, might have been her choice, I think, if she had been given a son. Yet Margaret buoyantly surfaced of its own accord in the certainty of Scottish public opinion. There had been a queen or princess of that name in Scotland almost in unbroken line, from the saintly wife of King Malcolm Canmore, the mother of three Scottish kings, through five centuries until the great grandson of Margaret Tudor became James VI, King of Scots, and James I, King of England. No heir so close in the British Succession had been born in Scotland since the day in 1600 that saw the birth of Charles I. Scottish newspapers were quick to remind their readers that the Duke of York was also titular Earl of Inverness and that the new princess was descended from the united powerful Scottish elements of Strathmore, Kinghorne and Bowes-Lyon.

'I am very anxious to call her Ann Margaret,' the Duchess wrote to Balmoral more fully. 'Elizabeth and Ann go so well together.' The King, however, did not agree, and the intended

Margaret still lacked a name on August 30th when the King and Queen called at Glamis to see their latest granddaughter. 'The baby is a darling,' Queen Mary noted in her diary. Another week slipped away, until on September 6th the Duchess wrote to her mother-in-law with some firmness, 'Bertie and I have decided now to call our little daughter *Margaret Rose* ... as Papa does not like Ann. I hope that you like it. I think that it is very pretty together.'

The name also prettily complimented her nearest sister in her own family, Lady Rose Bowes-Lyon, who was ten years her senior. It had a romantic ring, English and Scottish alike, a Rose of York, a Margaret born at Glamis, both unerringly popular. There remained only one final official hurdle. Under Scottish law the birth of the Princess should have been registered within twenty-one days except under payment of a penalty or fee. The local registrar of Glamis, Mr Charles Buchanan, who combined the role with that of village postmaster, postcard vendor and proprietor of the local sweet store, thought that he detected the reason for delay. Only twelve local births had been registered in his book that year, and the new Princess Margaret Rose would be the thirteenth. A man of resource, however, Mr Buchanan sent off a postcard to a Mrs Gevina Brown, whose baby boy, George, had been born within three days of the Princess, and she was persuaded to register the birth of her son forthwith. The practical wife of a tenant farmer, Mrs Brown was not superstitious and accepted Certificate 13 without a qualm. But it was not until September 30th that Mr Buchanan was summoned to Glamis Castle to receive his shilling fee for registration of the birth of Margaret Rose and to give in return Certificate 14.

In the care of her nurse, Mrs Knight, formerly nanny of Lady Strathmore's younger children and of the Duchess of York herself, the new Princess crossed the border three weeks later on the night train to London. By early morning the news of her coming had spread and an unusually large and warmly curious crowd welcomed her at St Pancras station. Not that they caught more than a passing glimpse of the wide-awake baby. On the pavement outside No. 145 Piccadilly, the London home of the Duke and Duchess of York, a small flock of 'newspaper cameramen' were waiting hopefully, but the cobbled forecourt beyond the tall iron railings remained royally sacrosanct and the tall, moustached policemen stood like sentinels.

At ten weeks old Princess Margaret Rose was christened by the Archbishop of Canterbury, Dr Lang, amid the flowers and potted palms of the old and rather ugly private chapel of Buckingham Palace, which the Nazi bombers were to oblige us by demolishing less than ten years later. The baby wore the creamy robe of Spitalfields silk and Honiton lace used for all royal baptisms since the first-born of Queen Victoria; the gold-plated lily font was brought up from Windsor and the flagon of Jordan water came from what was then the troubled British-administered territory of Palestine. Though ornate in setting, the ceremony was essentially a private family occasion. There were no crowned heads, save two of the grandparents, King George V and Queen Mary. The official sponsors were the Prince of Wales (the later Duke of Windsor), Princess Victoria (sister of George V), Princess Ingrid of Sweden, Lady Rose Leveson-Gower and David Bowes-Lyon.

Put so briefly, the godparents seem unadorned by any baptismal traits of significance. Yet the Prince of Wales found himself occupied elsewhere and was represented by his young brother, Prince George, the popular father of the Duke of Kent. Princess Victoria was a saddened spinster, who had moped for years after being forbidden to marry the man she loved, a commoner. Princess Ingrid (the Queen Mother of Queen Margarethe of Denmark) could not attend and her proxy was Lady Pat Ramsay, who had been the first of the modern Westminster Abbey brides when, as 'Princess Pat,' far removed from the throne, she had indeed happily married a commoner in 1919. Lady Rose Leveson-Gower, to whom the baby was niece and namesake, was the Duchess of York's sister, the former Rose Bowes-Lyon and subsequently Countess Granville, who as 'Aunt Rose' was ultimately to live in Kensington Palace and deeply attract Princess Margaret to the charms of this London environment. Then there was David Bowes-Lyon, youngest of all the Bowes-Lyon brothers, an extra 'Uncle David' to smile on the scene. The christening gifts, indeed — jackets and silver spoons, tiny slippers, rattles and toys — were tokens of family kinship or friendly affection more than symbols of regal birth.

The Times also noted the presence of four-year-old Princess Elizabeth, obviously well surrounded by 'members of their Majesties' Household in Waiting'. Many of the christening guests had also been at Victoria Station that morning, safely seeing off Queen Victoria's eighty-year-old son, the Duke of Connaught, on his way to the warmer climes of the Riviera. Immediately below the announcement of the christening, a special correspondent reported that the Duke of Gloucester had presented a gold sceptre to the newly-enthroned Emperor of Ethiopia, and the next column surely enshrines the royal atmosphere of the day in announcing a speed limit of twenty miles an hour in the Royal Parks. 'Police and park keepers have received instructions to enforce this limit rigorously,' the announcement fulminated, 'determined in the interests of users of the parks and of residents in the neighbourhood to use all possible means to prevent abuses by motorists whose inconsiderate conduct in the past has frequently been a source of annoyance and danger. Motorists using the Royal Parks would be well advised in future to keep within the speed limit.'

This was indeed the year 1930. And the world of the little Princess was hedged in truth by gold sceptres and policemen, keepers, speed limits and well-meaning advice.

III

In those days No. 145 Piccadilly was one of a terrace of stone-faced mansions, impressive and outwardly aloof, that looked southward over the plaza of Hyde Park Corner. It stood a little to the east of Apsley House, where the endless stream of London traffic now swings southward from the park, and whenever Princess Margaret passes nowadays she sees the red buses, the cars and trucks grinding across the site of her childhood home. Difficult to grow used to seeing a traffic island at the very spot where, in indoor quiet, she once played with her toys at her mother's feet! Difficult not to sense a twinge of the heart at the recollection of friendly 145, in another dimension of time, the budgerigars chirping in the hall, and the staircase coiling towards the nursery world on the fourth floor at the top of the house!

The young Duke and Duchess of York had been married only a year when they first viewed the house, then untenanted and dilapidated, with a warren of twenty-five bedrooms somewhere beyond the temperamental 'electric passenger-lift'. 'What should we do with twenty-five rooms?' the Duchess had enquired. But a number were mostly so small or ill-shaped that sets of two had to be knocked into one, and others adapted as bathrooms, dressing rooms and wardrobes. With such changes the house instantly became less cumbersome and more congenial. With the introduction of double-glazing, then a great novelty, it also became pleasantly quiet and tranquil. The assorted attics of the fourth floor blossomed into a nursery world, opening on to a bright glass-domed central landing destined to offer future stabling for thirty toy horses. The sunny day nursery overlooked the busy traffic of Piccadilly, and the night nursery at the back enjoyed morning vistas across the park. On the ground floor, a so-called ballroom with an outmoded conservatory became a spacious morning room, with French windows unexpectedly opening on to a garden shared with the neighbours. And this amenity in turn later proved useful when the two princesses were old enough to play with the next-door neighbour's children, the younger family of Lord and Lady Allendale at No. 144.

The Yorks had moved into 145 three years before Princess Margaret was born; and the house seemed to shrink, the Duke once said, from the moment he signed the Crown lease. The kindly Duchess found the numbers of her domestic staff constantly increasing. One of the building workmen was about the place so long that he remained to 'live in' as a telephone operator, and a plasterer's daughter became a housemaid. These were times of dire unemployment when it was laudable to give work to as many as possible. Even the butler, Mr Ainslie, required an under-butler; the cook, Mrs MacDonald, had three kitchen-maids. Early in the summer of 1930, in making space for the establishment of the then expected baby prince, the Comptroller's office staff had moved out, transferring their typewriters and filing cabinets to new quarters in Buckingham Gate, and the arrival of Princess Margaret as a surprise baby girl in no way diminished the household.

Mrs Knight — nicknamed 'Alah' from some baby difficulty with her Christian name, Clara — had 'managed' till then with an assistant nanny, Margaret MacDonald, then in her mid-twenties, who had been seconded from Lady Linlithgow's Scottish household and was now joined by her sixteen-year-old sister, Ruby, as a nursery-maid. These remained the nursery triumvirate for many years — the grey-haired buxom Clara Knight, a Hertfordshire farmer's daughter, and the auburn-haired MacDonald sisters from a railway cottage in the Black Isle. Ruby remained with Princess Margaret, eventually as nanny and later as personal maid, until after the birth of Viscount Linley.

Margaret Rose was just a year old when the Duke and Duchess of York embarked on their second and more personal and exhilarating home-building project in the rescue and rehabilitation of Royal Lodge, Windsor, which was then only a fragment of the present homestead, a house of grey stained stucco, formerly occupied by King George V's racing manager and scarred by all the usual symptoms of dilapidation and decay. The Duchess nevertheless realized what a wonderful home it could make for her family — enjoying solitude, yet close to London, and safe and circled within the limitless reaches of Windsor Great Park. The Yorks began to go down there on Saturdays or Sundays, taking a picnic basket and working in the keen autumn air, cutting back the overgrown shrubs while the chauffeur tended the bonfire. One Sunday, when the building work upon the house was fairly advanced, a pram was borrowed from a Windsor neighbour, and Alah and 'Bobo' — as Margaret MacDonald was becoming known — travelled down with the children on a family outing. Lilibet carried twigs of wood to the fire and Margaret sat woollen-wrapped in the pram, wide awake, her blue eyes watching all that went on.

The King and Queen sometimes came over unexpectedly from Windsor Castle, and passing near the Lodge fence one afternoon an elderly local lady noticed a bearded man, like the King, lifting a baby from her pram, sweeping her high in the air. 'I thought afterwards that it might really have been the King.' The old King indeed became intensely fond of his granddaughters, writing of his meetings with them with all the gravity of important events. 'Lilibet and Margaret came after luncheon,' he noted in his diary, on February 18th, 1932, when Margaret was just eighteen months old. 'My new little cairn, Bob, was fairly friendly to them.'

2: THE LITTLE SISTER

We were met on the doorstep by Princess Elizabeth and her little sister. A perfectly *delicious* pair. I have seldom seen such an enchanting child as Princess Elizabeth: and the little one bids fair to be the same.

Sir Miles Lampson, *September 1934*

I

Princess Margaret's earliest memory is of falling out of her pram, a vision of the sudden mischievous tilting of her cosy, cosseted, familiar world. She remembers 'the great to-do', the uproar of nannies, with a total recall that imaginatively elaborates the details, the gritty bump, the flurry of blankets, the barking dogs. 'I must have wanted to be noticed,' she says, with a disarming smile. The recollection need not be precociously early, for when Marion Crawford joined the household as a governess to six-year-old Princess Elizabeth in 1932 it rapidly became her firm opinion that Alah kept Margaret penned in her pram for far too long, 'long after she pined to run about'. In her eagerness for a playmate, it was Lilibet who urged the baby forward, compelling her to talk before she might otherwise have framed a word, helping her to walk almost as soon as she had learned to tug herself up from the floor, and harnessing her as a horse, swaying and tottering around the room, as soon as she had mastered locomotion on her own two legs.

Carrying Margaret downstairs from the Glamis nursery one day, Lady Strathmore heard her singing to herself and, on paying attention, discovered she was la-la-ing the *Merry Widow* waltz. 'I was so astonished,' the proud grandmama told Cynthia Asquith, 'I nearly dropped her.' The nannies similarly averred that from the age of two Margaret could hum in perfect tune any song she had ever heard. One gathers the picture of 'an enchanting, doll-like child', her face alight with mischief, once freed from that wretched pram. Miss Crawford's first mention is of a 'small fat face' appearing around the door of the dining room after lunch at Royal Lodge, holding out 'her small hot hand' to her father for a spoonful of coffee sugar crystals and pushing it all into her mouth. But we owe to others a minor footnote that Margaret — that reputed seeker of entertainment — was taken into the ballroom at Sandringham, aged two-and-a-half, to see her 'first talking film', *The Good Companions*, only to fall sound asleep in Alah's arms as soon as the lights were lowered.

The then Prince of Wales, her Uncle David, always fondly remembered her alert puzzlement in unravelling one of his Christmas gift packages; and some of her childish home-made greeting cards, drawn and painted when she was five or six, still remained among his last papers as Duke of Windsor. Queen Mary, 'Granny Queen', usually gave her little granddaughter Fabergé animal miniatures which were quickly locked for safety in a glass case, but Margaret played happily with an old doll cradled in a cardboard box, and quickly outgrew the phase of grabbing toys from Lilibet. 'Let her have it, Alah,' the elder sister would say. 'She's such a baby.'

Left to herself, Margaret preferred simple toys, picture books, crayons, as well as a few favourite dolls from among the constantly changing array that her mother brought home from afternoon engagements. A memorable success among presents one year was a scarlet child-size dustpan and brush, matching a set given to her sister. Thus equipped the two Princesses sedulously swept their mother's sitting room every morning, gathering a rewarding harvest of fluff. The younger child's vocabulary leapt ahead under her sister's teaching, though the words were not always exact. 'And what have you there?' asked a visitor, seeing her carrying a pencil box. 'Only my appendix,' came the reply, opening the box to disclose a pen.

On troublesome afternoons when the younger sister strayed into Lilibet's lessons, in the boudoir off the Duchess's sitting room, Miss Crawford kept her quiet and amused with her first kindergarten tasks, learning how to string beads or form long loops of coloured ribbon, happily immersed for an hour in making a necklet of paper flowers. One catches a hint of her future delight in fashion when the Duchess gave each of her daughters a necklace of corals and pearls, made up from a string of her own, to wear on special occasions, and Margaret, unbidden, chose to wear hers on her third birthday party at Glamis. Among the grown-up guests was Sir James Barrie, highly amused at the bright little face scarcely above the rim of her cup.

'Some of her presents were on the table, simple things that might have come from the sixpenny shops,' he wrote later, 'but she was in a frenzy of glee over them, especially one to which she had given the place of honour by her plate. I said to her as one astounded, "Is that really your very own?" and she saw how I envied her and immediately placed it between us with the words, "It is yours and mine."'

The charming courtesy deeply touched Barrie's sense of sentiment, so much so that he used the phrase some years afterwards in his play *The Boy David*. Yet the author of *Peter Pan* similarly made a decided impression on the Princess in turn. Hearing someone speak of him, she looked up brightly. 'I know that man,' she announced. 'He is my greatest friend and I am his greatest friend.' Reaching Barrie's ears, this phrase, too, remained in mind and was introduced into *The Boy David*. On meeting the young Princess again at Glamis, shortly before the London production in 1936, Barrie playfully confessed his guilt in taking her words and merrily declared he would pay a penny royalty for every performance.

The play was short-lived but Barrie remembered his promise and had a mock solemn Indenture drawn up, 'BETWEEN James Matthew Barrie so called Author and HER ROYAL HIGHNESS THE PRINCESS MARGARET WITNESSETH as follows: WHEREAS the said Barrie did write a play of short and inglorious life called *The Boy David* and basely produce the aforesaid play as exclusively the work of his own hand...' and so on. A bag of fifty glittering mint-new pennies was prepared, which it was intended Princess Margaret could acknowledge by counter-signing the document. Unhappily, Barrie died before they could be delivered, although the Princess believed they may have spurred her lasting enthusiasm for collecting the first proof of new coins of her sister's reign.

One gains from friends and mentors a beguiling impression of a child quick to pick up her mother's phrases or echo some private counsel from Lilibet. Taken to a children's party at which a stage had been arranged for a conjurer, she unexpectedly demurred at sitting in the front row. 'But you will see better in front,' she was told. 'No, thank you, I shall see *too well*,' said Margaret Rose. She was still only three when taken to church for the first time in the private chapel near Royal Lodge in Windsor Great Park, and we watch her through the amused eyes of Sister Catherine Black, one of her grandfather's nursing staff. Coached by Alah, listening to the hymns and music, 'her behaviour at first was exemplary.' But her intent interest could not remain bottled up and, during a pause in the prayers, a shrill little voice rang out, 'Are they all asking God for things out loud, Alah?' Alah deemed it wise to take her out before the sermon, and a ripple of amusement swept the congregation at her plaintive departing cry, 'Oh, must we go? I should so like to have heard *another song!*'

The Duchess of York had first taught her to say her prayers, telling her the story of the Christmas child and reading Bible stories, anxious to encourage her in the abiding religious faith she had herself gained at her mother's knee. Margaret's response was bright and enquiring: there were often 'questions about God and the angels', as her governess recalls, until at an early age 'her faith became so firm that she questioned no more'. The first book she ever managed to read quite by herself, at about the age of five, was *Tales of the Baby Jesus*. But her early visits to church also served the purpose of preparing the little Princess for her first appearance in public ceremonial, at the age of four and three months, at the wedding in Westminster Abbey of her Uncle George, the Duke of Kent, and Princess Marina. From the moment of the decision that Princess Elizabeth was to be a bridesmaid it became all too clear that Margaret could not be left at home.

'But she will make me laugh,' Lilibet protested. Her mother however felt confident that, after a simple explanation, Margaret would take the wedding seriously, and so it proved. The departure of the Duchess of York from 145 Piccadilly with her little daughter tightly clutching her hand was among the minor pleasures of Londoners on the wedding day and, owing to an assassination threat against one of the foreign guests, the crowds caught a better view of the Duchess's slow-moving car — and the Princess's merry, excited face — than of the bride's swift-moving cavalcade. In the Abbey, close to the High Altar, the Princess sat on a footstool at her mother's feet, a splash of colour in her pale rose coat and hat, quiet as a mouse and by contrast with the surrounding splendour almost as small. Watching her closely, Cynthia Asquith saw that she glowed at first glimpse of her sister but, as the bride's procession approached, she 'looked at her mother and then at her shoes until the procession was safely past'. The Duke and Duchess, with their two daughters, received one of the loudest outbursts of cheering of the wedding ride down the Mall.

Back at the Palace a nursery lunch sustained this youngest of guests while her aunt and uncle were being married by Greek Orthodox rites in the private chapel. The waiting crowds grew dense, and when the bride and groom and family group appeared on the Palace balcony one could also see a tiny hand mysteriously waving above the balustrade, until Brigadier Sir Hill Child bent down and lifted Princess Margaret high in his arms. The crowd roared with delight, and the King took her and stood her on the balcony plinth for all to see, while Queen Mary steadied her, the Princess all the while waving gaily. Amid the ovation for Princess Marina, the incident lasted but a few minutes. Yet in that pre-television, monarchy-worshipping era the effect was tremendous; and that moment, said *The Times*, 'was repayment enough to all who saw it, for whatever hours of waiting it may have cost them.'

II

In the 1930s — and earlier even than the Kent wedding — the phrase 'The little Princesses' had gained wide currency. It came new-minted into popular use on a surge of public affection and loyalty, and gave millions a benign sense of kinship with the Royal Family. Apart from the postcard child-portrait studies by Marcus Adams, the public at large could glimpse the little

Princesses only through occasional newsreel shots in the cinema, and yet an assurance of felicity glowed in the very words.

In London, in those calm and pleasant days, a small knot of onlookers often gathered in the early afternoon on the pavement outside 145 Piccadilly to see the little Princesses taken for a drive in one of the royal carriages with their nannies, a coachman and footman on the box. The policeman held up the traffic and the carriage turned at spanking pace into Hyde Park or south towards Battersea Park. The two were the best-known children in the world, and no one dreamed of security risks in the pretty pageant. On other days, people riding by on the upper decks of the red buses occasionally enjoyed a travel bonus in seeing the Princesses playing in the sooty enclosure of gardens behind the house. Then there were rainy afternoons when the Princesses in turn were the observers, gazing down from the day nursery windows, studying the Piccadilly scene so closely that they even noticed when the mounted traffic policeman had new stirrups. Horses still drew a number of passing carts and it was a triumphant moment when Margaret sighted 'a funny bus with a hat', one of the first of the covered-top fleet.

In the autumn, when the trees were bare, Grandpapa's window at Buckingham Palace could be seen from their own windows. At half past nine every morning a handkerchief flashed in the distant Palace window. The Princesses vigorously waved back, and this was their daily greeting. Such is the legend, and the old and ailing King may indeed have specially kept an ultra-large handkerchief for the signal. Yet Princess Margaret more vividly remembers him as a bearded giant, greeting her hilariously, prepared to play horses or making indulgent promises that were always reliably kept.

Having begun dancing lessons with Madame Vacani, she danced for him, to his jovial applause, during the New Year at Sandringham in what was to be the last full year of his life, and his journal at the time makes frequent affectionate mention of his granddaughters.

On May 6th, 1935, King George and Queen Mary celebrated their Silver Jubilee with a processional ride to a thanksgiving service in St Paul's, an occasion of immense rejoicing in which the little Princesses again took part. With the exciting clatter and jingle of a Captain's Escort of the Royal Horse Guards, they rode with their parents in the first open carriage to leave Buckingham Palace, dressed exactly alike — as so often — in pink frocks and hats. 'It was a glorious summer's day,' the King wrote afterwards, 'the greatest number of people in the streets that I have ever seen in my life, the enthusiasm most touching.'

The York family at the head of the procession, received the brunt of the deafening welcome, 'Princess Elizabeth and Princess Margaret waving to the people and enjoying the spectacle as only children can,' as *The Times* recorded, and when the return journey was made along the Thames Embankment, where many schoolchildren were gathered, 'the cheers rose to a tumult for the little Princesses, and Princess Margaret delighted all with the enthusiasm and daintiness of her handwaving.' At the Palace, when the King and Queen appeared on the balcony, a little hand was once more seen waving beside them until a footman brought a stool. And then, added *The Times*, 'as she peered over the balustrade the people shouted with joy and, as the royal group withdrew into the Palace Princess Margaret lingered awhile and enjoyed the scene by herself.'

Such was the measure of the phenomenal popularity focused upon her as a child. Some might say that the Princess was taking her first step in monarchy, in that distant and very different day and age, showing every future promise of sharing her sister's measure of understanding. That evening the King broadcast his thanks to the nation and the Princess was allowed to stay up to listen. 'I am speaking to the children above all,' said her grandfather. 'Remember, children, the King is speaking to *you*... As you grow up, be ready and proud to give to your country the service of your work, your mind and your heart.'

During the week, the King and Queen drove to different parts of London to see the street decorations, accompanied on two or three occasions by the Princesses; and the King, who was fond of repeating his jokes, no doubt echoed the jest he had already enjoyed with a friend. 'I suppose,' he said, 'you think these flags are hung out for you? Let me tell you' (with a bow, his hand on his heart) 'they are for me!' But probably Margaret Rose already understood that the friendly cheers and gay decorations were for her grandparents, a beneficial spectacle in which she was included. Many years later, when asked if she had not found it embarrassing to be stared at so much, she responded, 'It's strange, but somehow, right from the beginning, I don't seem to remember noticing.'

III

At the age of five, Princess Margaret could be trusted to behave at any ceremony, whatever the pressure of grown-up tedium. After the family commemoration of his forty-second wedding anniversary, the King particularly noted, 'All the children looked so nice, but none prettier than Lilibet and Margaret.' From Balmoral that summer the engagement was announced of the King's third son, the Duke of Gloucester, and his future bride — Lady Alice Montagu-Douglas-Scott — lost no time in deciding that she wished to include both Lilibet *and* Margaret among her eight attendants. The dress of the younger Princess must have been one of the smallest Norman Hartnell had ever designed.

It was 'of palest pink satin, short skirts bordered with three graduating bands of ruched pink tulle,' Mr Hartnell recollected, 'tiny sleeves and a tulle-bordered bodice.' This feature particularly gave difficulty in measurement, the little figure fidgeting and dancing about so much that her mother eventually had to hold her feet still. 'I don't suppose,' she said sympathetically to Mr Hartnell 'that you often have to kneel to fit the necks of your customers.' A later fitting was held at the Hartnell salon in Bruton Street, nearly opposite the house where Princess Elizabeth had been born, and the couturier methodically noted the little blue jackets, silver buttoned, worn by the Princesses, with 'tiny grey hats wreathed in forget-me-nots'. But the children were more interested in the close-up view of the scintillating cars and the life of the street below his windows. As they left, passing through the showroom with their mother, the designer was long to remember that all the women there 'rose as one and tendered a lingering curtsy ... a beautiful and moving sight.' Probably only the two children could take the homage for granted, a customary obeisance for their mother, and to the magic always surrounding her, still inexplicable to them ... the mystic gleaming magic of the Crown.

At the last moment, the scene of their 'Uncle Harry's' wedding was changed from Westminster Abbey to the Palace private chapel owing to the death of the bride's father, and Princess Margaret was not to become an Abbey bridesmaid

32

until her sister's wedding twelve years later. The curtailed festivities nevertheless left the ardour of the crowds undiminished. Great cheers welcomed Lady Alice as she drove from her London home. During their balcony appearance, all the bridesmaids wore white fur capes over their dresses, none more enchanting than the white snowball that was Princess Margaret and, apart from the bride herself, as *The Times* acknowledged, 'As always, it was the little Princesses who had the warmest greeting.'

At yet another ceremony in the private chapel, two weeks later, the Princesses saw their new baby cousin of Kent christened Edward George Nicholas Paul Patrick, a very long name indeed to Margaret Rose, struggling just then to write only one name of her own. Every ceremonial event had its intimate domestic aspect. At the family party, her Uncle George of Kent sat down to play the piano, whereupon Margaret had cause to confide that she was having music lessons with Miss Lander and was lifted to the piano to demonstrate her scales. Her fingers had difficulty in spanning four keys, so small were her hands. Her gloves, Alah proudly claimed, had to be specially made because they were below the smallest stock size.

The wedding and the christening, followed as they soon were by the renewed story of the Christmas child, all flowed together into the firm continuity of a child's unquestioning faith. As a Christmas gift to various relatives that year, the Duke and Duchess of York had commissioned a gramophone record of Margaret singing a carol duet with her sister, and the two voices echoed through the Sandringham drawing room, seeming to the then Prince of Wales to emphasize all the more the closely-knit family fabric now wrapped his three brothers in the security of their married life. 'I felt lonely and detached,' he wrote later. 'A fourth generation had begun to assert itself... Bertie's two children, Elizabeth, who was then nine, and her sister, Margaret Rose, romped around the twenty-foot tree...' From little Margaret, had he but known, he gained a response of warm affection. Years after the Abdication, she recollected the sense of missing him when he had gone and, among all her elaborate presents, she remembered that this 'Uncle David' had given her a set of A. A. Milne books, *Winnie the Pooh*, *When We Were Very Young* and, with a ring of coincidence, *Changing the Guard at Buckingham Palace*.

IV

King George V died at Sandringham on January 20th, 1936, a few days after the children had returned to Royal Lodge. The Duchess of York, who had been in bed recovering from pneumonia, had to go to London to rejoin her husband, and the two Princesses quietly passed through the transition of the reigns in Alah and Crawfie's tranquil company, playing endless games of noughts and crosses. Lilibet had to attend the funeral and could understand that 'Uncle David' was now King Edward VIII, but Margaret was merely mystified when Alah from time to time burst into tears. After her first pony, Peggy, had died, she had said confidently, 'Now I expect Jesus is riding him, instead of that silly old donkey', and one day she was overheard similarly explaining, 'Grandpapa is in Heaven now, and I'm sure God finds him very useful.' Heaven was fully consistent with Windsor Castle or Balmoral or other royal homes into which some of the grown-ups disappeared from her ken for months on end. Listening to her lengthy prayers one night, Alah pointed out that it might not be thought possible to grant all she was asking. 'Oh, that will be quite all right,' Margaret said firmly. 'Grandpapa is up there now and he will see to it.'

With the scope of royal influence thus borne in mind, the younger sister also began 'real' school lessons with 'Crawfie'. Miss Marion Crawford has been sadly maligned for the sentimental journalism in which she briefly took part after her elder pupil had come to the throne, yet one day posterity may equally hail her as the Fanny Burney of the era. In her early twenties on coming to 145, she had studied at Moray House in Edinburgh, and the poverty in the poorer parts of the city had fired her to be a teacher and so do what she could against some of the misery and unhappiness she had seen. After concluding her training, she had taken what was meant to be only a holiday post as coach to the Countess of Elgin's little boy when word of her reached the Duchess of York through her sister, Lady Rose Leveson-Gower. 'I had certainly never intended to be a governess,' wrote Miss Crawford, on looking back at the workings of fate. But perhaps it was as well that the Princesses were to have a mentor who did not always see life through conventional rosy spectacles. Indeed at times, when they were older, she would speak out savagely to remind her startled royal pupils that outside a palace conditions and ideas could have a harsher social reality.

But for a time she coped simultaneously with a girl of ten and a child of five, striving to follow Queen Mary's suggestion that history was as important for these children as arithmetic, and that writing and reading were the rudiments of their future profession. Now and then their father joined in games of hopscotch on a gravel path in the gardens of 145 during the morning break, puzzled that 'Windsor rules' seemed different. The Duke little realized that Crawfie's rules were based on the flat stones and chalk markings she had seen used in the teeming courts and closes of old Edinburgh.

Now, of course, there were occasions when the two sisters were at odds over their different lessons or toys. Books were banged, tears shed, and Crawfie reminded Alah that they would not have been normal healthy children without quarrels at times. Lilibet would cry, 'Margaret always wants everything I want.' There were moods when Lilibet wielded a hefty slap and Margaret was known to bite. When they had to wear hats, which they both detested, ill-tempered elastic-snapping sessions could develop unsuspected by the people who saw them in their pretty bonnets, all sweetness and light. Alah knew that Margaret could quickly kiss and be friends, and storms begun with a sidelong look of defiance swiftly subsided. There was never any real or memorable naughtiness. When under rebuke, tantrums dissolved into giggles. Reproving adults could not repress smiles, though pretending to be stern with the bouncy little figure, when she opened her eyes wide and began singing, 'Who's Afraid of the Big Bad Wolf?'

To Miss Crawford we owe innumerable glimpses of Princess Margaret as a child, the born comic, the impulsive, endearing, affectionate personality who would become the woman. 'She was warm and demonstrative … her father would be almost embarrassed, yet at the same time most touched and pleased, when she wound her arms round his neck, nestled against him and cuddled and caressed him.' In contrast, Lilibet was the reserved and quiet one. She would emerge from the lift at 145 to meet guests with a touch of hesitant dignity, while Margaret scampered forward in a rush, usually getting there first.

Arriving on a rainy afternoon, one guest noticed every door in the house standing open while wild shrieks of laughter came down the staircase. The children were playing hide-and-seek.

Margaret's official bedtime was only thirty minutes ahead of her sister, but she would be romping with her parents at bath-time or hilariously out of bed in pillow-fights until an hour later. Ensconced unseen on their upper landing, the children revelled in a staircase view of guests arriving for a party, 'Lots and lots of lovely ladies, but none as lovely as Mummy.'

In the spring of 1936 the photographer Lisa Sheridan visited Royal Lodge with her camera, to note the simple and well-contrived detail that the Duke of York opened the front door himself, to discover the two rocking-horses side by side in the hall, to admire the effect of light and sunshine everywhere and then to meet the 'two little girls who came running down to shake hands'. This notable domestic experiment in public relations was also the first photo-camera session within Princess Margaret's remembered experience, and for the hungry and unsatisfied public the resulting pictures savoured of enchantment. The little Princesses were truly in focus. They had rushed about, posing the two corgis, Dookie and Jane, rather than themselves, taking the visitor to see their own special gardens, their budgerigars and their miniature Welsh play-cottage. 'I found out later', wrote Lisa Sheridan, 'that anyone new to them always excited their interest very much. They were full of enthusiastic curiosity.'

'We've got everything except a telephone,' Princess Margaret had asserted, as they entered the miniature cottage, and Mrs Sheridan noticed the sharing 'we' of the two sisters and the elder sister's care for Margaret which seemed 'more from love of doing things for her than from actual solicitude'. The younger child posed at one moment 'with attractive self-importance'. Then presently the ponies were brought for a riding session, and the photographer must have become aware of the minute-to-minute maternal planning that had ensured the success of her visit.

V

In the new reign, when Margaret alleged herself 'nearly six', their Uncle David was seen infrequently at Royal Lodge. Now that he was the King, his young nieces were told, he had more business to do and less time to join in the games after tea, like Snap and Happy Families. One Sunday afternoon indeed he came to tea, but brought with him a slim and elegant American lady, who went to the window to see the view and asked with a strangely proprietary air whether it would not be improved if one or two trees were cut down. When tea was over the Duchess of York suggested to Crawfie that the children might be taken out for a walk in the woods for a while, and this was Princess Margaret's only meeting with Mrs Simpson until many years later.

Certainly Margaret was too young for the incident to make any impression. The two sisters were more concerned just then with a prospective visit to the Royal Tournament and with the thrills or chills of their first swimming lessons at the Bath Club. 'You mustn't be a limpet, Margaret,' Lilibet adjured, as her sister clung to the side, looking in her swimsuit like 'a plump navy-blue fish'. The antics of the other children, however, soon lured the novice farther out and, a season or two later, she emulated Lilibet by winning her life-saving certificate with a test that involved plunging into the water 'fully dressed', wearing an old frock over her swimming costume. Earlier that year, there had been a lovely seaside holiday with their parents at Compton Place, Eastbourne, although Alah took no chances with Margaret's colds and judged the water as too chilly except for a brief paddle. The little Princesses had long since been initiated into the mysteries of building castles and making sand-pies on the shore at Hunstanton, near Sandringham, but now their ponies were also brought down for long rides along the Sussex beaches, almost deserted at that time of year; and during the family motor-drives around the Sussex countryside Margaret first saw the sweeping hills and woods and timbered cottages where one day she would have a country cottage of her own.

Over that Easter of 1936 Queen Mary also spent a holiday at Royal Lodge, staying nearly a month, an exceptional novelty to Margaret to have Grannie sleeping in the house. A party was held for Lilibet's tenth birthday, followed the same week by the social bewilderments for the younger child of a family luncheon party for her parents' thirteenth wedding anniversary. For Margaret's sake, at about this time, the Duchess of York revived a game that had helped Lilibet to understand how to behave with different people. The Duchess would move about the room saying, 'Now I'm the Prime Minister ... now I'm the Archbishop of Canterbury ... now I'm Grannie' and the Princess would echo, 'Good morning, Mr Baldwin ... Good morning, Your Grace...' Now that the Duke of York was next in succession to the Throne, newly appointed ambassadors, government ministers and bishops alike would call to pay their respects at 145 Piccadilly and occasionally chanced to meet the children. The pleasant family atmosphere of the house remained unchanged. The canaries and budgies still sang in welcome. But an over-talkative parrot had to be given away to the London Zoo, where the Princesses were welcomed like State visitors when they sought the first opportunity to visit him in his new surroundings to make sure he was quite at home.

At Royal Lodge, with their parents more preoccupied than of old, the children were encouraged to take a closer interest in their gardens. One might add that they needed little encouragement; they had always tilled the little two-by-four plots around the Welsh Cottage and near the budgie cage, and a gardener who attempted in their absence to make good their mistakes heard indignant protests afterwards that 'someone had been there'. Crawfie seized the occasion for some first lessons in botany; a gardener and the cook also added practical instruction. One day when lamb was served for lunch, the Duchess of York mentioned with pride that Margaret had gathered the mint, and the Princess sometimes presented guests with her 'own home-grown radishes'. As well as being a considerable expert on rhododendrons, the Duke of York found that his daughters expected him to be well-informed on potatoes, not merely potatoes but also the desirable varieties. When nearly six, Margaret solemnly announced that 'King Edwards' were best, although 'Arran Chiefs' lasted longer. Peeled and cut up by Alah, her new potatoes would be placed in a pot on the cooker of the Little House for make-believe boiling. And as soon as she could use a knife safely, Margaret became an expert potato peeler.

If at Glamis pea-plants still spring up in unlikely spots, they are the successors of peas that the Princess would experimentally pop into any soft patch of ground during the summer weeks spent with her Strathmore grandparents. Margaret giggled, heedless of Lilibet's reprimands, because Grandfather Strathmore's silky moustache tickled when he kissed her. There were always young Bowes-Lyon and Fife cousins on hand, and a favourite excursion was to ride down on the ponies to Glamis Station to watch the Aberdeen fish train go through. Being reputed an express, this often attracted quite a crowd of children on the platform, and the chewing-gum slot machine did a roaring trade, chiefly because Margaret Elphinstone knew of magical possibilities. If crossed pins were bound together with gum, and the stationmaster could be prevailed upon to put them on the lines, the roaring train would transform them into tiny pairs of scissors. 'You ask him, Margaret,' cousins would insist. 'He always does it for you.'

On days of Scottish mist and rain, the Glamis dressing-up chest came into its own. There were wonderful old robes that Mummy had worn, and people everywhere had fascinating stories to tell of 'when your Mummy was a girl'. The Princesses also undertook a separate journey with their mother that year to stay with old friends of the Pierpont Morgan family, at Gannochy, overlooking the river gorge. And so to Birkhall, the old Jacobean house in its own saucer of hills near Balmoral, which the Yorks had come to regard as their true Scottish home. But in 1936 the children missed the customary tea-party visits to Balmoral Castle, where the King's house-party presently included Mrs Simpson. At Birkhall, in somewhat sharp contrast, the Archbishop of Canterbury, Dr Lang, came to stay — and little Margaret bowed her head deeper because the Archbishop was saying grace. After tea one day, as Dr Lang jotted in his diary, 'Lilibet, Margaret Rose and Margaret Elphinstone sang some action-songs most charmingly. Strange to think of the destiny which may be awaiting the little Elizabeth, at present second from the Throne! She and her lively little sister are certainly most entrancing children.'

Margaret's impressionable attention was also showered on a newlywed couple, her elder cousin, the former Jean Elphinstone and John Wills, who came to stay shortly after their honeymoon. The little Princesses had attended their wedding at St Margaret's; they and the young couple clambered up to the viewpoint of the Eagle's Nest and went for long walks along the rim of Loch Muick. In the evenings the log fires blazed and the sound of piano music reached the children in their nursery bedroom. Mrs Wills was to prove a true friend and counsellor to Princess Margaret at a later and crucial stage in her life.

So passed the late summer and autumn of that 'Abdication year' when the world bristled with rumours. At some stage Lilibet had to be told of events, and when they returned to London and could see the newspaper placards 'The King and Mrs Simpson — Crisis', as Miss Crawford has said, 'Both the children asked questions, and some sort of explanation had to be made... I explained that unfortunately Uncle David had fallen in love with someone England could not accept as their Queen, because she had been married before and her husband was still living.' Princess Elizabeth could understand this broad black and white picture and no doubt painted it, simplified yet more, for Princess Margaret. A six-year-old was unconcerned with adult perplexities, although the iron inevitability of royal duty became summed up in the chilly remembered phrase that 'Papa might *have to be* King'.

Meanwhile, the children became preoccupied with the tasks of choosing and making their Christmas gifts, and with the fun of Christmas cooking, too. In the warm and mysterious semi-basement regions of No. 145, Mrs MacDonald, the cook — otherwise known as 'Golly' — allowed them to stir the Christmas puddings or to help decorate the iced cakes she made for blind soldiers, which had to be trimmed with paper horse-shoes and silver bells and other charms to please the seeking fingers. A doughy smell of baking pervaded Golly's domain and under her tuition, the Princesses donned large aprons, rolled their sleeves to the elbows and made little scones and pastry rolls, with Golly's continuous reminders that 'It is always so *much* easier if you tidy as you go.' They had to wash up the dishes they used, replace everything back in its drawer or cupboard and scrub the table afterwards. Years later a neighbour unexpectedly calling with a message at Princess Margaret's country cottage was startled to find her wielding a scrubbing brush.

Ill in bed with influenza that December, the Duchess of York was unable to come down to Golly's private sitting room as usual before Christmas to have tea there with her daughters and approve their home-made fare. On December 9th, when the crisis of the Abdication fever was approaching, nothing could keep the two children away from the nursery windows overlooking Piccadilly, peeping down at the crowd that had collected on the pavement. While keeping an eye on Margaret, Lilibet procured a sheet of Buckingham Palace notepaper from her private store, which she headed Abdication Day — prematurely as it happened — and sent a message to a friend. 'Mummy says we may not swim tomorrow as the crowds will be rather big and there are no cars… It's a great pity.'

It was not until two days later, on the Saturday, in fact, that the children saw their father in his uniform as an Admiral of the Fleet, when about to leave for his Accession Council at St James's Palace. They gave him a hug as usual, and Crawfie afterwards gravely explained to them that when he returned home he would be King of England and they should curtsy to him. 'You, too, Margaret, and try not to topple over.'

When the time came, the people were cheering outside as he came through the door and the two Princesses swept him a beautiful curtsy. For a moment he stood taken aback and touched with emotion and then kissed them warmly. Their mother, the new Queen, came down to lunch and they were all still at table when a message came 'to tell His Majesty that he had just been proclaimed'. With the emotion and uncertainty of the morning now safely behind him, King George VI looked at his daughters with twinkling eyes. 'Supposing someone comes through on the telephone,' he asked. 'Whom shall I say I am?'

By an engagement made several days before, and thus not entirely by chance coincidence, Cynthia Asquith came to tea with the Princesses and their governess that same afternoon. Little Margaret knew that the guest was an authoress and considerately felt that she had to turn the conversation to the subject of writing. 'Just think,' she said. 'I've just learnt how to spell York — Y-O-R-K — and now I'm not to use it any more. I'm to sign myself just Margaret, all alone.'

3: SECOND IN SUCCESSION

The younger girl was gifted, impish, overflowing with the personal. There was an echo of Queen Victoria's youngest daughter who, at the age of four, told a lady-in-waiting, 'I was very naughty last night ... but it doesn't signify much!' Now there came tales of salt found in 'Lilibet's' tea and tapioca in her bath.

David Duff, *Mother of the Queen*

I

In the first week of her father's reign, the six-year-old who was now second in succession to the Throne inveigled nursery visitors into incessant games of demon pounce. Her quick wit gave her an advantage over bemused grown-ups, and the exultation of winning amended the slight daunting sense that can beset a younger child. On the Monday the Princesses heard the guns in Hyde Park saluting their father's forty-first birthday, which came only two days after his Accession, and the day was in fact conveniently celebrated on the Sunday with a tea-party of family and friends at Royal Lodge.

The two girls learned with dismay that before long they would all have to live in Buckingham Palace. 'You mean for ever?' said Elizabeth. 'You mean we've got to leave our own house?' said Margaret. On the hall table at No. 145 Lilibet noticed letters addressed to 'H.M. The Queen' and murmured in awe, 'That's Mummy now.' From the nursery windows Margaret descried some new significance in the Royal Standard floating over Buckingham Palace, raised as soon as the King reached his office desk and rarely lowered until he returned home, no longer her Uncle David's Standard but her 'Poppa's'. The King and Queen dined at 145, but the rush of official business sometimes forced them to abandon the hour usually spent with their children.

The storm of change fretted the nerves of everyone in the house, adults and children alike. The staff particularly suffered an untoward sense of insecurity that communicated itself to the younger child. Every King she had ever known had disappeared, her grandfather, her uncle, and now her own Poppa was mysteriously involved in long daily absences. The abandonment of her family name of York seemed to go on rankling, Cynthia Asquith considered, 'as though it involved some mysterious loss of her own identity'. At morning service in the Royal Lodge chapel Margaret heard the new form of prayers, 'for the King's Majesty ... our most gracious Sovereign Lord King George ... our gracious Queen Elizabeth ... the Princess Elizabeth and all the Royal Family ... endue them, enrich them, prosper them with all happiness...' Childlike, she must have waited, vainly yet not in vanity, for her own name. 'Since my Poppa turned King,' she complained, 'I don't seem to be anyone at all.'

The calm of Christmas and New Year with Grannie at Sandringham created new vistas, however, and presently even the preparations to move to the Palace turned into fun. The Princesses wrapped up and packed their own toys in wicker baskets, gleefully avoiding the hazards to favourite toys in a ruling that surrendered *every other toy* to a hospital crate. 'It's quite impossible to decide,' said Margaret, shaking her head. Alah firmly responded that nothing was impossible if one tried hard enough. 'Oh, Alah,' cried the child, 'have you ever tried putting toothpaste back into the tube?'

The Princesses also noticed that nursery callers were more apt to 'bow and bob' than of old, which led to the revelation that as the King's daughters they were entitled at times to a curtsy. Deciding to try this out when their next visitor, Miss Daly, arrived to take them for a swimming lesson, their victim found her hand firmly grasped and pumped up and down to solicitous cries of, 'How do you do, Miss Daly, how do you do?' Catching her cue, Miss Daly said, 'I believe you're trying to make me curtsy?' 'That's right, that's right,' cried her captors, and Miss Daly obliged amid peals of laughter.

The new King and Queen moved to the Palace on February 18th, where the children followed them a week later. The schoolroom windows overlooked the Mall, and lessons were at first disturbed by the music — and to Margaret the irresistible spectacle — of the Changing of the Guard. Ultimately a more peaceful schoolroom was devised looking west over the gardens, like the one level with the cedar branches at Royal Lodge. Before long, too, the Princesses made familiar territory of the endless corridors, where all manner of strangers were to be encountered, from friendly policemen and saluting postmen to upstairs maids and the silent 'clock man', who went from one clock to another, winding, listening and testing chimes. In one direction lay a desert of State apartments, the furniture hunched spookily beneath the dust sheets, an unexplored realm until young Mr Kenneth Clark, then Surveyor of the King's Pictures, led them through the State rooms to the Picture Gallery one afternoon to tell them the stories of many of the paintings.

Some of the people they met in the Palace corridors were so starched and solemn that Margaret discovered the amusement of jumping out at them with a 'Boo!' from behind columns or curtains, a pastime quickly discouraged. But at night the vast rambling edifice grew silent. During those first winter evenings the wind moaned in the chimneys and Alah, who shared Margaret's bedroom, sat with her knitting in an armchair near the Princess's bed until she fell asleep. 'I had a nightmare,' Margaret would sometimes say with great conviction, embroidering a story she was clearly inventing then and there. Sternly told to sit quiet one day, she heaved a massive sigh and said, 'I do wish we could all go home.'

Then the daffodils bloomed in the Palace garden; the first flotillas of baby ducklings on the lake provided a new magic, and the preparations for the Coronation moved decisively forward. One morning the King took Margaret with him round to the Mews, where he wished to discuss some improvements to the Gold State Coach with the superintendent, Major Hopkins. Intently listening to the King's instructions, the Major ignored a tiny sting at his ankle. The irritation increased, and he tried to scratch it with the other foot, this time to feel another nip and an unmistakable tug on his trouser-leg. Looking down at last, he met little Margaret's impish smile as she peeped from beneath the coach, her suppressed mirth now exploding in delight.

'What are we to do with her?' Lilibet would say, in mock despair, and worried lest Margaret should not behave during the Coronation, only to be reminded of all the special occasions when she had comported herself very well indeed. 'Even so,' said the elder sister, 'she *is* very young for a Coronation. I do hope she won't disgrace us all by falling asleep in the middle.'

The Queen had decided that her daughters should wear long dresses of ivory lace over satin, with three rows of gold lace on the train, under robes of purple velvet, edged with ermine. 'But of course,' she explained, outlining these formalities to the designer, 'Margaret need not have a train.' From the corner of the room piped a crestfallen small voice, 'But I must have a train.'

The Queen, indeed, needed little persuasion that the two Princesses should be dressed precisely alike, with trains and complete with coronets of the lightest silver-gilt. When the robes and coronets were ready, both girls assiduously practised wearing them. 'And what did you do today, Margaret?' her mother enquired one evening. 'I put on my coronet,' Margaret explained with glee, 'and walked and walked about, just like Johnnie Walker.' With Queen Mary's help, Miss Crawford meanwhile ensured that each day's reading gradually prepared the children in understanding of the ceremonial. Though not yet seven, Princess Margaret was painstakingly taken through H. E. Marshall's juvenile history *Our Island Story*.

The Coronation was to take place on Wednesday May 12th. During the weekend, at Royal Lodge, the King set aside time to talk to each of his daughters, earnestly and separately, to tell each in turn of the nature of his dedication and the need of them all for the help of God. The King gave Margaret her own copy of the 'Order of the Service of the Coronation' with her name embossed in gold, to be treasured until one day she could read it all for herself. 'But I can read most of it already,' the Princess told the Dean of Windsor, with great conviction.

The week before the ceremony, the two Princesses were taken to the royal rehearsal in the Abbey, dressed alike in their flowered straw hats and pale-blue coats, taking their due place in the procession, 'most attentive, and intelligent', as one of the high officers thought them. Both then and on Coronation Day, Princess Margaret was the youngest person in the Abbey. Too young to chronicle her impressions as Elizabeth did, she was probably, like Lilibet, awakened at 5 a.m. by the band of the

Royal Marines striking up just outside. 'Bobo made me put on an eiderdown as it was so cold … every now and then we were hopping out of bed looking at the bands and the soldiers.' Later on, when Crawfie saw the Princesses dressed and ready, even Margaret seemed shy for once 'a little overawed by their own splendour and their first long dresses'.

At 10.30 the two children rode to the Abbey in the glass coach with Queen Mary and Queen Maud of Norway, Margaret perched upon a seat specially built up to enable her to see and wave to the crowds, 'which she did with much enthusiasm'. All along the route, the double spectacle of Queen Mary and the Princesses evoked cheers and applause of intense affection. In the Abbey itself a most happy photograph captured the two children in procession, so small and endearing in their robes and coronets, the taller girl tightly holding her young sister's hand, bending over her with tender caution.

In the Royal Box, wrote Queen Mary, 'I sat between Maud and Lilibet, and Margaret came next. They looked too sweet in their lace dresses and robes, especially when they put on their coronets.' With closer precision, the artist Frank Salisbury chose for his official painting of the ceremony the culminating moment when the Archbishop faced the newly crowned King and raised his hand in the benediction. All eyes were upon the King except Princess Margaret's who, the artist painstakingly noted, 'had fixed her gaze on the noble figure of the Primate as if saying to herself, "I can see Papa any day!"'

Back at the Palace, after that fantastic ride in the second State coach through the tumultuous crowds, Lilibet was asked how six-year-old Margaret had behaved. 'She was wonderful,' came the heartfelt reply. 'I only had to nudge her once or twice when she clattered the prayerbooks.' In the Throne Room,

Dorothy Wilding expended a hundred films for the official photographs and this time it was the elder sister who gave trouble. Miss Wilding wished the Princesses to stand with one hand holding their trains. 'I simply couldn't get Princess Elizabeth to pose as I wished,' she wrote. 'Her idea was that she would look better with her hands folded in front of her, and I was compelled to give way... But little Princess Margaret was most amenable.' In the group photograph with her parents she stands close to her father with serene composure, while Lilibet has a look of strain.

II

The King and Queen leaned over backward to treat their two children exactly alike, but differences inevitably arose, less through the age gap of four years than by the imperative needs of Elizabeth's future training as heiress presumptive. When the King and Queen sailed down the Thames by royal barge to open the new maritime museum at Greenwich, Elizabeth alone travelled with them, while Margaret stayed at home and so did not glide past the old house at Rotherhithe where she would one day find the romantic love of a young photographer. At the review of the Fleet at Spithead, it was Princess Elizabeth who appeared at her father's side on the royal yacht, while the younger sister, even if privately aboard, was nowhere to be seen. At a tea for disabled Servicemen in the Palace riding school, the King and Queen cut the centrepiece cake, and Princess Elizabeth cut an official cake of her own, though sweetly encouraging Margaret to help, and guiding her hand to cut the second slice.

The quality of strangeness, looking back, is not that the two Princesses were occasionally apart but that they so frequently appeared together. Two days after the Coronation both the children stood beside their parents on the dais during the King's presentation of Coronation medals to leaders of his vast contingent of overseas troops, and both stood admirably immobile while the King took the salute of the prolonged march-past. Ten days more and they rode with their parents in the carriage procession to the thanksgiving service in St Paul's. What can the impressions of the younger child have been, shaking hands dutifully with files of solemn dignitaries? What disciplines were astonishingly already implanted there? After the Garter procession at Windsor Castle, both children braved the crowds, tightly holding hands. And at the Palace garden party there they were again, dressed alike in sprigged muslin, all but swallowed up within a sea of eight thousand guests. Steering her sister, Lilibet noticed her smallest fault but reserved comment until later. 'If you see anyone in a funny hat, don't laugh and point,' she cautioned. 'And you mustn't be in such a hurry to reach the tea-table. That's not polite, either.'

Alah followed a rule of thumb that the two Princesses in public were dressed alike as twins. Fortunately, they were seldom interested in what they wore until 'Aunt Rose' (Lady Rose Leveson-Gower)[1] gave Margaret a little hat of frilled velvet which she persuasively wore as often as possible. Hats were *always* worn. One afternoon, when the Princesses were subjected to the intense noise of the Aldershot Tattoo amid an audience of 70,000 shrilling schoolchildren, their hats were padded with cotton-wool as protection. When Elizabeth alone accompanied her parents, extra time was found for junior lessons; and Queen Mary softened the earlier Greenwich disappointment by taking Margaret by car to see Greenwich

---

[1] Elder sister of Queen Elizabeth the Queen Mother, Lady Rose Bowes-Lyon married the Hon. William Spencer Leveson-Gower, who succeeded his father as the 4th Earl Granville in 1939.

Palace, no doubt telling her of two other little princesses who once lived there, one also named Elizabeth, the other Mary. Precocity, though not entirely avoided, was diminished by taking all the richness of royal event for granted.

And when still only six, a month after the Coronation, Margaret incredibly rode with her sister and parents to make the State entrance into Windsor and to shake hands with all the masters of Eton, a muster of Goliaths. The ceremonial of the similar State entry into Edinburgh called for youthful endurance, and a letter from Lilibet effectively mirrors the child's point of view. 'The Scottish Horse was great fun because one company was on riding horses and the other on some of Lord Ancaster's deer-ponies ... very rough and shaggy and all pulling like steam-engines.' At Holyrood, the two children once watched a march-past of four thousand men. It was 'very tiring', Lilibet wrote, 'because we stood for an hour and dust continually blowing in our eyes.'

Just after Margaret's seventh birthday at Balmoral, another of Lilibet's letters hints at the problem of finding companions of the right age. 'We had Margaret Elphinstone for only a long weekend for *our* Margaret's birthday... We have Georgina here, which is great fun.' Yet differences of only a few years are the immeasurable chasms of childhood, and since Margaret Elphinstone was twelve and Georgina Wernher nearly eighteen the scarcity of age-equals is obvious. As so often with young children isolated among elders, Margaret filled the gap by improvising her own make-believe friends, particularly a 'Cousin Halifax' whose exploits and shortcomings were to be recited with gusto for several years. If dog-leads were missing, Cousin Halifax had mislaid them. If a school task were unfinished, the Princess would explain, 'But, you know, Cousin Halifax has been bothering me.' And an unwanted invitation was dismissed with, 'Of course, we cannot go — because Cousin Halifax has a cold.'

The Coronation season sapped even the children's energy, and the Princesses were whisked to Glamis as soon as possible. Somewhere in an old chest Margaret found a turn-of-the-century children's paper, its tiny print disclosing a thrilling tale of piracy and derring-do in which she immersed herself by the hour. As her governess has said, she was remarkably secretive about it, and a new element of blood-and-thunder bolstered the exaggerated breakfast-table accounts of her dreams. Lady Helen Graham, who often accompanied the children on minor excursions, considered her at times too imaginative for her own good. Patiently listening to the dreams with analytic interest, Crawfie worried on occasion lest the threads of her pupil's 'restless, inquiring and imaginative brain' might be too tautly spun. Many a stress with Alah had to be soothed with, 'She is so highly strung.'

Glamis was also littered with months-old illustrated magazines which the Princess read omnivorously, taxing the adults with questions afterwards — what did televising mean, who was Ivor Novello? But even her governess was startled when, aged seven, Margaret enquired, 'What is the Regency Act?'

Miss Crawford explained that if her father should ever fall seriously ill and be laid up, someone would be appointed to act in his place, 'perhaps the Duke of Gloucester, your Uncle Harry'.

'And supposing Papa should ever die, like Grandpapa?'

The governess explained that the Duke of Gloucester would probably look after things until Lilibet was old enough to reign. 'I see,' said Margaret. 'A Regent is in lieu of the King.' Miss Crawford remembered that nearly perfect definition for long afterwards. The question arose in a different form in the early summer of 1939 when the King and Queen visited Canada and the USA, and Counsellors of State were appointed to act in the King's absence. It was explained to Margaret that she might well be appointed a Counsellor of State herself when she grew up. The children travelled with Queen Mary to Portsmouth to see their parents off, and a blurred photograph shows eight-year-old Margaret, examining a map of the journey with some puzzlement. 'We waved handkerchiefs,' wrote Queen Mary in her journal. 'Margaret said, "I have my handkerchief" and Lilibet answered "to wave, not to cry", which I thought charming!' But another photograph reveals the younger Princess after the leave-taking, self-controlled, yet tight-lipped and sadly woebegone.

III

It was a strange, a unique childhood, then, for the two little Princesses, the two most popular little girls in the world. A childhood totally without precedent and all the more astonishing in retrospect: in private, an affectionate family life which everyone around them strove to maintain at a normal everyday tenor ... and in public the adulation, the cheers, the cameras, and the compulsion and enforcement in the grown-up world of being always on one's best behaviour.

When still only seven, Princess Margaret and her sister rode to the State Opening of Parliament and watched the pageantry from the royal gallery of the House of Lords, listening to the King's speech — that legislative programme of which Margaret could have scarcely understood a word — with every appearance of intent interest. The following year, more by accident than design, she became the central figure at the launching of the liner *Queen Elizabeth*, when she clambered on to a chair between her mother and sister and so stood head and shoulders above everyone else, almost over-balancing with excitement at the sudden cry of 'She's away!', at the vast cheer and the din of steam-whistles as the great ship reached the water.

All this and the heavens of childhood, too: the visits to the zoo, to the Royal Tournament, the Braemar Gathering, the fun of visits to the London Museum and to the British Museum with 'all those wounded statues'. Disney's *Snow White and the Seven Dwarfs* was shown in the Palace ballroom, and not least Margaret saw her last pre-war pantomime, *Red Riding Hood*, with no one afraid of the big bad wolf now that Mr Chamberlain had gained the promise at Munich of peace in our time. Shortly before the Munich crisis, Sir Miles Lampson visited Balmoral and his journal records one of the last pictures of carefree peacetime childhood. 'Just a really nice domestic scene, the two little girls, sweet both of them... After lunch, played with a television set just installed, which the King had no idea how to work, much to the amusement of the little girls.' And then again, 'Princess Margaret was fascinating with the gramophone this afternoon. A real pet!' She had accompanied all the songs in silent mimicry.

When guests took their leave, the two girls went ahead to open the door, and Margaret could echo her sister precisely in saying with a grown-up air, 'We are so sorry you are going...' Even Mrs Knight, the firmest of nannies, was not always proof against that unashamed persuasion. On the evenings when the Courts were held, those glamorous yet slightly absurd occasions when hundreds of debutantes came to be presented to the King and Queen, the Palace throbbed with excitement. The two Princesses watched the Royal Family, in all their evening finery, forming the procession to enter the Throne

Room, and then had no difficulty at all in cajoling Alah to allow them to ensconce themselves in their quilted pink dressing gowns at their 'fly's-eye view'. From behind a grille, they could hear the music and gaze down on the sea of curled white ostrich plumes worn by the 'debs' and sponsors in their hair. 'Never mind, Margaret,' Lilibet would say, 'one day we shall be down there, sharing the fun.' But these were evenings, too, when Margaret was 'kept awake by Cousin Halifax' and Queen Mary would grumble to Lady Cynthia Colville that 'yawns in the morning certainly seem all wrong.'

Meanwhile lessons went forward, on a curriculum kept as close as possible to Queen Mary's suggestions. There were tranquil days when Margaret knitted industriously, ultimately producing a neat and unblemished scarf which was placed on display for Queen Mary's London Needlework Guild. From the balcony at Buckingham Palace, the children watched the enthusiastic demonstration of welcome to President Lebrun of France and then ran off to nursery lunch, unaware of anything extraordinary in their share in public event. Without too much public fuss, the King and Queen were again able to take their daughters to Eastbourne for a few days, and the two girls rode their ponies along the sands and built splendid sandcastles (with the aid of policemen). But Margaret longed above all else to have afternoon tea at an hotel, and the treat duly took place, her child's view of unimaginable luxury ruined in the tame disillusion of tea served in a private room.

Far more satisfying was the famous adventure of travelling on the Underground when, for days beforehand, Margaret questioned everyone on the correct method of stepping on and off the 'moving stairways' or the safest distance to 'stand back from the doors'. Lady Helen Graham and Miss Crawford were for once not the best of mentors, for Crawfie had never been on a tube train in her life and Lady Helen was no less vague. They made the initial mistake of commencing the journey at St James's Park, a station involving nothing more subterranean than a short stairway, but the thrill of 'the train rushing out of the tunnel and the sliding doors opening as if by magic', was authentic, as Lady Helen recollected later, and at Charing Cross the explorers changed by way of the escalators to the true deep-level Underground.

'I was amused to see how few people noticed the two children,' wrote Lady Helen. 'There came a time when an old gentleman became conscious that he was the target for all eyes right down the carriage. It took him a few bewildered minutes to realize that it was two demure children sitting next to him, holding their tickets very ostentatiously, who were the real centre of attraction.'

When they surfaced at Tottenham Court Road, however, a posse of cameramen were waiting, having gained word of their adventure and the exploit was completed by 'walking very quickly indeed' to the nearby YWCA headquarters for tea. Princess Margaret next campaigned in vain to be allowed to ride on a bus but this ambition was not realized until seven years later, and then only on a single-decker on special hire to their group of Sea Rangers. (Margaret rushed gleefully to the 'Devon General' driver, however, to tell him of this 'first time' distinction.) In contrast to the social freedom of royal children nowadays, the two Princesses were as segregated and contained within their community of cousins as any Dalai Lama of old. Miss Vacani's circumspect Palace dancing class; Miss Daly's swimming lessons at the Bath Club and riding at Windsor under Horace Smith's tutelage were the compass points of their sheltered private world.

The richer fun of being a 'Brownie' and then a Girl Guide quickened later and in fact it was not until wartime that Miss Violet Synge felt that the Princesses were truly 'taking guiding in their stride'. Although an announcement that Princess Elizabeth would join the Girl Guides had been promptly made weeks after the Coronation, Margaret was too young to enrol and her status remained in doubt. Lilibet vigorously pleaded her sister's cause. 'She has a fine pair of hiking legs, haven't you, Margaret? Pull up your dress and show Miss Synge.' When enlisted as a junior Brownie, however, Margaret's rosy visions of cooking sausages on sticks at a campfire quickly faded. The Guiding took an unpromising turn, Miss Synge had to confess, when nannies brought their charges to the Palace meetings in party frocks with white gloves. '*They* won't be able to race about and get dirty,' the Princess agreed and scornfully noticed that in a scramble game when the children had to sort out their shoes from a heap on the floor some of their companions did not know their own shoes.

The fun improved as more children of Household officials enlarged the group and nannies became better informed on Guiding. Margaret also ultimately showed an unexpected aptitude in waving signal messages down long royal corridors and particularly enjoyed patrol marching through the Palace grounds, a zestful change from riding horseback or in carriages or cars. 'I had lovely Christmas presents,' she wrote from Sandringham, at the New Year of 1939. 'I got a pedometer but it is awfully complicated, and lots of books, *Tony and the Dragon* and many more besides.'

IV

When morning lessons were over, Princess Margaret liked to play the piano, and her miniature keyboard model stood in a nook of the corridor near the staircase above the Privy Purse entrance. Arriving dignitaries downstairs would hear the distant strum of 'Little Sir Echo' or 'Whistle While You Work', often without realizing that the player was so young. She liked to greet members of the staff as they hurried by, chaffing them with 'Hurry up, you'll be late for lunch!' or welcoming others with their favourite tunes. She could improvise anything she had ever heard. Thus the half-hour was filled sociably, particularly when Lilibet had gone off on tasks of her own.

With her ninth birthday drawing near, Margaret tried as usual to catch up by pretending to be older, 'nearly ten... I'll be in my tenth year.' Wearing a new dress, she solemnly claimed, 'Look, Mummy, I'm quite a good shape now, no longer like a football.' Learning that Lilibet was to visit an exhibition of 'Royal and Historic Treasures' at none other than 145 Piccadilly, she pleaded, 'But I must go, too. I'm nearly old enough.' Taking a cue from Lilibet, she asserted, 'It's a public duty!', which quite won her mother over, and so in due course her first public duty was indeed carried out.

This proved to be an extremely strange experience, bizarre as any dream she had ever recounted. Some months earlier, during a childish misdemeanour, she had amused and touched Crawfie by saying 'I do wish we were all at home again', meaning back at No. 145. And now 'to find the familiar old rooms stripped of much that was remembered, to see the old doorways newly labelled *Their Majesties*, *Dining Room*, *The Queen's Boudoir*, *Princess Margaret's Room*, *The Royal Nursery*, to move through crowds of whispering people and find one's old dolls scattered on the nursery floor, which Alah would never have allowed, must have been an intimidating adventure', as a sympathetic observer wrote later. Princess Margaret clung tightly to her sister's hand. All around her were murmurs, 'Isn't she sweet! Oh, what a darling', and she naturally tried to oblige by looking as sweet and darling as possible.

Happily, this traumatic experience was quickly forgotten. Within a few days there followed the thrilling excitement of the cruise on the royal yacht *Victoria and Albert* from Cowes to Weymouth and the 1939 visit to Dartmouth Naval College which was to have such momentous consequences when Princess Elizabeth met Prince Philip. Or did Margaret perhaps meet Prince Philip *first*?

Even the Royal Family, one suspects, have forgotten the occasion five weeks earlier — on May 2nd — when Philip with his sister, Margarita, and their mother, Princess Alice of Greece, went to Buckingham Palace to tea with the King and Queen. Did they hear the lively strains of *The Lambeth Walk* drifting down the staircase? Was Margaret perhaps introduced, in Lilibet's absence? When touring Dartmouth, Crawfie noted that Philip 'spent a lot of time teasing little Margaret', as if both were already acquainted. The Princess in any event had no firm recollection of a first meeting: it seemed to her that Philip was always there. And Dartmouth memories in turn were quickly succeeded by the fun, a week or two later, of joining her father's boys' camp at Abergeldie Castle. Photographs show her, beaming with merriment, singing 'Under the Spreading Chestnut Tree', suiting the action to the words, packed beside her mother in the teenage crowd, and as usual the youngest person there.

4: PRINCESSES IN THE WAR

'Who is this Hitler, spoiling everything?'
Princess Margaret, *aged nine, 1939*

I

'Well, we're here!' Princess Margaret wrote triumphantly from Scotland in the mid-August of 1939, as the train-loads of children left London and the anxious clouds of war darkened over Europe. The King and Queen travelled south in great haste on August 23rd, leaving their daughters at Birkhall, that old Jacobean house in a secluded cup of the Highlands, east of Balmoral and south of the Dee, which the two Princesses had known all their lives as their family home of high summer. They were there on the Sunday morning when the BBC so strangely played a record of *The flowers that bloom in the Spring, tra la* as interlude music to introduce the Prime Minister with his announcement of war. Alah considered that the music must have been specially chosen not to frighten the children. 'I don't think we should talk about battles and things in front of Margaret,' the thirteen-year-old Princess Elizabeth confided to her own small household of governess, nurse, cook and equerry. 'We don't want to upset her.'

The nine-year-old Margaret was confused and apprehensive. 'Why had Mummy and Papa to go back to London?' she demanded of Crawfie. 'Will the Germans come and get them?' She waited anxiously for the reassuring six o'clock telephone call that punctually came through every evening from London and was hardly able to contain herself while first Crawfie and then Lilibet talked to the Queen. Life at Birkhall, however, soon settled down with lessons as usual in that country calm. Day to day, it was like any other summer, except that the stay in Scotland extended into an indefinite future and the children began to feel a deeper sense of separation from their parents. As the tints of autumn deepened, the Princesses would return from their afternoon walk along Glen Muick to find the rooftops glowing with rose in the early evening light, and Mrs Montaudon-Smith, their French teacher, liked to pretend that they were truly princesses in an enchanted castle, with the scream of a power-saw seeming quite like a dragon in the woods.

Princess Margaret discovered with fascination that some of the Canadian lumberjacks working on the royal estate were Red Indians and whenever near their encampment of Nissen huts she looked out for them. Her day was made if they stopped work to give her a friendly grin. There were more mundane visits with her sister to a dentist in Aberdeen, enlivened by shopping in Woolworth's for future Christmas gifts. By arrangement with their equerry-comptroller, Sir Basil Brooke, who gravely presented them with their shilling pocket money each week, they borrowed the necessary cost of a cricket set for the crew of their local anti-aircraft gun. These young soldiers comprised their immediately military defence force, and also came in for their full share of 'comforts' and cakes from the weekly sewing parties in the Birkhall schoolroom at which Alah was hostess. Margaret had the duty of choosing records and winding up the gramophone. The schoolroom in reality was a wooden-walled extension heated only by an iron stove in the middle of the room, and her repeated choice of 'Thy tiny hand is frozen' was highly appropriate.

Adequately warmed by stoves and log fires in early autumn, Birkhall congealed in the frosts and first winter snows. Margaret carefully carried her face-flannel down to breakfast one day to show with great glee that it had really become a slab of ice, and she was soon repeatedly catching cold. The Queen in London heard this with misgivings; fearing that there might be 'a family liability' and remembering the winters of her own childhood when she had been swaddled in shawls and scarves and yet had caught every cold going.

For fresh interest, Miss Crawford and 'Monty', as the children called her, got into touch with the local Girl Guides and arranged meetings in a nearby village hall. The Princesses were puzzled at not always understanding the thick accents of the Glasgow evacuees, the children who had been brought from the city into the countryside for greater safety, and the bewilderment was mutual. Partly to break down this dialect barrier, a nativity play was planned with the Guides in which Princess Margaret would take the part of a child rocking the Holy Infant in a cradle. But at an early stage a rehearsal had to be cancelled when Margaret caught another cold, and then an outbreak of mumps in the village caused the entire plan to be abandoned. With nearly every phone call, however, the Queen seemed to grow more alarmed lest the Scottish winter proved too severe. And then, only seven days before Christmas, her voice was bright as any carol as she announced that, after all, Christmas could be spent at Sandringham.

This was the time of the 'phony war', of the calm — except in the U-boat campaign — as foes and allies prepared for the onslaughts of the future. As if debating the matter with himself, the King mentioned in his diary that many children had returned to the cities, and in February the Princesses went back to Royal Lodge. Attending the little school in Windsor

Great Park, and billeted around the estate, were thirty London children, some so intensely Cockney that they afforded Margaret a new range of Bow Bells mimicry. Her impressions were exact yet kindly, and they were soon 'all sisters together' in a reformed and greatly enlarged troop of Girl Guides. Nine years later, when about to take off for Italy on one of the first flying holidays of her life, the Princess found it a happy augury that one of the hostesses at the airport was a girl whom she had last met 'in camp'. 'Why, hello, Jo. Fancy meeting you!'

II

After several years of every form of news media's over-stressing the happy family life of the King and Queen, it can be counted a blessing in one sense that their daughters were restricted now to an orderly and placid tempo, set to the calm of a seldom changing pattern. They had been exposed to the plaudits of royal processions, flooded with admiration at garden parties, unflinchingly introduced to thousands of strangers. How long could this artificial and unrealistic fervour have gone on without ill-effect on their characters?

Invited to Royal Lodge to photograph the Princesses at this juncture, Lisa Sheridan sensitively recorded her renewed impressions of the two children, 'Princess Margaret had lost most of her charming puppy-fat, though the sparkling little face was much the same ... the younger sister's clever brain and the older sister's lack of selfishness bridging the gap of their ages, Elizabeth the more contemplative of the two, the more reserved, Margaret somewhat older than her years yet still showing a spontaneous self-assurance and a delightfully quick response.' Mrs Sheridan photographed the Princesses with their dogs and ponies and working in their garden 'growing vegetables as well as flowers'. Many people imagined that they had already been sent to the safety of Canada. But when Mr Neville Chamberlain first raised the possibility, it is indeed true that the Queen responded, 'The children could not go without me and I could not possibly leave the King.' Except for a secret plan to fly them out under extreme emergency, the matter was never raised again.

Then on May 10th, 1940, overwhelming enemy forces invaded Holland, Belgium and Luxembourg. Nazi paratroops rained on Rotterdam, and the next day Winston Churchill became Prime Minister of Britain. The seclusion of Royal Lodge could obviously offer little protection against the imminent danger of paratroop kidnapping, and the Queen telephoned instructions that the children were to be taken 'anyway for the rest of the week' to Windsor Castle. This 'country house somewhere in England', as it was styled under wartime censorship, was to be their home for the rest of the war.

Yet Windsor Castle in wartime was a fortress, a haven, not a home, and — as Crawfie recollects — 'we were always very much aware of this'. The furnishing in the larger rooms remained muffled in dust sheets, the glass-fronted cabinets turned to the walls, and there were fixings in the ceilings where the chandeliers had been. The pictures had gone, leaving only their ghost marks, and carpets had been removed as a fire hazard along the stone corridors. Princess Margaret shared a room with Alah in the Lancaster Tower overlooking the park. It took time to acclimatise to the new atmosphere, the footfalls of the guards and air-raid wardens patrolling the passages and cobbled courtyards at night, the depressing low-powered lighting and, later on, the moan of the air-raid sirens.

Princess Margaret was indeed 'nearly ten' in that first early summer of war, and when hostilities at last ended she was within a week of being fifteen. The years all but merge in retrospect, although the different phases of the war were very definite as time went on. The children had been at the Castle only three days when Lilibet could enter in her diary that the first company of Grenadier Guards had arrived. Later, the Castle garrison formed the core of an easy and sociable community. Three officers always came to lunch with the Princesses, and Margaret found she could turn on their laughter as if at a tap. 'If you sat at Princess Margaret's end of the table,' one Grenadier Guards officer recollects, 'the conversation never lapsed for a moment. She was amazingly self-assured, without being embarrassingly so.' Ultimately three hundred officers passed through the Castle during the war years, and Margaret is said to have known them all by name.

In the early days, the first urgent 'red alert' saw the Princesses descending fully-dressed down to a dungeon where beetles scattered away from the lamplight and, later on, bedrooms complete with bathroom amenities were fitted within the Castle cellars. In June they heard the tremor of the guns of Dunkirk, and who did not in southern England? In July they watched one of the dogfights of the Battle of Britain from the doorway of Queen Victoria's favourite summerhouse in the Home Park. Even Alah had not understood the danger of shrapnel from the smoky puffs around the zooming, distant planes in the sunlit sky. There was no need after all to keep talk of battles from Margaret who in her tenth birthday week could read for herself the news of three hundred enemy planes destroyed over Britain. As the hazard of invasion threatened, she took up, without prompting, the calm defiant assumption of every civilian, adult or child, 'They will not come here.'

The Queen's sister, Countess Granville, was staying at Windsor one Sunday when an exceptionally heavy air-raid occurred, as if the Castle itself were the target. The anti-aircraft guns were barking and the Queen — who was staying for the weekend — ushered Alah and the Princesses down to the shelter. 'She made it all rather a picnic instead of alarming.' Another guest was amused by the elegant little cases, one pink, the other blue, which the Princesses carried with their night-things. These were in fact the travelling cases of the two French dolls presented to them from the French people before the war, unexpectedly proving most useful months after the fall of Paris.

At the height of the Battle of Britain, Princess Elizabeth herself suggested that she should broadcast to the children involved in the war. 'Oh, yes, we must!' said Margaret and, as soon as the King gave his consent, she had to be cautioned that it could not be entirely a joint effort. Young as she was, she read the script and 'gave her opinion'. Accepting that it was Elizabeth's broadcast, yet promised that she, too, would play a part, she sat in, quiet as a mouse, at the last two rehearsals. The broadcast was given 'live' from Windsor during the five o'clock Children's Hour on October 12th, in a week when a force of 450 enemy planes had attacked London. 'All we children at home are full of cheerfulness and courage… We are trying, too, to bear our own share of the danger and sadness of war.' So the message went out ultimately, to millions of listeners throughout the world. 'We know, every one of us, that in the end all will be well,' Princess Elizabeth concluded. And then she added, 'My sister is by my side, and we are both going to say goodnight to you. Come on, Margaret.' Margaret needed no second bidding and ended the programme with the words, 'Good night, and good luck to you all.'

At Badminton, where she had taken up residence, Queen Mary's customary self-restraint gave way to tears. In

Amsterdam, the present author once visited the Anne Frank house where, for two years, a young Jewish girl kept her diary while concealed with her family from the Gestapo. Still pasted up at eye level on the wall beside that child's desk are the postcard photographs of Princess Elizabeth and Princess Margaret, her quiet inspiration day by day as she entered up her immortal journal of courage, and just as they were when the Gestapo at last broke in, to take Anne Frank to the concentration camp where she died.

III

At the time of the invasion alert in the summer of 1940 the Queen — the late Queen Mother — was sometimes hard put to conceal how desperately worried she was lest the Princesses should be captured in a paratroop raid and held hostage. She rarely spoke of her fears and I believe that an unexpected telephone call from Windsor only once made her disclose her nervousness and she quickly recovered. The Queen was never alarmed for herself, but she had written separate letters to both her daughters in case anything happened to her. Both the children agitated to be allowed to join their parents in London, pleading that they would be as safe as at Windsor, and they were not told until long afterwards of the bombing of Buckingham Palace. Whenever a warning of 'enemy aircraft overhead' was given while the Princesses were out in the park at Windsor, a tank sped to wherever they were taking shelter. Watching eagerly for this unusual transport, almost keeping a time check, Margaret would cry, 'Here he comes!' Getting the dogs into the hot cramped interior took time and, as Crawfie noticed, Margaret usually tried to be the last inside, risking penalties for disobedience rather than miss seeing anything that might be happening in the sky.

The events of war went on side by side with the prosaic happenings of every day and, as a reassurance during the heavy air raids late that autumn, plans were resumed for the Nativity play abandoned in Scotland the previous year. As before, Princess Margaret was cast as the little child, not at all shy and indeed in her element, and Hubert Tanner, the Windsor Park schoolmaster, leapt with buoyant Welsh enthusiasm, at the opportunity of staging the production in the Castle in the long beamed vista of St George's Hall. His schoolboys made a wonderful procession of shepherds. Princess Elizabeth in a gold crown was one of the three kings, while two London evacuees completed the trio.

The King and Queen could not restrain their tears as they watched their younger daughter singing 'Gentle Jesus, Meek and Mild' all alone before the large audience. 'I wept through most of it,' wrote the King in his diary that night. But Margaret was delighted to learn that a collection plate raised thirty pounds. In an unguarded moment, Crawfie happened to say, 'I almost believe we could do a pantomime' and from that moment, as she noted, 'We had no peace.' Princess Margaret, who seemed to know everything about showbusiness, announced that London producers had to prepare their pantomimes a year ahead. She did sketches of stage-sets and costumes for both *Aladdin* and *Cinderella*. 'Margaret knows what she wants,' wrote Crawfie, 'and she never lets go.' The King readily agreed to the idea, well content with the suggestion that it would help to improve the girls' self-confidence, and so the amusing and memorable Windsor pantomimes became a reality.

'They'll pay anything to see us,' Margaret said, when production costs were discussed. By 'they' she meant the immeasurable crowds of her pre-war memories, the people packed outside Buckingham Palace, the throngs that stared from the pavements, and Lilibet was no doubt the first to point out a wiser perspective. The audience would be drawn from the people around the Castle and their friends, from Windsor soldiers who might be off-duty, the estate workers and landgirls and perhaps a few friends from London who might be on leave. 'Well, it is for the Queen's Wool Fund,' Margaret amended, having already made up her mind that she would be principal girl, and her sister, being taller, 'obviously principal boy'.

These were now the years of intensive food and clothes rationing, and everyone enjoyed the incidental fun of ransacking the Castle for useful items for props, scenery and costumes. Velvets and brocades were found in unlikely cupboards. Band-parts were provided from a Royal Marines store brought inland from Portsmouth. The Queen curbed Margaret's wilder enthusiasms by insisting on economy to help the Wool Fund, and the Princess pointed out in an amusing letter that the lavish production of *Cinderella* was 'regardful of cost and with every expense spared'. As in Queen Victoria's day, the large Waterloo Chamber in the Castle was converted into a theatre seating nearly four hundred. The hire of some necessary costumes from Nathan's produced some unforeseen expenses, but Margaret urged, 'We mustn't skimp for the soldiers.' Lilibet also wished to keep her tights as a souvenir. With the dress rehearsal, each production ran for a week — *Cinderella* (1941), *The Sleeping Beauty* (1942), *Aladdin* (1943) and *Old Mother Red Riding Boots* (1944) — and the Wool Fund benefited from the series by nearly a thousand pounds.

It has often been said that in an ordinary walk of life, Princess Margaret could have become a fashion designer, and for the first pantomime she sent Nathan's her own drawing of a costume which they then precisely copied. When she had to wear a charming Victorian frock, all white muslin and lace, she spent hours going through old photograph albums from the Royal Library to make sure all her accessories were right. Needing a fan as Cinderella, she 'purred with satisfaction', as a family guest said, when her Aunt Marina lent her a fan that had belonged to Marie Antoinette.

Entering her teens, however, the tap-dancing principal girl was in no way the unselfconscious child of the Nativity play a year or so earlier. The first morning of the pantomimes invariably found Margaret almost green with stage fright and excitement, and acutely feeling so sick that she took to her bed. 'But I shall be quite all right,' she reassured Alah, and she always was. One onlooker remembers her in Cinderella's gold coach — in reality Queen Charlotte's original sedan chair — 'looking so lovely that she brought down the house'. Lisa Sheridan who took scores of photographs of every production, made her own private comments in a letter to a friend. 'I don't think Princess Margaret was quite so merry this year. She is taking herself a little seriously but I'm sure *that* won't last! Her ability on the stage is quite outstanding — slick, self-possessed and a really charming voice. She is quite exceptionally musical...'

This was in fact the year when Princess Elizabeth registered for national service under a voluntary youth scheme, being aged sixteen, and her twelve-year-old sister felt herself annoyingly left behind. She was 'pleased as Punch' when her father appointed Lilibet a Colonel in the Grenadier Guards, but one of her cousins felt that Margaret 'detected for the first time some of the difficulties of being a younger sister.' Her mentors, indeed, coped for a while with all the symptoms of going through a difficult phase. 'I was born too late,' Margaret once stormed dramatically, on being told she was not old enough to go to an officers' dance. 'You've no idea what I have to put up with!'

Most of the grown-ups, however, felt that she accepted her junior limitations rather well. If she were spoiled, she was also disciplined to overcome that fault and the wartime difficulties were exceptional. She had long since enjoyed the freedom of a bedroom of her own, and some replanning of the accommodation to give Princess Elizabeth a separate suite left Princess Margaret free to adapt the old nursery as a sitting room. Yet she preferred to share Lilibet's rooms, drifting in and out with gramophone records or settling down there with a book, and reluctantly leaving only when 'outside' visitors were expected. Growing up under clothes rationing, she took it for granted that apart from two new frocks — or the equivalent — a year, she should inherit her sister's wardrobe. Much ingenuity was exercised in suggesting how some outfits could be altered to her own much smaller figure, with sketching and pinning-up to illustrate her ideas. Later on, she contented herself with designing dresses she would like to have 'if only we had the coupons'. But on viewing Lilibet's cast-offs, it became a scathing verdict when she remarked, 'That's not for me!'

IV

There were times when the war atmosphere lightened, and in the late summer of 1941, when the German armies had plunged into the catchpit of the Russian front, the Royal Family snatched a brief holiday in Scotland. Among the Balmoral guests, the Canadian Prime Minister, Mr Mackenzie King, gives us a picture of a picnic at the Queen's little cottage on the moors, 'only two rooms, one used as a sort of dining

room with a little table in the centre, the other the kitchen with a huge open fireplace with equipment for cooking food. The Princesses had gone on ahead to arrange the tables, with lettuce leaves for decoration, quite pleased with everything they had done to make things look nice. There were no servants...'
None were necessary, with the tables laid and the King's two daughters happily heating a kettle over the brushwood fire for the washing-up. When the King wished to go out walking with his guest, Margaret took it as her social responsibility to see them off, suggesting to the Canadian visitor that he would surely wish to see a little more of the countryside.

Lunch at Balmoral Castle next day proved harder going and the Princess did her best to lighten the atmosphere, 'entertaining in the way she laughed at different subjects', as Mr Mackenzie King solemnly chronicled. 'She tried to amuse others and made her eyes looked crossed: the Queen and later the King told her to stop for fear they might become fixed.' Yet she succeeded in making the table talk rather more casual.

As if by instinct, she could mask her father's preoccupation, her mother's occasional fatigue, even her sister's rare timidity. If the King were in carefree mood, she could reduce him at times to helpless giggles. Portraying every scrap of Castle gossip with a cavalcade of mimicry, she could entertain him by the hour, but would switch off her vivacious mood like a lamp at any sign that he needed to deal with official business. His scarlet leather boxes arrived one day when the photographer, Mrs Sheridan, was present. Turning over the papers, he 'very earnestly' explained one document to Princess Elizabeth and 'the Queen and Princess Margaret meanwhile sat silent with their books and knitting'. For the King the personalities of his daughters were complementary, two sides of a coin.

As his biographer, Sir John Wheeler-Bennett, has said, 'in Princess Elizabeth King George saw certain of his own traits: his own combination of humour and dignity, his common sense and eagle eye for detail.' His younger daughter had 'the same quick mind and with it a vivacious charm, a sparkling sense of wit, an appreciation of the ludicrous. She it was who could always make her father laugh, even when he was angry with her.' Yet she could talk with him most seriously at times: there was nothing she felt they could not discuss, even to his innermost view of the arts of statecraft. It frequently troubled him that Margaret was deprived, even more than her sister, of the companionship of youngsters of her own age with whom she would have been good friends but for the social dislocations and separations of wartime. He shared her pleasures, riding, music, card games such as Lexicon, whenever he had the time, but always felt concerned about the problem of finding more friends for her.

It was a great event, for instance, when Pamela Mountbatten reappeared at Windsor after being at school in America. She added a transatlantic verve to the Guides, and shared a tent with Margaret during the camping weeks. The two girls couched down with their sleeping bags in a summerhouse during a night of thunderstorms, vied in baking cakes and scones for their cookery badges and practised unremitting cajolery on their elders until the Frogmore boathouse with its dinghy became an official base for a Sea Rangers unit.

The Guides, it must be said, usefully provided Margaret with a nucleus of giggling companionship and extra scope for larking about. Crawfie was persuaded one morning to press the Castle alarm bell, with wonderful results. Bells rang everywhere, and the courtyards and passages filled with running soldiers, although everyone took for granted that it was a routine drill. Another time, when the Guides were cooking sausages, one of the terrifying Nazi V1 guided missiles came trundling over. Everyone threw themselves to the ground, as they had been drilled to do, and Crawfie flung herself across Margaret but the 'bomb' passed low overhead and exploded harmlessly on the racecourse some miles away. 'We've been under fire,' said Margaret, not without satisfaction. 'Doodle-bugs are fired, are they not?'

Presently the formation of a Madrigal Society also played a sort of social counterpoint to the pantomimes. Mrs Montaudon-Smith took pride in the high standard of the singing, some of the young Castle officers joined the group and a few boys came over from Eton, among them young Angus Ogilvy, a certain Willy Smith (4th Viscount Hambleden), Lord Hertford, Colin Tennant, and Douglas Montagu, a nephew of the Duchess of Gloucester. Yet they were mostly considerably older than Margaret: the invitations, for instance, rarely included any Eton newcomers, and so passed over Antony Armstrong-Jones, not six months older than Margaret, who was in his first term in 1943.

The Duchess of Kent gave small parties and gramophone dances at Coppins now and then, and Princess Margaret is amusingly chronicled 'tethered to a young officer in a three-legged race'. Then there were 'clump parties' at Windsor, for which Miss Crawford had the task of compiling equal lists of young men and girls for charades, treasure hunts, games of 'sardines' and dancing ... with Margaret sometimes torn between the piano and her partners. In the guest lists can be found names such as Billy Wallace, Lord Blandford, Peter Ward and so on, friends later to shine in the widely-chronicled sociabilities of the group of young people later known as the Princess Margaret set, a good-natured and pleasant, well-born and well-meaning, monied yet not leisured set, it seems, on looking back. But these were as yet the early stages of acquaintance, and the closer friends were still with Lilibet's group. 'Did you have a happy Xmas?' Margaret wrote from Windsor Castle in 1943. 'We did. Philip came! On Xmas eve we all had dinner together. There were nine of us only.' By the following evening, Philip's cousin and later best man, David Milford Haven, had joined the group and, Margaret recorded, 'He and Philip went mad. We played charades, clumps and then we danced and danced until one o'clock. It was the best night of all … we danced four nights running.'

She was very much thirteen at the time, a teenager, elated at staying up later, and so it was all the more disconcerting, early in the New Year, to find that Lilibet would soon join the ATS, sharply relegating her sister, yet again, to junior status. 'Margaret was very cross' noted her governess, though it was later 'a great treat' to be entertained in Lilibet's mess at Camberley. Amused at the heartiness of the lady officers drinking sherry and smoking, she returned with a repertoire of fresh mimicry impressions. The younger Princess decided, too, that khaki uniform was not particularly becoming. On the next visit to Balmoral, the King gave Lilibet a first lesson in the finesse of deerstalking and lent her a pair of his own plus-four trousers. Margaret comically pretended to be jealous, resentful and horrified. But she thought shooting unfeminine and considered that the plus-fours looked 'not at all nice'.

Keeping up with Lilibet indeed still presented insoluble problems, the age gulf inelastic as ever. When Lilibet, aged eighteen, drove off to the ATS, Margaret, rising fourteen, was appeased only by being allowed to undertake her own first solo public engagement, accepting purses on behalf of charity from girls of the school named after her in Windsor. A month or two later, while the King visited his troops in Italy, Princess Elizabeth was appointed one of the Counsellors of State to undertake certain of his nominal duties in Britain. 'Now I'm floored, I'll be put in my place,' said Princess Margaret, good-humouredly, but was concerned for her sister on learning that one of the documents in the red dispatch box had concerned a murder trial, 'a rather haunting one'. She keenly enjoyed accompanying Elizabeth on extra official duties to airfields and so on, 'supporting Lil', as she privately called it. Scouring the newspapers for photographs of the event, she often found herself cut out of the picture, usually owing to shortage of space. 'I've been censored again,' she would clown, acting comic mortification. But her sister saw the hurt behind the comedy, and a round robin went to Fleet Street, 'Please do not cut Princess Margaret out of pictures unless unavoidable.'

Elizabeth learned to drive, and Margaret, too, had lessons on the private roads of Windsor, but the younger girl now unmistakably went through her school lessons alone. There was a bookworm phase when she was seldom without a book or magazine in her hand, reading at high speed, and remembering everything almost indelibly. Taking tea with 'the happy little family group', Field Marshal Alanbrooke noticed that the King's younger daughter 'remained on the sofa reading *Punch* and emitting ripples of laughter at the jokes'. *Carnival, Ivanhoe, David Copperfield*, the novels of Angela Thirkell and Evelyn Waugh were all omnivorously devoured.

Then the last of the rocket bombs fell upon Windsor Park and suddenly, after the years of endurance, the months of suspense, the war ended. The sirens had always been a signal to halt any German lessons and now Margaret excitedly flung all her German books to the floor and declared she would never learn another word of Hitler's language. On Sunday May 6th,

1945, instead of waving goodbye as usual to her parents when they returned to London, the Princess discovered that incredibly she would be going with them. As they arrived at Buckingham Palace, workmen were placing loudspeakers and flood lamps in the forecourt. There ensued a day of uncertainty before the Allies could fix the hour of final surrender. And as ever in such great moments of history the people of London converged on the Palace, clamouring for the King and Queen.

Looking from the Palace windows on the Tuesday, the Princesses felt they had never seen such multitudes. For Margaret it was like the dimly remembered scenes of her childhood, of the Coronation. The cheers grew deafening when Churchill's car arrived, while she watched the police struggling to make way for him and kept up a commentary from a curtained window, 'They can never do it!' Then the crowds parted and began singing 'Happy V.E. Day to you!' After lunch the Royal Family went out on the balcony, again and again, to face the rejoicing tumult. 'We went out eight times altogether during the afternoon and evening,' wrote the King. 'We were given a great reception.' Then he added that Lilibet and Margaret had gone out after dark in the care of two young officers to see what they could of the excitement and enjoy themselves in the crowds. 'Poor darlings,' the King closed his wartime journal. 'They have never had any fun yet.'

It was a night of nights. With no more disguise than scarves and old country coats, the Princesses went down the Mall to Trafalgar Square and round to Piccadilly, quite unrecognized in London's mood of delirium. Like everyone else, they ducked under the chains of linked hands formed by the revellers, watched air-raid shelter signs blazing in impromptu bonfires and joined in little groups of song.

There ensued an interlude of rejoicing when Margaret found it hard to concentrate on her school books in any language. The two sisters joined their parents on the State drives through the hard-bombed areas of East and South London, and Margaret saw for the first time all that the war had meant in the destruction of homes and the dogged endurance of the people. They rode to the Service of Thanksgiving in St Paul's Cathedral, receiving a wonderful ovation, and journeyed to Edinburgh for similar celebration in St Giles'. Undertaking her own programme of duties, visiting schools, hospitals and Army camps, the Queen was now frequently accompanied by her daughters, and occasionally by Princess Margaret alone, as if for a graduate course in royal duties.

Then, on August 15th, the King and Queen drove to Westminster accompanied by their daughters, to open the first peacetime Parliament. The Princesses had already attended a ceremony under the ancient oak beams of Westminster Hall, and perhaps vaguely remembered a visit to the Houses of Parliament in childhood; but this was Princess Margaret's first visit to the House of Lords to take part in the memorable procession of the State Opening and to take her seat, composedly, in a chair of state to the left of the Thrones. She was just six days short of her fifteenth birthday. Moreover, August 15th was also V.J. Day, marking the cessation of hostilities in the Far East and thus the first day of total peace for the whole world after the six years of war. That afternoon the Princesses appeared with their parents on the Palace balcony but, after nightfall, they bettered their Arabian Nights adventure of V.E. Day by slipping out of the Palace and cheering the King and Queen from the heart of the rejoicing throng outside.

'It was absolutely wonderful,' wrote Princess Margaret. 'Everybody was knocking everybody else's hats off, so we knocked off a few, too. Everybody was absolutely marvellous… I never had such a beautiful evening.'

V

At Balmoral late that September Princess Elizabeth suffered one of her rare riding mishaps, being heavily thrown against a tree, so severely bruising her legs that she could scarcely move. Her chief concern was her inability to attend a youth rally near Aberdeen, and fifteen-year-old Margaret deputized for her, not merely reviewing a march-past of 4,000 young Scots on Dyce airfield but also capably making a speech to a prepared script which she had both rehearsed and revised. On returning to London, the King must have mentioned this effective debut with pride when dining at Marlborough House with Queen Mary and the Duke of Windsor. This was his first meeting with his exiled brother since the Abdication, and the safe topic of his daughters must have relieved some of the embarrassment of the conversation.

Princess Margaret was then at Glamis, visiting her Uncle Patrick, Lord Strathmore, and so, on this occasion at least, they did not meet — the former King who had relinquished his Throne for love nearly ten years earlier and the Princess, his god-daughter, who ten years hence was to relinquish love for duty. (Undiscerned as in a mirror darkly was also the underlying significance of the fact that the Princesses that November attended the christening of the younger son of Wing Commander Peter Townsend, the ace RAF fighter pilot who was fast becoming the King's favourite 'Equerry of Honour'.) But perhaps Queen Mary, nearing her eightieth year, confided in her granddaughter some of the bygone family emotions of the Windsor affair and explained her own life's dedication of 'putting my country before everything else.'

The old lady and the impressionable — and irrepressible — Princess companionably went about a great deal together that autumn, both equally overjoyed at being in London, visiting exhibitions and picture galleries, all such a novelty to the young girl who had been immured so long at Windsor. They found a mutual interest in 'unpacking the palaces', with the excitement of constant discoveries of recognition as the furnishings and treasures of the royal residences emerged from the packing cases in which they had been stored through the war. A friend has told of Princess Margaret singing in her richest 'village choir voice', plunging her hands into the wood shavings and dusting fine pieces of crystal and china with her handkerchief as she unpacked. The dismantled rooms of Buckingham Palace and Marlborough House all invited exploration and, at the Palace, Margaret loved to carry off some small object, a bibelot, a lamp, a picture, back to her own room for an hour or two just to try the effect.

In the midst of these pleasures she fell ill, and was in such pain late one night that the doctors had to be summoned through the fog. Her health had often caused concern, but now appendicitis was diagnosed and an operation was imperative. A royalty of today would be rushed to hospital, but grand traditions still lingered and surgeons and nurses of the Great Ormond Street Hospital performed the operation in her own room. In that pretty pale-pink ambiance the Princess was soon sitting up in bed, reading her well-wishing letters and enjoying the 'hoosh-mi' — a mix-up — of cards and telegrams that began to make 'a great mound' on her large round table. After a short convalescence at Royal Lodge, she quickly regained her high spirits and had her impressions of the doctors, nurses and more officious visitors perfect as ever in imitations to entertain the family. Her grandmother defined her as *espiègle* — mischievous, arch, roguish — in confidences to her old friend Lady Airlie. 'All the same,' Queen Mary added, 'she is so outrageously amusing that one can't help encouraging her.'

Lady Airlie was at Sandringham to welcome the New Year of 1946 and alertly enjoyed 'the new atmosphere', the King begging 'Meg' to turn down the blaring radio, the jigsaw puzzles set out on a baize-topped table in the hall, and the younger members of the party, the Princesses and 'several young Guardsmen congregated round them from morning to night.' It was amusing to hear the King say 'You must ask Mummy', as any father would, or to see Margaret's pout if sent back to the house to 'put on a thicker coat'. Only upstairs, in Queen Mary's rooms — or perhaps in the little sitting room where everyone visited 'Alah' (Mrs Knight) — was it possible, wrote Lady Airlie, 'to recapture the past'.

The old nanny had always been part of Christmas and New Year for as long as anyone could remember, but of late she had tired easily and on the evening of January 2nd she did not stay up to watch the country dancing. The strains of 'Hicky Hoo' and 'Sir Roger de Coverley!' rang through the house and to the echoes of the old music Alah quietly slipped away from this life, as she would have wished. Only her untouched breakfast tray next morning conveyed the truth, and Princess Margaret wept for her, not knowing how strangely the circumstances presaged the death of the King six years later.

5: THE TEENAGE INTERLUDE

Our family, us four, the 'Royal Family' must remain together, with additions of course at suitable moments!

King George VI, *November 1947*

I

It was difficult for King George VI to realize that his daughters were growing up. He had not long written to King George of Greece that Princess Elizabeth was still too young to think of marriage when he learned that Prince Philip had found a London lodging at the Mountbatten house in Chester Street, and there were soon 'high jinks' in the Palace corridors. The Princesses and their distant cousin raced about like a bunch of high-spirited children, as Mrs Buthlay, the former 'Crawfie', remembers. The card slotted into the door of Princess Margaret's suite still bore the word *Nursery* and Philip replaced it with another card announcing *Maggie's Playroom*. There was often dinner for three in the 'playroom', with hours of jazz and dancing, unless their elders thoughtfully summoned Margaret away on one pretext or another.

She was still very much the young sister, 'fond of Philip in an entirely sisterly fashion', Crawfie noted, yet anxiously concerned, too, to take up her own royal tasks in the post-war world. Early in 1946 the King was mildly astonished when she showed him an invitation from the Save the Children Fund for her to visit some of their London centres ... and with it, for his approval, her own draft letter of acceptance. There was no question here of merely deputizing or touring the settlements

84

on a 'private' visit. Delighted at undertaking her first public duty in her own right, and accompanied only by Lady Delia Peel as lady-in-waiting, she charmed the Labour mayor of St Pancras, delighted the Socialist aldermen of Bethnal Green, said all the right things at the 'Hopscotch Inn' and other youth centres, made happy little jokes to the children and returned flushed with success. This was on March 26th, 1946, and she was not yet sixteen.

Next morning Margaret was again the student, sitting down as usual to her schoolbooks, again content to play her everlasting role of second fiddle, and she seemed very small and young indeed when accompanying the uniformed Lilibet and a considerable group of army officers around the overseas military encampments in Hyde Park. She was also an extra onlooker on the royal dais close to the King for the spectacular march of all the Commonwealth contingents in the victory parade, and in the autumn an extra passenger during the speed trials of the liner *Queen Elizabeth*, when her mother steered the great ship over the measured mile. In April, in the private chapel at Windsor, there had also occurred the ceremony of her confirmation into the Church of England, a renewal of baptismal vows which she regarded with deep seriousness, greatly impressing the Archbishop of Canterbury, Dr Fisher, during his talks with her, by the personal quality of her firm religious faith. Sources of strength were developing within her personality of which few outside the family were ever aware, and concealed beneath the froth of gaiety was an ingrained pertinacity and courage.

Sir Dermot Cavanagh, who controlled the royal stables, once stood watching the Princess exercising a difficult horse over the jumps at Holyport. She was thrown heavily and remounted and was thrown again. 'This can't go on,' said Sir Dermot, but before he could dissuade her she had remounted and was thrown a third time. From the corner of her eye the Princess saw that the exercise was about to be brought to an end, but she picked herself up, caught the horse and this time took the jump and went on at a canter. Passing Sir Dermot, she flashed a triumphant smile that spoke volumes.

With more leisure at Royal Lodge, the King and his younger daughter often went riding together, while Lilibet that summer usually preferred long walks with Philip in the recesses of the park. The King's scheme of appointing young war heroes as 'equerries of honour' had been wound up, but two of this select band still remained, 'the two Peters', cheerfully ready among other duties to squire or escort the Princesses when needed. Wing Commander Peter Townsend was the better rider, but openly anxious at times to get home to his wife and children at Adelaide Cottage. Lieutenant Peter Ashmore, who had won the DSC for his gallantry in a destroyer naval action was a bachelor of twenty-five, an enthusiastic tennis partner and a keen fisherman who did his best to initiate Princess Margaret into the subtle techniques of the Dee. When the Princesses wished to arrange an impromptu theatre party of eight to see *The First Gentleman*, a play about the Prince Regent, Peter Townsend excelled at the art of charming seats out of an apologetic management who claimed there was not a seat in the house. Peter Ashmore shone in the detailed work of organizing a large and congenial party for an Army pageant; and Major Harvey, the Queen's secretary, commended him as 'always so reliable'. On a rainy afternoon in Edinburgh, Princess Margaret proposed 'Let's go to the pictures' and leafed through the newspaper to hit on a film called *Scarlet Street*. Neither of the Princesses had ever been to a public film show, and Peter Townsend obligingly took them into the two-and-nines. It would not have been Ashmore's scene.

For Princess Margaret the freedom of being able to go to a play was perhaps greatest of all the exhilarating new pleasures of peace. She discovered the theatre with rapture, from the wit of *Private Lives* to the marvel of Olivier and Richardson in *Henry IV* at the Old Vic. Wartime security had forbidden even visits to the little Theatre Royal in Windsor town but, of a sudden, all the horizons were expanding fast. In February, 1946, the royal box at Covent Garden was packed for the re-opening gala performance of the Sadler's Wells ballet *The Sleeping Beauty*, a theatrical event hailed as a symbol of post-war recovery, and none watched the youthful Margot Fonteyn with more ardour than Princess Margaret. A week or two later she saw another performance with her governess and indeed returned a third time with such unquenched enthusiasm that the family teasingly dubbed her 'Margo'.[2]

In quite another field, the Princess coaxed the King into reviving the 'royal command' variety performance, and the staff of the Coliseum Theatre showed their appreciation of the royal visitors by pooling their ration points to buy a huge presentation box of chocolates. At the ceremonial moment, alas, the bottom fell out of the box and the chocolates cascaded on to the floor. 'May I have one?' the Queen instantly asked, to soften the blow. 'Oh, goody,' echoed her younger daughter, kneeling to help pick up the chocolates. 'They'll be none the worse, you know, for a tinge of glamorous theatre dust.'

---

[2] A nuance of the production escaped us at the time, in that the scenery and the decoration of roses that embowered the royal box had been designed by Oliver Messel, uncle of Lord Snowdon.

Wartime shortages were to continue for years under the softer, more palatable guise of 'austerity', and Margaret wore her first very own evening gown — as distinct from Lilibet's hand-me-downs — only a week or two before her sixteenth birthday when she first went out dancing at the Savoy and displayed 'a very very good rumba'. The Royal Family had been invited to visit the then Dominion of South Africa early in 1947, and the question of whether they should be allowed extra clothing coupons was solemnly discussed in Parliament. The South African Wool Board stepped in to present the Queen and the two Princesses with two outfits each, of their own choice. Whereupon, in concert with Norman Hartnell, Margaret set down her design ideas for a coat and dress of peach-pink wool which, if not her first practical essay in *haute couture*, was certainly the first to be generally discussed and widely copied.

II

A reigning monarch and his consort had never before left Britain, together with the two next in line to the Throne. They were sailing into waters not yet exempt from the risk of floating mines, and Princess Margaret impishly conjured up visions of the four of them adrift on a raft. Wildly excited as she was about every prospect ahead, some of her elders considered it just as well that she had quietly to get through a great deal of reading about every place she would visit. Her mother asked her to list some of the films that should be taken aboard and said to an Admiralty adviser, 'Margaret will know as well as anyone.'

The largest and newest battleship afloat, HMS *Vanguard*, was adapted and equipped to take the twenty-nine members of the royal party, and when the warship sailed from Portsmouth on

February 1st, 1947, the Princess could hardly wait to escape from public view and inspect her cabin, delighted to find real portholes and eager that everyone should see the pretty effect of the rosebud green chintz, a pattern she had chosen herself. And for a time it was a joke of the two Peters that this was almost all she did see, for they quickly ran into rough weather and in the Bay of Biscay the battleship 'stood on her stern'. Waves lashed the portholes, and indeed some of the cabins were flooded. Sensibly advised to take it lying down, Margaret retired to her bed, a divan-bed matching the one in Lilibet's cabin next door. 'I tried to hold the bedpost,' she said, 'and there wasn't one.'

It was no comfort to learn that the three ladies-in-waiting — Lady Harlech, Delia Peel and Margaret Egerton had formed a 'crisis rota'. 'I for one would willingly have died,' Lilibet wrote home. 'I wasn't actually seasick but everything hurtled about so much. I found my eyes gave out and it was exhausting trying to keep one's feet. However, as soon as I could stand upright without too much effort, I was perfectly all right.' Hearing that her mother was playing Chinese Checkers, holding on to the pegged board with one hand, Margaret said, 'Well, if Mummy can, I *must*,' and all the royal group presently struggled up to the saluting platform to acknowledge the untimely courtesies of the passing French battleship *Richelieu*. From the Canaries however Margaret wrote that the sun was shining and that she had her sea legs ('How does one fix them on?').

'The officers are charming, and we have great fun with them,' wrote Lilibet in turn. 'There are one or two real smashers ... and three delightful Scottish subs!' The two Princesses delighted the ship's concert with their party songs, and there were lively deck games, especially deck tennis and tag; while the King preferred to rest, encouraging Margaret to amuse him at the piano. She feigned extreme nervousness at the Crossing the Line ceremony, as a novitiate who had never before left Britain, but on biting at Neptune's order into a cherry 'made of soap' it proved delectably to be the real thing. The King worried about the privations his people were enduring at home, in a winter of blizzards and fuel shortage, and Princess Margaret tried to console him, 'They couldn't even send us a snowball.' Lilibet was alarmed on studying the impending South African programme. 'It is absolutely staggering how much they expect us to do and go on doing for so long at a stretch. I hope we shall survive, that's all.' But at Cape Town their first impression was of crowds all in white formed up on Signal Hill to spell the word Welcome and Princess Margaret — 'the youngest lamb to the slaughter' — began a fresh series of impetuous and vivid letters home to her friends.

The Governor-General, Major Brand van Zyl, and his staff wore 'the vastest smiles' on discovering that the Princess spoke a little Afrikaans: she had, in fact, been coached in London and had dutifully observed daily study sessions aboard *Vanguard*. It was by no means a minor accomplishment, and initial Dutch Nationalist scowls melted in smiles as the tour progressed. The Princess had already learned from her mother the good sense of scanning beyond the immediate crowds, with the result that while inspecting Basuto Girl Guides she noticed a group of lepers sitting apart in a bus and thereupon visited them with Lilibet, an unexpected gesture against superstition that gained wide praise. At one of the racecourses it was felt that the Princesses would seem stuffy if they did not visit the betting-ring, and Margaret's subsequent dance of triumph proclaimed that she had not only placed the first bet of her life but had moreover backed the winner.

In those days, the 10,000-mile itinerary would not have been possible without the special White Train, with its fourteen coaches, the longest, heaviest and most luxurious train ever run on the South African railways. At one point, the two Princesses were duty-bound to don dustcoats and scarves and ride a few miles on the footplate. Lilibet found it sufficient to sample the dirt and noise; but Margaret politely asked the driver if she could come again, and later wrote with ecstasy of a long musical ride when she had sole charge of 'pulling the whistle'.

An early sightseeing visit was paid to an ostrich farm where the Princesses were shown how to cut soft white feathers for themselves from under the wing, 'like clipping the trees at Royal Lodge!', wrote Margaret. A display of 5,000 Zulu warriors became, in her own words, 'a kind of dance-past', culminating in a tribal rush towards the royal dais when the warriors flung themselves down 'just in time'. After flying in a plane for the first time in her life, on a trip with her father in the Northern Transvaal, she reported with delight that their aircraft had been dented by colliding with a vulture. At a firework display, the sparks fell so close that they burned a hole in Lilibet's dress as if, in Margaret's comic imagination, they were being prepared for burning at the stake.

From the Rand she wrote of her longing to go to a goldmine and her disappointment that this was not on the programme, but it was soon proved that her powers of persuasion had lost none of their guile. The Easter rest-break offered a free day and the Princess described the adventure of descending one of the deepest shafts in the world, looking down through binoculars two hundred feet farther to where the miners at the lowest level were singing at their work like a heavenly choir. Ten days later, in Rhodesia, the Princess found herself drenched in warm spray, a swimsuit under her dress, walking through the rainforest to view the spectacle of the Victoria Falls, 'a burning bubbling mass looking rather like a cold hell.'

This was the most northerly point of the tour. The journey through Africa had occupied fifty days, including the 'lost days', as Margaret impatiently termed them, when she alarmed her parents by developing a temperature of 102 and reluctantly had to stay in bed under doctor's orders. But there were the delectable days also beside the Indian Ocean, when the Princesses went out riding along the sands in the early morning with the two Peters. The four-day return train journey to Cape Town seemed to pass in a flash, the tedium forgotten in the discussions and reading for Lilibet's twenty-first birthday dedication broadcast in Cape Town. Princess Margaret listened thoughtfully and is known to have suggested amendments. 'If we all go forward together with an unwavering faith, a high courage and a quiet heart, we shall be able to make of this ancient Commonwealth, which we all love so dearly, an even grander thing...' There are echoes perhaps of the toast to England from Noël Coward's *Cavalcade*, which Margaret knew by heart and could recite with moving conviction.

Yet the tour had been desperately arduous and fatiguing and when the Royal Family returned to England on May 11th, their appearance shocked their friends and kinfolk. The King and Queen appeared worn out, Lilibet was thin and drawn, but 'Margaret looked ill and tired out, the worst of them all' and Miss Crawford was 'quite horrified' and 'secretly very anxious about her', as she wrote at the time.

III

While all the world took an interest in Princess Elizabeth's romance with Prince Philip, Princess Margaret nevertheless returned to her 'finishing' studies with a new serenity, arriving for lessons with her pens and pencils in the same pencil box she had used as a child and sitting down with her books with an obviously enhanced enjoyment of those quiet morning hours. Proposals that she should study constitutional history under Sir Henry Marten, as her sister had done, were brought to an end by that old gentleman's illness, but instead she contentedly embarked on the broader waters of European history and literature: constitutional history had always been more in Lilibet's line. Margaret took great pride in being Princess Elizabeth's younger sister, watching the official side of her work with an admiration totally devoid of envy, but apparently her own position as second in succession to the Throne seldom crossed her mind.

In South Africa she had beamed with an onlooker's pleasure when her sister was presented with a square casket of twenty-one fine diamonds as a twenty-first birthday gift, and the next minute was utterly astonished and delighted when given a round casket of diamonds of equal quality for herself. Lilibet found it difficult to decide how her stones should be mounted, with the result that alterations were being made to a necklace many months later, but Margaret sketched her own designs on the homeward voyage on *Vanguard* and produced very definite ideas for a necklet in readiness for the jeweller.

It was a happy link that her own 'seventeenth summer' coincided with Elizabeth's betrothal. She was more woman now than child and responded to her sister's happiness with a tender and intuitive understanding. 'Poor Lil,' she once murmured, at the early stage when engagement rumours were being denied. 'Nothing of your own. Not even your love affair.' These few words have become well known, and her attitude was sympathetic and compassionate in turn. She knew when to disappear tactfully and welcomed the invitations from her Aunt Marina, from the Duke and Duchess of Marlborough, Viscountess Hambleden and others just then, enabling her to keep out of the way.

Things were different when Lilibet and Philip went out in a group, to the theatre and perhaps to Giro's or the Savoy afterwards, and Margaret leapt at the opportunity of fun. There was an unwritten rule that the party should break up at midnight, and Jean Nicol, of the Savoy publicity, noticed with amusement that, as the Cinderella hour approached, the younger sister would choose to dance with her tallest partner 'with downcast eyes and hidden by his protective shoulders' while Carroll Gibbons at the piano ran through a mélange of her favourite songs. Musicians were not infrequently puzzled at her knowledge of the dance scene. 'It's very simple,' said her elder sister. 'She sleeps with the *Melody Maker* under her pillow.'

Miss Crawford still considered that her young charge was not strong and tired easily, though she would never admit to tiredness. Margaret, on the other hand, felt that Lilibet undertook too many public duties, leaving too little leisure to spend with Prince Philip, and she never wearied of persuasive argument that some of the 'little jobs' could be diverted to herself. 'When you've passed your driving test,' the King would say, turning his daughter's own trick of making light of everything. Her test was however undertaken at Balmoral with Mr George Scott, chief testing officer for northern Scotland, shortly after her seventeenth birthday and the L-plates were removed with good-natured family celebration.

It had in fact been arranged long beforehand that in October Princess Margaret should visit Northern Ireland to launch the liner *Edinburgh Castle* at the Harland and Wolff yard. Princess Elizabeth had launched her first ship, the *Vanguard* itself, when eighteen (the same age as Princess Anne, for those who enjoy such comparisons, when she similarly named a Tyneside tanker). At Belfast airport she was welcomed by the Earl and Countess Granville, the Governor-General of Northern Ireland, and his wife, who was of course her Aunt Rose. The liner was to serve on the Cape run, and it is said that the Princess herself proposed that the ship should receive its baptism with South African wine, a neat sequel to her African journey, and so it was. The event was also graced by another regal and poetic touch which was 'distinctively Margaret'. Spotless in white overalls, the youngest of all the shipbuilders, a fifteen-year-old joiner's apprentice named Tommy Smith, shyly presented a bouquet of roses, and for a puzzling moment the Princess seemed to fumble with the bouquet. Then she placed a single rose in the young lad's buttonhole. The resulting cheers were tremendous.

With this decisive debut, lessons petered out. On her seventeenth birthday, the King had appointed his younger daughter Colonel-in-Chief of the Argyll and Sutherland Highlanders, the first of her military distinctions, and as the Princess was quick to point out, a C-in-C could not still sit in nursery class. There was suddenly so much to do in preparation for Lilibet's wedding. Besides, Crawfie herself had been quietly nursing a romance throughout the war years until she decided that the Royal Family could at last spare her; and in Scotland in September she was married 'without fuss' to George Buthlay, an Aberdeen bank manager, 'Governess beats Liz to the altar,' proclaimed an American headline.

Princess Margaret said, 'I intend to continue brightening your life, Crawfie,' and chose three bedside lamps as a wedding present. The governess agreed to stay on while still needed, and her pupil was instrumental in finding Nottingham Cottage, an enchanting little redbrick house at the back of Kensington Palace, which the King gifted on a grace-and-favour lease. Meanwhile, Margaret pondered the riddle of just the right wedding present for Lilibet. She was, needless to say, to be chief bridesmaid at her sister's wedding, but what could she usefully give, amid the jewels and silver, the crystal and porcelain ... something that had to be 'perfect and happy'? 'I've thought of something Lil needs and doesn't have,' she mysteriously hinted, and the solution to the riddle proved to be a picnic set.

In some degree all the family joined in opening the presents as they arrived, and the old schoolroom became snowy with tissue paper. Dr McKee, the Abbey organist, found the two sisters singing part-songs together in 'a cavern of wedding gifts'. Princess Elizabeth particularly wanted her wedding music to include a descant of *The Lord is my Shepherd*, which she and Margaret had often sung, and the two sisters hummed and played it over and over, while the organist took it down note by note to get it right.

Norman Hartnell similarly noticed how charmingly the younger sister deferred to the bride-to-be. Princess Margaret always knew her own mind in matters of fashion, but preferred to say nothing on seeing the designs of the bridesmaid's dresses until the other seven bridesmaids had been consulted. There were indeed some suggested amendments and the dresses, in Mr Hartnell's description, 'were finally made of ivory silk tulle with a full flowing skirt and a tulle *fichu* swatched across the shoulders... On the skirts a milky way of small starshaped blossoms repeating the motif of the bridal train.'

Though carried manfully by the two small pages, the Princes William of Gloucester and Michael of Kent, that train, fifteen yards long, caused trouble. The pages proved unequal to the task as the newly-wedded pair were about to walk down the aisle, and Princess Margaret hurriedly stepped forward to take the middle of the hem until her two young cousins recovered. 'I just had to help the wedded pair on their way,' she said afterwards, gleefully exaggerating, to Queen Alexandra of Yugoslavia. But behind the small-talk and laughter of the wedding reception, practised bridesmaid as she was, she had found herself more moved by the ceremony than she dared to confess.

At the end of the day, tired and a little doleful, she returned to the familiar upstairs rooms and sighed, 'I can't imagine life here without Lilibet.' Then she added, with a flash of her usual spirit, 'Ah, well, Papa and Mummy need me to keep them in order. What would they do without me?'

IV

Happily, the disconsolations of youth are quickly forgotten, and the solitudes rarely noticed, except by perceptive elders. A visit to Sandringham served to fill the interlude, for Margaret, of Elizabeth's honeymoon and, although she made fun of the menfolk 'popping horrid guns at silly birds,' she enjoyed the off-duty atmosphere of easy sociability. In London she adored helping Crawfie to get straight in her new Nottingham Cottage, singing about the rooms and 'making many a useful suggestion', as the governess found, on colour schemes and arrangement. Just across the green, outside the garden gate, was a small formal double-fronted house with the number '10' on its front door, shabby as so many houses still were more than two years after the war, and yet undeniably fascinating. The Princess admired it as the kind of house she would like to live in, and little guessed it would one day be her first married home.

The charm of Kensington Palace, moreover, seemed at its best early in 1948 when Elizabeth and Philip moved for two or three months into the Clock House, borrowed from Princess Alice of Athlone, who was absent in South Africa. It was fun to go to tea with Crawfie and then to dinner with Lilibet and Philip — and highly novel to find her sister also installed at least nominally in a house of her own, with some of her wedding gifts around her. Now that Princess Elizabeth was married, she was accorded on all sides the deference due to the Heiress Presumptive, and it was noticeable that Princess Margaret treated her sister with enhanced respect, with less of the old teasing and none of the mimicry, often discreetly changing a subject rather than give a pert reply as of old. Far from the frivolous girl of the public image, some people about the Court considered Margaret level-headed beyond her years.

When the hunt for a suitable permanent London establishment for Princess Elizabeth presently narrowed to Clarence House, the elder sister first inspected the dilapidated old mansion with her husband and then toured it again with Margaret, who immediately immersed herself in furnishing magazines and was soon tireless in ideas and suggestions. Clarence House was 'quite ghastly' and 'replete with labour-making devices', and yet Philip could walk home down the Mall from the Admiralty and the views from the upstairs windows were among the best in London. When Margaret knew that Elizabeth was going to have a baby, she was briskly solicitous, urging her to wear comfortable flat shoes *and* put her feet up. Watching the mother-to-be exercising the corgis in the Palace gardens one day, she chided reprovingly, 'Really Lilibet, you mustn't run with the dogs like that. Not now!'

Princess Elizabeth did not retire from public engagements until June, while Princess Margaret lost no time in adopting a maxim of 'It's up to me now', proclaimed less in words than by her own considerable official calendar. She busily opened exhibitions, visited schools and charities, named ships, presented Colours to RAF cadets, adopted patronages — and she was still only seventeen. An American magazine enhanced its global circulation with an article 'The Blooming of Princess Margaret Rose' which asserted 'She is Britain's No. One item for public scrutiny. People are more interested in her than in the House of Commons or the dollar crisis', and this was no more than true. Her official solo royal visits ranged from Bath, where the huge crowds broke the police cordons, to a more workaday visit to open a trade exhibition in Sheffield. The King, in giving consent to this early emergence into adult activities, had needed little persuasion. Looming on the royal horizon for 1949 was a projected visit to Australia and New Zealand by the King and Queen and their youngest daughter, which made Margaret all the more eager to gain every crumb of public experience.

Yet she was not strong. She caught cold too readily and had a tendency to blinding headaches, of which the public knew nothing. On an official visit to Glasgow she went through the ceremony of accepting the Freedom of the City on behalf of the Highland Light Infantry in spite of an intense migraine and, although some lesser events were cancelled, she resumed her duties later in the day much to the concern of those who could see she was still in pain. Two months later, she had a severe attack of measles and pretended dismay that her two nursing sisters came from the Great Ormond Street Hospital for Sick *Children*. The nurses had expected a spoiled and difficult patient and were completely won over, taking merry lessons from her in Scottish reels when she was convalescent and joining a happy tea party at Nottingham Cottage. 'She's a charmer, a sweet, considerate person,' one of them privately said afterwards. 'Why does one ever believe mere gossip?'

Next, the Princess suffered a bout of acute fibrositis, her neck held rigid, 'first a child and now a cripple', as she ruefully claimed. The public rumour was that she had caught a chill while sitting out at a dance. But the chills of the English summer were professionally more suspect, after a weekend visit to Windlesham Moor, the country house not far from Windsor which Elizabeth and Philip had rented until Clarence House became ready.

Whenever her programme thus went awry, Princess Margaret made a point of apologizing by telephone or letter to everyone thought to have been inconvenienced. Although her engagement book was filled, most of her official correspondence was handled by Princess Elizabeth's secretary, John Colville, and she had no staff of her own except her personal maid, 'Ruby' MacDonald, younger sister of Lilibet's 'Bobo'. Even her dress expenditure derived from the £1,000-a-year bequeathed her a year or two earlier by the Queen's friend, Mrs Ronald Greville. Three more years were to elapse before the Princess received an official Civil List income of £6,000-a-year. But on August 21st her eighteenth birthday was celebrated with a family picnic on Loch Muick and the King jocularly mentioned that in recognition of growing up he proposed to ask her to undertake a special mission the very next month to represent him in Holland at the installation of Princess Juliana as Queen of the Netherlands.

The surprise secret had been well kept, despite the advance travel arrangements that had to be made and some amusing subterfuge around the timely birthday gift of a glamorous white fur wrap. Princess Margaret was overjoyed, both at the nature of the task and her first opportunity to visit Europe.

Confident and far from shy, her official duties could still cause 'a sick feeling in my tummy, just as before our pantomimes', yet this adventure was pure pleasure. Her suite included her sister's lady-in-waiting, Lady Margaret Egerton, and the King's equerry, Peter Townsend, who was always good fun.

They flew out in a plane lively with wedding guests to find the road into Amsterdam lined with crowds in a gala mood, and the Athlones were waiting at the deluxe Amstel Hotel to greet her arrival. The Princess was delighted with her first glimpse of the spires and domes of the city, and that evening the Dutch royal family took their guests for a cruise through the mesh of illuminated canals where every building and every tree sparkled in floodlighting. Next day, Princess Margaret was principal guest at the investiture banquet, wearing for the first time the diamond and pearl diadem given to her by Queen Mary barely three weeks earlier. And still there followed a wonderful day of sightseeing, a visit to Delft, an Aaslmere flower auction, a glimpse of the Rembrandts at the Rijksmuseum. The Dutch were delighted with their guest, and the Duke of Beaufort reported home on 'how beautifully the Princess carried out her duties ... how composed and dignified she was.'

Yet she returned to a number of family anxieties. She fussed and worried around Elizabeth, regardless of calmly reassurances that there were still two months to go. She became deeply concerned about her father, who for some months past had been troubled by an increasing numbness in his left leg and was now on the point of consulting his doctors. There were family activities, implied in visiting old and ailing friends of her mother, which never became public news. In her eighty-first year, Queen Mary seemed to depend upon her very much for news of Lilibet, and meanwhile Margaret prepared eagerly for the Australian tour, her taste for travel considerably whetted.

There was also the pleasure of being bridesmaid to Margaret Egerton at her wedding at St Margaret's to John Colville, a match which Princess Margaret enthusiastically felt she had fostered. At the Palace the pulse of family life had never beat stronger, and Princess Elizabeth had consulted Princess Margaret, as well as her parents, on the chosen names for the new baby, Charles for a boy and Anne if a girl. Early in November the Queen was to have unveiled a window of remembrance in Westminster Abbey and at the last moment had a severe cold, and Princess Margaret deputized for her, placing the traditional cross also in the Field of Remembrance on the Abbey green. Then the Princess left London to fulfil engagements in Yorkshire and on Sunday November 14th was staying with the Earl and Countess of Scarborough at Sandbeck Park near Rotherham. It was a congenial weekend party, the son and four daughters of the house being mostly all of her own age group, but Princess Margaret is remembered 'constantly dithering around the telephone'. A celebration beacon ready for lighting had been piled in the grounds. And then at about 9.30 p.m. the news came. 'Hurray!' said Margaret, turning from the phone. 'I'm Charlie's aunt now.'

They stayed in the house to hear the BBC news bulletin and, curiously, the announcer giving the news was the same John Snagge who eighteen years earlier had announced the birth of Princess Margaret. Prince Charles was christened in the Music Room of Buckingham Palace a month and a day later, with Princess Margaret as one of the sponsors. And to be the baby's godmother was, she said, her proudest title of all.

6: THE PRINCESS MARGARET SET

Princess Margaret was simply dressed. But already she is a public character, and I wonder what will happen to her? There is already a Marie Antoinette aroma about her…

Henry (Chips) Channon, *18th June 1949*

I

In the Royal Ascot race-week of 1949, this disarming social diarist, Mr 'Chips' Channon, found himself among the house-party guests at Windsor Castle and noted that 'there must have been 50 or 60 people, mostly young friends of Princess Margaret.' The Queen, he added, 'though unfortunately very, very plump, looked magnificent in a white satin semi-crinoline … and the King had his foot up on a footstool to rest, though he seemed quite well and often danced.' Three months had elapsed since the King had undergone the operation to improve his circulation which first caused public alarm for his health, and later that year Chips commented that 'the King now dotes on society and parties'. It was as if the ailing monarch drew new vigour and resilience from his beautiful younger daughter and all the young people whom she now drew about her.

Early on the Saturday morning of the operation, the Queen and her daughters had taken Holy Communion in the Chapel Royal, St James's Palace, and in a characteristic letter Princess Margaret wrote, 'When Papa decided he could no longer struggle to keep going, he went to sleep for two days.' Yet she nowhere mentioned her intense disappointment that the projected Australian tour had been cancelled. Her mother had taught her always to look on the bright side, and instead of the tour the Princess presently found herself with an unforeseen reserve of free time, 'a positive ocean of unrestricted hours', as one friend remarked.

When her father grew 'tired and bored with bed', as he said in a letter to Queen Mary, Margaret had her old piano strategically placed near his door and played to him by the hour. As soon as he could walk a little, she remarked, 'It's a blessing I'm not very tall. I make a good walking stick.' She entertained him one evening with an hilarious account of having her fingerprints taken at Scotland Yard: she had no criminal record, but when she visited them, the police had obliged. On turning eighteen and being accorded her first lady-in-waiting, the choice fell on Jennifer Bevan — later to become Mrs John Lowther and one of the Princess's closest friends — who was then only twenty-two and found agreeably that her 'waiting' included adventures that had hitherto never found space in the schedules. The Princess wished to see a Fleet Street newspaper 'put to bed', and so they visited the old *Daily Graphic* offices late one night to watch the whole process, the reporters tapping out their stories, the clamour of typewriters and telephones, the compositors setting type, and finally to hear the urgent roar of the presses. No member of the Royal Family had visited the Central Criminal Courts since they were first opened, but Margaret and Jennifer sat behind the barristers' table in No. 1 Court at the Old Bailey during a murder trial. They visited the House of Commons, and the Speaker in his wig and gown met them in the lobby to conduct them to the Chamber.

Above all, after the King's safe recovery, Princess Margaret gratified one of the burning ambitions of her life by visiting

Italy. Queen Mary had always painted a glowing picture of her own girlhood travels when she had gone picking flowers in the Florentine hills or sat eating 'brown cherries brought by peasants'. The modern reality needless to say, was not like Grandmama's reminiscences at all. The Italians fell into a fever of excitement at the prospect of seeing *La Bella Margherita*. When the royal aircraft touched down at Naples, the young Princess was greeted by the President of Italy; the Prefect and Mayor of Naples; the British Ambassador, Sir Victor Mallet and his wife; the Italian Air Force band and a full guard of honour.

Such courtesies were unfailingly due to a King's daughter in those years after the war. Her own suite of five, with Jennifer Bevan, Major Tom Harvey (the Queen's secretary) and his wife, Lady Mary Harvey, a personal maid (Robina MacDonald) and a detective, seemed scarcely that of a private visitor. And if the State reception was daunting, when Margaret climbed to the roof terrace of her hotel to enjoy the famed view of the Bay of Naples, from smoky Vesuvius to the hunched rock of Capri, she saw that the road was packed with police and photographers, and beyond them, at the mere distant glimpse of her, a dense crowd of waiting sightseers began to clap and cheer. Her own first sightseeing drive in Naples involved speeches and presentations and signing a Book of Honour. She wrote home, however, of being serenaded by *Santa Lucia*, comically followed by *You are my Sunshine*. The Isle of Capri proved to be something of a dogfight between carabinieri and cameramen. In the Blue Grotto she laughed on discovering that two or three swimmers accompanying the boat were neither guides nor guards but press photographers.

In the vaulted alleys of Capri town, she took in good part the police swarming everywhere — and, despite their protection, the bouquets impulsively thrust into her arms. One develops a sixth sense of sightseeing, despite the press of people and the flash of photo-bulbs. One afternoon Lady Mallet plucked a rose for the Princess but caught her hand among the thorns and, at the risk of missing a picture, a photographer gallantly went to her aid. Noticing the incident, Margaret rewarded him with a special pose.

The Rome newspaper, *Giornale d'Italia*, complained that she was seeing nothing but the backs of policemen, instead of the beauties of Italy; the Italians themselves cursed the police and reporters and within a few days, with the help of the Princess's unsparing smiles and patience, matters improved. Gradually the Italian holiday in the hot May sun became all she had hoped. She had longed to see Sorrento, Amalfi, Pompeii, the temples of Paestum, and spoke afterwards of being 'absolutely enchanted'. Other official ceremonies awaited her, but she seemed to the Italians to impart to them her own poetic dignity. The roses given to her amid the ruins of Pompeii were laid on a grave in the cemetery of British and Canadian troops killed at Salerno.

In Rome, Princess Margaret had been invited to a private audience with Pope Pius XII and welcomed the prospect. Queen Mary had been similarly received at the Vatican, and no new precedents were established, although some Protestant voices seized the opportunity 'to deprecate and deplore'. Rome was inevitably a feast of sightseeing. (In the countryside, a restaurant proprietor, alerted by Thomas Cook's, prepared a royal menu. But Margaret asked to see the kitchen and there observed the traditional pot of haricot beans and macaroni for the staff. Richer dishes were declined, and the Princess had two helpings.)

The Communist mayor of Florence rightly judged the spirit of his citizens when he presented the royal visitor with a bouquet of orchids, but among them she also carried a nosegay given her by a child. Inevitably, Venice was encapsuled in the news heading 'Serenades and Gondolas', though Margaret made a point of visiting Torcello, on which Philip had enthused so much. As it chanced, the battleship *Vanguard* lay off the Lido, and the Princess attended Divine Service on deck and stayed to lunch with the officers, among them many old friends of the South African cruise.

And so to Stresa on Lake Maggiore and over the Simplon Pass to the Lake of Geneva, where she visited the romantic Castle of Chillon and stayed for a night or two with Queen Victoria Eugenie of Spain, who was living in retirement at Lausanne. Queen Ena irresistibly remembered the rather lonely young girl whom she had once invited to tea at Claridge's, enquiring if she would prefer to have it upstairs in her apartment or downstairs in the salon. 'Oh, downstairs, please,' Margaret had responded eagerly, 'where I can see the people.' 'She has blossomed out deliciously,' wrote the Queen. 'What a success she will be in Paris!'

Still the same at heart, the outwardly sophisticated Princess indeed chose to travel on the midnight train to Paris in order to sample the delights or otherwise of the *wagon-lit*. Margaret wished also to seem Parisian to the Parisiennes. Jennifer Bevan had telephoned ahead to ask the British Ambassador's wife, Lady Harvey, to recommend a hairdresser, and they went straight from the Embassy to a coiffeur in the Rue St Honoré. A photo session in the Embassy garden was followed by lunch with the President and Madame Auriol at the Elysée Palace — Margaret 'with so much to tell', to the delight of her hosts. Into the rest of the day was crammed a reception at the Canadian

Embassy and a ball that night at the British Embassy, where she danced happily until 3 a.m. Next day, fresh-eyed, she was at morning service at the English Church, made an excursion to Barbizon for lunch, and explored the Ile de la Cité before going early to bed.

And so Princess Margaret saw Paris, from Notre Dame to the heights of Montmartre. She went to Versailles, where she was particularly charmed by the elegant Petit Trianon, returned to visit the British Hospital and still had time to attend dress shows at Jean Dessès and Christian Dior. The fashion writers noted appreciatively that for nine public engagements she wore nine different outfits, and her final day was spent unashamedly shopping, her most obvious purchase a large teddy bear for the little Prince Charles.

II

After only five weeks' absence, and a brief weekend with her parents at Midhurst, Miss Bevan was startled at the business that had accumulated. There were plans for Princess Margaret to undertake a tour in Lancashire, from Manchester and Salford to St Helens, Warrington and Wigan. There were proposals for her to launch a tanker at Wallsend-on-Tyne, to inspect a Sea Ranger training ship at Portsmouth, to visit schools in Canterbury and a children's home in Sussex, and to attend the 'Camp Fire' of the world conference of Girl Guides. All these engagements were to be duly fulfilled and many more. The Princess spent a happy afternoon opening her 'welcome home' mail, and from one end of the Palace to the other sped Elizabeth and Philip's written invitation for their house-warming at Clarence House. While working with Lady Alexander at Government House, Ottawa, Jennifer Bevan had learned the art of slotting every prospect into a convenient pattern, and for two or three years — indeed, until her marriage — all the intricate threads of the Princess's life flowed through her fingers, like silk to a loom.

There were some friendships, just then, that sparkled more brightly in the firmament than others, and some six or seven friends whom the telephone switchboard could always unhesitatingly put through. The bright American voice of Sharman Douglas, the daughter of the US Ambassador, was never refused. Two years older than Margaret, the blonde Sharman had breezed into London for a holiday with her parents at the Embassy, a vacation, so to speak, at the Court of St James's, and had quickly scrapped her intended two further years as a Vassar college girl in exchange for a morning secretarial course at Queen's College, which would keep her in London. 'Sass', as her friends called her, had the considerable gift of treating the Princess as an equal, though greeting her with respect. Over coffee in her own room at the Embassy at Prince's Gate, they could be ingenuously 'two girls together'. Fleet Street also found her approachable: she had a smoothly deceptive technique of chatting blandly about the Princess, although in fact she never betrayed a confidence.

Sass lacked the inhibitions, widely shared till then among the royal cousinhood, that made it plebian to go to see the Crazy Gang except for the royal charity performance, or to book seats to see Danny Kaye at the Palladium. After the show, Sharman marched her friends right into his dressing room, and Margaret added an impersonation of Danny Kaye to her theatrical imitations. She persistently urged her parents to see the show until, to humour her, the King said he would order the royal box. 'But you can't see properly from there,' said Margaret. 'It's much better in the stalls.'

Sharman's father, Mr Lewis Douglas, similarly possessed an incautious social verve, rare among ambassadors, which rapidly won him the friendship of the Royal Family, and the news of a fancy-dress party at the Embassy rang round the world with an absurd air of scandal. Prince Philip, Lord Milford Haven and Princess Elizabeth went dressed as 'The waiter, the porter and the upstairs maid', Philip capered about in his role wearing a dapper French moustache ... and Princess Margaret danced the can-can. To be precise, eight young ladies, Sharman and Jennifer among them, lined up in the most decorous can-can ever performed, their high kicks merely knee-high. 'May I? Does it matter?' Margaret had asked the Queen, and had been reassured. Danny Kaye was enlisted to teach them the steps. The Offenbach music was authentic. 'Rehearsing was more fun than the show,' said Sharman. 'We were giggling all the time. But it wasn't going very well until Danny helped out.' It was at best no more than an amateur party piece. Yet unexpectedly the headlines blazed and in thousands of suburban homes youngsters countered parental strictness by claiming, 'Look what Princess Margaret does!'

The Palace did not subscribe to a press-clipping service, and the Princess only casually saw the news and gossip printed about her, although a newspaper comment occasionally made her pull a rueful face. 'You must grin and bear it,' advised an older friend. 'It's the penalty for being a princess,' and many of the 'unrealities' made her laugh. 'Look into my eyes,' she advised a dance partner, 'The *Express* says they're the most beautiful eyes in the world.' Pirouetting before one of the large mirrors in the powder room at the Savoy, she enquired in Jean Nicol's hearing, 'Now what fur would you say this coat is? The papers always get it wrong.'

Later on, it was said that Sharman Douglas had been a founder member of 'the Princess Margaret set', but one doubts whether this collective phrase was coined until the 1950s; and it flourished, with its undertone of asperity, only after Elizabeth came to the Throne. For the gossip columnists it provided a facile definition of Princess Margaret's close-knit coterie of friends, though over-focused on the late-nighters, 'drinking champagne and eating cocktail canapes,' the supper parties, and particularly the 'escorts', all of whom were made to seem suitors to the Princess's hand. As Princess Elizabeth's romance faded, for the public, into the equilibrium of married life, intense speculation developed around every 'eligible bachelor' sighted within talking distance of her sister.

'Who CAN She Wed?' ungrammatically demanded the now extinct *Sunday Dispatch*, thereupon listing the Earl of Dalkeith, the Marquess of Blandford, Mr 'Billy' Wallace and a quartet of also-rans. While *Life* emphasized to its five million subscribers the diversities of Lord Ogilvy 'taking her to a fox-hunt', Tom Egerton 'escorting her to the races', Mark Bonham Carter 'at a ball', Julian Fane 'taking her to the opera' and Michael Tree 'going with her to church'; the young men pretended not to notice the cameramen or columnists, chivalrously endured the conjectures, and shrugged at these more difficult aspects of the pleasure of accompanying the King's younger daughter.

The incessant and varied rumours were a new phenomena of royal reporting, much followed and discussed, even if news values had rarely been stacked upon such fragile foundations. The King's press secretary, Commander Colville, who regarded his role as one of protective reticence, rarely issued a denial or rebuke, except when the Princess was said to have visited a disreputable nightclub which in fact she had never been near, and minor mistakes accrued by default to the mass of royal folklore. It was widely supposed, for instance, that Princess Margaret could not marry a commoner. In consequence, the studious Prince Henry of Hesse found himself pictured in every picture magazine in Europe after squiring his distant cousin for a night out in Rome. Romantic eyes were turned on young King Michael of Rumania on the slim basis that they both bent their heads over the same theatre programme. In reality, Margaret found him 'exceptionally hard to talk to'.

In this insubstantial whirl of nonsense, the constant stress was on 'suitors' and 'constant companions' (of the opposite sex) with seldom a mention of Princess Margaret's women friends, or of any serious purpose. There were young women whom she had known since childhood, such as Laura and Katharine Smith (Lord Hambleden's daughters), Rosemary Spencer-Churchill and Lady Elizabeth Cavendish. There were the daughters of Sandringham neighbours, such as Lady Anne Coke, from Holkham, and friends stemming from families who were three-generation friends of royalty, as with Lady Caroline Douglas-Scott, the Duchess of Gloucester's niece (and sister of the young Earl of Dalkeith). There was Rachel Brand, a banker's daughter, who devoted a great part of her week to volunteer hospital work, and whose brother married Laura Smith. By way of Coppins introductions, Margaret was also drawn to Judy Montagu, seven years her senior, who like Rachel came of a banking family and had developed great gifts of fund-raising for charities, always glowing with ideas which the Princess found irresistible.

One may create a false impression in listing these diverse personalities as Princess Margaret's friends, if we omit to mention that the Princess was their friend also, equally playing her own part in the give-and-take, the magnetic attraction and mutual support of friendship. Colin Tennant, son of the chemicals and shipping magnate, Lord Glenconner, first made her acquaintance during the wartime Windsor and Eton sociabilities, an unconventional schoolboy who found Princess Margaret an unexpected sympathizer in youthfully radical views. Simon Phipps, son of an honorary Court official — an old naval friend of the King — and cousin of Joyce Grenfell, was briefly posted to Windsor with the Coldstream Guards, and it may be that conversation with the forthright younger sister clarified his views upon one day entering the Church. (He was subsequently a chaplain at Trinity College, Cambridge; an industrial parson in Coventry and Huddersfield, and later Bishop of Horsham and Lincoln.) Princess Margaret seemed unconvinced when I once mentioned that she had inherited her mother's genius for friendship. Yet there are glimpses of the same virtuoso flair for people, the same responsive delight in their idiosyncrasies, and one considers the Princess has always felt particularly drawn to those who have undergone some Balzacian buffeting of fate.

Billy Wallace, for instance, had faced the tragic death of his father, the highly regarded politician Captain Euan Wallace, and within the next three years, three of his brothers were killed in the war, and the fourth died shortly afterwards. Too young himself to enlist in the Services in wartime, he worked in an aircraft factory and later served as a post-war Guards officer. He had however suffered from childhood from a liver complaint, and few of the gossip paragraphs mentioned the amount of time he compulsively devoted to the Invalid Children's Association. Happily his mother — a daughter of Sir Edwin Lutyens, the architect — was married in 1945 to Herbert Agar, the American historian. Margaret was among the early young guests at their home in Sussex, and Billy Wallace remained one of the Princess's staunchest friends.

The so-called Princess Margaret set, then, was never the whoopee-making assembly of young 'men about town' and 'gadabout girls' of popular legend. In so far as any generic link existed, it was a group of young men and women well-born, wealthy, the majority at the beginning of their careers and vocations, fond of dancing — and perhaps enjoying themselves best of all in making up a table together at a charity ball. Their pleasures would seem tame enough by present standards. Even Queen Mary, that rigid upholder of the highest royal standards, raised no eyebrow of objection, except to comment drily on the health and beauty hazards of late nights. Probably the old lady heard with affectionate amusement that Dominic Elliot, the grandson of one of her ladies-in-waiting, had taken Margaret to supper at a Soho restaurant, that Mark Bonham Carter had partnered her at the 400 Club, and indeed she took for granted the preponderance of the grandchildren of her own lifelong friends in her granddaughter's circle: the descendants of the Gore sisters (the Ogilvys and Hambledens), of the Tennants, of Herberts and Devonshires. One gained a sense of *déjà vu*, so close was the pattern.

In the early 1920s the newspapers had bristled with rumours that the Queen's daughter, Princess Mary, was to become betrothed to the Earl of Dalkeith. In the 1950s, the headlines seethed around his son, a successive Earl of Dalkeith, for whose companionship Princess Margaret was said to have cut short her Scottish holiday. The fogs of rumour centred upon the New Year house-party at Sandringham, and crowds of romantic-minded onlookers were densely packed around the church on Sunday. The headlines overflowed prematurely with the gush of a royal betrothal. But the much watched guest, it transpired, was more concerned with presenting his future wife, Miss Jane McNeill, later the Duchess of Buccleuch, whose engagement to him was announced not long afterwards.

And so what happened to 'the Margaret set'? They married, they settled down, they grew older, and each followed their paths of separate destiny. In 1951, when Lord Blandford married Susan Hornby, and the playwright, William Douglas-Home, married Rachel Brand, I noted in my personal journal, 'One sees now that Princess Margaret is as skilful a matchmaker as her mother', a conviction fully confirmed when Lady Anne Coke married Colin Tennant, and again perhaps especially in 1965 when Billy Wallace married Elizabeth Hoyer Millar, whom I believe he first met at a function for the Invalid Children's Association. Her sister, Annabel, was subsequently the Princess's lady-in-waiting, and in 1973 married another acquaintance of the Princess in Mr Christopher Whitehead.

III

Princess Margaret moved from her teens into her twenties through her galaxy of young company and, as she once insisted, 'through sneezes and spots as well'. Influenza prevented her from taking part in the festivities of the State Visit of President Auriol of France in 1950 and German measles laid her low soon after the official visit of King Haakon of Norway in 1951. The frequency of her colds became a continuous joke with her father in pretending that 'we are both very prone'. Yet my notebooks depict the usual schedule of formal royal activities, visiting Barnardo homes and Sunshine schools, taking part in a royal tour of Cornwall, accompanying her mother on a four-day visit to Northern Ireland, and so forth, with little hint that there were occasionally physicians in the background. And the bygone repetitive events filled her calendar more regularly than the theatre and dance parties on which the Fleet Street gossip columnists so continuously relied.

'Have a good time while you're young,' said the King, and the Queen echoed, 'We are only young once. We want her to have a good time.' With her appreciation of the ludicrous, Margaret would cheer her father up with a lively account of events. Touring the Ideal Home exhibition she was trapped in a lift which refused to budge further than two feet from the ground, and the lattice doors similarly remained firmly closed. 'We were near the food counters,' she said. 'I was hoping the people would pass us sandwiches through the bars.' Before going to the theatre with Mark Bonham Carter she mentioned that they would be having supper after the show at Joyce Grenfell's flat above a shop in the King's Road, Chelsea. 'Well, it's *my* road,' said the King, 'but will you find the flat all right?' The Princess repeated her chauffeur's instructions, 'It's above a sweet shop near a bus stop!', highly amusing the King with visions of his daughter searching for sweet shops.

The birth of Princess Anne in August, 1950, caused some light-hearted conjecture beforehand lest the baby should create Margaret doubly a maiden aunt on her twentieth birthday, but in fact Anne was born on the morning of the 15th, and Prince Philip arrived at Balmoral in time to join in Margaret's birthday celebrations the following weekend, armed with the developed reel of his own first family snapshots of her little niece.

'First a boy and then a girl, heavenly!' Margaret intimated to a friend and, early in December when the young parents were in Malta, she flew out to visit them and help arrange some of their own domestic treasures in the Villa Guardamangia, which they were planning to make their settled island home. Lilibet was full of ecstatic stories of her cruise to Greece on the frigate *Surprise*, and there was a proposal from Queen Frederica that

Margaret might also enjoy a visit but the Princess regretfully felt that 'one couldn't leave Papa just now'. She flew home to Sandringham in time for Christmas, exhilarated with the fun of travel, but the King was unwell, and racked through the early months of the New Year by a troublesome cough. At the opening of the 1951 Festival of Britain exhibition on the south bank of the Thames, his appearance and obvious fatigue caused public concern. 'The incessant worries and crises through which we have to live got me down properly,' he wrote to a friend.

There is evidence that he tried to lessen the anxieties of his impressionable younger daughter by concealing the true state of his health, so far as he knew it. With an easy mind, she drove out one night to a fete at the Hurlingham Club, gaily urging the chauffeur to hurry, 'We don't want to miss the fireworks.' Thanking her acting hostess, the Duchess of Devonshire, she said, 'It's been wonderful fun. I'll tell my father about it. He's much better tonight.' But the doctors had detected 'a shadow' and inflammation in the left lung, and in reality the King had no idea how ill he was. The link between cancer and tobacco was not then generally realized, and Princess Margaret herself smoked, albeit decoratively with a cigarette at the end of a long jewelled holder. The fact that this indulgence was reserved for private occasions led to a press inquisition on the vexed question — did she or did she not smoke? — until at a public luncheon it could be reported that she had indeed accepted a light.

The undeniable beauty of the Princess at twenty is evidenced in a thousand news-shots and photographs: youthful loveliness has never been better documented. The King liked to have the newspaper pictures marked up and pointed out to him; he would smile at the more absurdly flattering captions or read them aloud with clowning emphasis, and yet was secretly proud that his daughter had the gifts of glamour, innovation and style that won public admiration. He was pleased when someone mentioned that Margaret's ankle-strap shoes had started a minor boom in the leather trade. He evidently winced at a bare-shouldered Dior evening gown, and the Princess mollified him by later wearing it with shoulder-straps. Deeply admiring the taste and chic of her Aunt Marina, it may be true that she complained, 'I can't really be elegant, but wait till I'm thirty.'

Norman Hartnell nevertheless took great pains with a strapless crinoline-skirted dress for the Princess's twenty-first birthday at Balmoral, 'the prettiest dress we have ever made'. Decorated with delicate gold flowers of sequins and tracery in flecks of mother-of-pearl, the design foreshadowed like an intuitive dream her sister's Coronation gown of not two years later. Yet one recollects also that the birthday party was deliberately quiet, with only the closest personal friends, and ten days later the King's doctors were urgently summoned to a consultation.

A week later, after fuller examination and X-rays, their patient was told that a blockage of one of the bronchial tubes necessitated the surgical examination and possible removal of his left lung. So far as we can tell the King was never aware of the truth of his condition, and neither of his daughters fully knew it at the time. While the Queen attempted to conceal her anxiety and suspense, the operation was to take place at the Palace on Sunday September 23rd; and the family travelled south on the 18th, except that it was agreed that Princess Margaret should remain with Charles and Anne at Balmoral. In reality, she found she could not endure being so far away at such a time, and accordingly flew to London on the Saturday.

Early next morning she drove with her mother and with Elizabeth and Philip to pray for the King's recovery in the chapel of Lambeth Palace.

When Margaret returned to Scotland to rejoin the children at the end of the week, it was taken as a favourable sign of the King's recovery. In fact, he was strong enough after four days to sign the warrant authorizing the Queen, Princess Elizabeth, Princess Margaret, the Duke of Gloucester and the Princess Royal to be appointed Counsellors of State. The Edinburghs were however due to leave on October 8th for a long-projected tour of Canada, and it was decided that the journey should not be postponed. Both the Queen and Princess Margaret were at London airport to see them off. For five weeks both mothered the royal children, and when the King was able to leave his room, 'Aunt Margo' and Nanny Lightbody ensured him a peaceful afternoon by whisking the noisy small fry off to Coppins.

The Duchess of Kent (Princess Marina) was shocked to see how thin and wan her niece had become, and only then realized how much the King's illness had taken out of her. The Duchess knew how deeply the Princess longed to revisit Paris, and sympathetically proposed a recuperative holiday there, just for a few days. Reluctant as Margaret was to leave her parents, the prospect had to be sugared with a pretended need of official engagements, attendance at a gala ball in aid of the British Hertford Hospital and the diplomacy just then of accepting a luncheon invitation with President Auriol at the Elysée Palace. Marina's sister, Princess Olga, who lived in Paris, revelled in ensuring the smooth running of the arrangements and, shortly after Elizabeth and Philip's return home, Margaret and her aunt flew to Le Bourget in a Viking of the King's Flight.

Once transplanted across the Channel, the Princess of course enjoyed it all tremendously. She had determined to catch up on the sights missed on her first visit, a breezy trip to the uppermost open deck of the Eiffel Tower, lunch in a Left Bank restaurant, visits to art exhibitions, a shopping expedition and finally a supper party with Prince Paul and Princess Olga at Maxim's. She returned bright-eyed and refreshed, not least to cheer her father with a lively account of having tea in Paris with General and Mamie Eisenhower, American style, cream or lemon.

When the Royal Family settled at Sandringham for Christmas, and the New Year of 1952, it was with a false sense of security. 'An operation is not an illness,' said the King. 'I am all right now.' There were comforting plans ahead for a convalescent voyage to South Africa aboard the *Vanguard*, sailing on March 10th. At the end of January they all briefly returned to London, the King to see his doctors, who were pleased with his progress, and the Queen and their daughter enjoyed the dress fittings of their new summery frocks. On January 31st Elizabeth and Philip were to be seen off on the first stage of their intended tour to East Africa, Australia and New Zealand, and on the previous evening, as a *bon voyage* party, they all went to see the musical *South Pacific* at Drury Lane.

On the afternoon of February 5th, while the King was out shooting, the Queen and Princess Margaret visited Edward Seago's studio at Ludham, returning with a painting which the Queen wished to consider on her easel. That evening, with a few friends, they sat together relaxed and contented. Princess Margaret played the piano a little until her father turned on the radio to hear the commentary of the welcome given to Elizabeth and Philip in Kenya. Then the King went to his room along the corridor while the Queen and Margaret took their guests to the ballroom for a movie show.

In the morning it fell to Sir Harold Campbell, the King's equerry-in-charge, to tell the Queen that the King had died in his sleep, a task she made curiously easy. She went to the King and, after giving instructions that he should not be left, she went to Princess Margaret's room. 'I never knew a woman could be so brave,' Sir Harold wrote that night to his wife.

7: THE QUEEN'S SISTER

The rigid left arm, draped and unseen, represents her unshakable strength; the right arm her volatility and impulsiveness.

Pietro Annigoni, *on his portrait of Princess Margaret, 1957*

I

After the initial abandonment to desolate grief, it was noted by one of the King's Household that the Queen Mother and her daughter stayed close to each other, often slightly leaning towards one another, as if sharing strength and encouragement. The Queen Mother began writing letters and encouraged Princess Margaret to follow her example. The Rector of Sandringham, the Rev H. D. Anderson, came to kneel in prayer with them and was struck by the fact that each had separately sent him a message to pray for the Queen. The difficulties of telephone communication with the new Sovereign at Sagana Lodge, in Kenya, proved to be all but insuperable, and mother and daughter each wrote a letter to the new Queen to be handed to her on arrival in Britain.

From the first, Princess Margaret found her own sheet anchor in the thought of what her father would have wished her to do. When her self-control faltered, she still schooled her hands and eyes to the task before her 'as if there were two people, not one'. On the second day, so far as emotion allowed, she listened to Mr Churchill's broadcast on the late monarch, 'He was sustained by the sincerity of his Christian faith. In the end death came as a friend.' On the third day, in the late afternoon, when the Queen and the Duke of Edinburgh arrived at Sandringham, Princess Margaret curtsied to her sister for the first time as Queen, and then the two sisters and their mother went slowly up the staircase out of sight.

About an hour later, in the February dusk, the Queen and her husband, with the Queen Mother and Princess Margaret, walked behind the estate wagon that conveyed King George VI from his Norfolk home to the little church in the north-west corner of the grounds. The Princess now knew what she had to do: to help the Queen, to comfort her mother, and in public, whenever possible, to show the calm certitude of her religious faith. This deep and abiding certainty was to carry her through the prolonged and grievous journeys with the funeral cortège, from Sandringham to Wolferton station, and again through London and from Buckingham Palace to the all but overwhelming beauty of the Lying-in-State in Westminster Hall. The Princess shirked nothing. On February 14th she stood with the Queen and the Duke of Edinburgh, almost unnoticed in the shadows at a side door, watching the silent flow of the people past the catafalque of their King. And on the next and last day she stood behind her mother during the committal in St George's Chapel, Windsor, before they returned home to Royal Lodge with all its memories.

Dr Ansell at Sandringham had prescribed sedatives which, I am told, his young patient did not always take in case her mother should need her. 'To think I have to wait so long before I see Papa again,' she wrote to one friend; and to another, 'Life has seemed to stand still'. Simon Phipps, that old friend, then a curate in Huddersfield, was a helpful correspondent, who then visited London to share the consoling philosophy and unashamed prayers that he knew she craved. He may have noticed, as others did, that messages of condolence were tendered by Parliament to the Queen, to the widow and to the bereaved Queen Mary, but neither publicly nor directly to the younger daughter. Yet all her friends who had seemed to the unthinking world so facile and shallow now truly proved a sure source of strength and comfort.

Lent was drawing near, and when one of her circle recommended a series of eleven half-hour lectures which were being given on Monday evenings at St Paul's, Knightsbridge, the Princess was immediately interested and the then Bishop of Kensington noted that the small attentive figure never missed a session. He would no doubt have been further impressed had he known that some of his topics, ranging from prayer and the Sacraments to the arts of Christian living, were often discussed at Lambeth Palace with the Archbishop of Canterbury, Dr Fisher. 'Every meeting with her was a sort of friendly argument,' said Dr Fisher, years later. 'She was always friendly, always intelligent, but would state her views and would let me state my views, which we would discuss and argue, talking things over in this free and open way... I came to be especially devoted to her: I knew what a genuine concern she had in the life of the Church and the life of a churchwoman.'

Amid these discussions, it was perhaps ironic that, at home at the Palace, at Royal Lodge and when visiting friends, the Princess found her chief lay confidant in Group Captain Peter Townsend, with whom the clear-cut tenets of the Church were later to cause her unhappiness and solitude of spirit. Like many who have repeatedly faced death, Townsend was a sincerely religious man. He knew his Bible and would often quote it, and from these deep springs she drew the assurance and solace of which both Margaret and her mother stood in need. The Princess had often gone to her father to debate quite trivial problems, 'to help talk things out', as she put it, and now more and more, increasingly, she turned to Peter. Both were also aware, at a different level, of a curious dovetailing of events. The breakdown of the King's health under the burdens and aftermath of war had matched, in a more qualified sense, the breakdown of Peter Townsend's wartime marriage.

'We had only known each other for six weeks,' he once said, apropos of this union. 'Ridiculous, wasn't it?' It had been a marriage of constant wartime partings until the Townsends settled into their grace-and-favour cottage in Windsor Great Park — and little eased even then. As an equerry to the King, the Group Captain underwent the separations of any married man whose work often takes him away from home, with an added strain of irregular hours and barely predictable absences, often for weeks at a time, while his wife was left with the children. He faced with others in this the constant dilemma of many engaged in personal duty to the King. The Royal Family can be all-demanding, unaware that they are being so. That tug-of-war of duty and fealty versus one's private life had intensified in 1950 when Townsend was appointed Deputy Master of the Household. Henceforth, wherever the Court travelled, he would travel. Wherever the King and Queen were, he would be not far from their side. And to their younger daughter this good-looking, lean and reliant man in his forties had seemed increasingly a 'gentyl parfait knyght' in modern guise.

He was at once modest, considerate and attentive and, although sixteen years older than Margaret, he was among the few men at court whose quick wit and high spirits could match her own sallies. Whatever his private moods, he was always good company and utterly dependable. When the King's illness came to its crucial phase, shortly after the Princess's twenty-first birthday house-party at Balmoral, Peter Townsend was both a guest and by virtue of his official position an adept and unhesitant assistant host. And as the King submitted to his surgeons, so Peter Townsend submitted to his lawyers' advice to commence a divorce action against his wife; and the King knew of the inevitability of the proceedings months before that last Christmas at Sandringham.

It would have matched Townsend's orthodox outlook if, although the innocent party, he had tendered his resignation. The Royal Family, in any event, felt that they could ill spare him at that juncture, Princess Margaret youthfully considered the breakdown of his marriage a terrible pity and hoped that it might yet be put right. There was bewilderment in the situation. Yet she was full of sympathy; Peter had long been a dependable and indispensable friend, and when she returned to London after the first shock of her father's death, his was inevitably a protective shoulder to cry on.

II

The Queen Mother had drawn guidance from some lines of William Blake, which she commended to Margaret, 'Labour well the Minute Particulars, attend to the Little Ones, And those who are in misery cannot remain so.' Mother and daughter took turn to visit Clarence House to be on call from the nursery while the Queen was at the Palace, working, at first, at her father's desk. Playing with the two children on the sitting room floor, as they had grown accustomed to doing with their mother, Margaret taught Charles his alphabet; and every other afternoon, she visited the grieved Queen Mary, who fell ill that April and took to her bed for a month. The secretaries gently initiated their new Sovereign into the unremitting desk-work, the audiences, and the first investitures of her reign, while the younger sister experienced an untoward sense of futility; a constant fret and frustration, at being able to do so little of practical help.

Court mourning was ordained until the end of May, but when a 'calendar committee' met in April to consider the shape of future royal engagements, the Princess had indeed laboured the particulars so well that she was ready with proposals for duties that would take her to Devizes, Portsmouth, Folkestone, Ruislip, Plymouth, Norwich, Worcester, London's dockland and so on, visiting hospitals, opening Service clubs, attending youth organization rallies and so forth. 'Well done, Margaret!' the Queen had cause to say, scanning the list with the chief of her secretaries, Sir Alan Lascelles. The chores were moreover ingeniously leavened with future social occasions, a visit to the Buccleuchs at Boughton, a weekend with the Blandfords, a stay with Billy Wallace and his family, the Agars. Friends were never more loyal and reliable than in those months of transition.

Then, in May, an unforeseen pleasure came literally, out of a blue sky. Queen Elizabeth the Queen Mother was lunching with Lord and Lady Salisbury at Hatfield House when the inaugural flight of the world's first passenger jet airliner, the Comet jet to Johannesburg, came under discussion. 'Why don't you try it, Ma'am?' Lord Salisbury enquired.

'You mean there's a Comet to spare?' his guest replied. The upshot was that on a brilliantly sunny day shortly afterwards, Princess Margaret and her mother boarded the plane with the Salisbury's, Sir Geoffrey and Lady de Havilland, Sir Miles Thomas, Group Captain Townsend and other guests, and within ninety minutes were over the Alps, with the snowy peak of the Jungfrau clearly visible. After finishing lunch Margaret went into the pilot's cabin to see all the Riviera coastline presently glistening on the starboard side. 'Can we go as fast as a Meteor jet?' the Queen Mother asked, on accepting an invitation to take the controls, and the pilot, John Cunningham, showed her how to push forward the control column and hold it until, as the needle approached red, the plane began to porpoise up and down at the limit of aerodynamic stability. 'I still shudder every time I think of that flight,' Sir Miles Thomas wrote later, after a then unsuspected weakness in the early Comets had proved the cause of two cataclysmic disasters. Yet from the edge of hazard the passengers returned exhilarated, their hearts lighter, and for Margaret the clouds of bereavement were at last moving away.

Embarking on her programme of official engagements, she continued to wear black, but had noticeably recovered much of her old gaiety, her old mischief. When the Queen agreed to attend the Royal Ascot race meeting, Margaret paraded an 'advance view' of the dress she would wear on opening day, with the deep *décolleté* of the least modest Lely ladies. The Queen began to protest and then realized that her sister was teasing, having planned all along that the plunging line should be suitably vested with grey tulle.

The Queen and the Duke of Edinburgh had formally moved into Buckingham Palace on May 5th, installing themselves in the Belgian Suite on the ground floor as if they were guests, and within the month all the family, with the Queen Mother and Margaret, found themselves actively enjoying the renewal of all living together under the same roof. It would be winter again, they imagined, before Margaret and her mother could move to Clarence House; and in reality the transfer was completed only two weeks before the Coronation. They met as a family group as often as possible at the same table, companionably exchanging domestic gossip. The Queen smiled when telling a friend that Margaret was spending a weekend with the Wills at Binfield; Lady Jane Willoughby's coming-out ball was being held nearby at Cliveden; it meant that Margaret would be dancing again.

Then, in the summer calm of Balmoral, they played charades one evening, and the Princess triumphantly leapt to the right answer and looked jubilant at discovering that she and her sister still understood each other's thoughts. 'It's no trick,' she had said. 'It's telepathy. We really can do it.' In the autumn, a more convincing demonstration of their rapport occurred a few minutes before an investiture when the Queen was taken ill with a sharp attack of abdominal cramp and Lord Scarborough's assistant telephoned Margaret in her suite upstairs to alert her to be ready to act as deputy. 'I was just getting ready,' she said. 'I felt I might be needed.' The Queen, however, felt that she could continue, and Margaret waited, so to speak, in the wings.

Again, shortly before Christmas, Norman Hartnell went down to Sandringham with a bevy of models, first to display the sketches and designs of the proposed Coronation gowns and then to submit dresses newly prepared for the spring from which the Queen might express ideas for her projected overseas tour in the autumn of 1953. The dress show took place 'in a large bedroom of old-fashioned charm', as Mr Hartnell wrote afterwards, and the mannequins entered 'through a door that led out of a capacious white bathroom'. The Queen and her mother, with Princess Margaret, all watched the display side by side on a slender Victorian sofa at the foot of an enormous bedstead. But again and again, as one of Mr Hartnell's assistants noted, 'the Queen and her sister often made appreciative comments in the same breath, as much in unison as if they had rehearsed beforehand'.

III

The Coronation year of 1953 began, on an unusual note, with wedding gaiety in Scotland, and for six months the light and shade of family events alternated strongly as the rain showers that were to lash the gold Coronation coach. Early in January the Queen and Prince Philip were in Edinburgh with Princess Margaret for the wedding in St Giles' Cathedral of the Earl of Dalkeith to Miss Janet McNeill, that same 'Johnny Dalkeith' whom, twelve months earlier, many leading newspapers had rumoured might marry the Princess. Back at Sandringham, gales littered the paths with fallen branches. 'When it is night, and the wind and rain beat upon the window, the family is most truly conscious of the pleasant fireside,' wrote the Queen, observing her axiom that as soon as one broadcast is finished the next script should be drafted. But at the end of the month the winds roared with exceptional ferocity, the tides rose, sea defences were breached, and the east coast suffered appalling inundation. For three days, members of the Royal Family toured the flood regions, while Margaret and the Queen Mother particularly visited Canvey Island, Benfleet and Tilbury to give what comfort and encouragement they could to the thousands evacuated from their homes. Yet February 6th, observed by the family as the first anniversary of George VI's death, was a day of calm sunlight.

The Queen and her sister approached the Coronation with reverence. During Lent the Princess attended a series of post-confirmation classes at St Paul's vicarage to help renew the vows of the Confirmation service, 'to keep God's holy will and commandments' and perhaps to seek interpretation on the puzzling pledge of renouncing 'the vain pomp and glory of the world'. With Iris Peake, who had recently succeeded Mrs John

Lowther as lady-in-waiting, Margaret attended every Tuesday for six weeks, never missing, and accepted gladly when the Vicar suggested that a pew should be reserved for Sunday worship if she were in London. 'My sister has asked us to pray for her,' she told Peter Gillingham, the Chaplain at the little chapel at Royal Lodge, and added, 'That is terribly important.' Meanwhile, visiting Marlborough House, she found Queen Mary eager as ever for news of outside events, yet realized that her grandmother had not long to live. Queen Mary died on the evening of March 24th, and once again Margaret watched the panoply of a funeral at St George's Chapel, Windsor. It was the significant end of an epoch, as if brooms had swept the family paths clear for the new reign.

Princess Margaret had been due to fly to Luxembourg a week later to attend the wedding of the Hereditary Grand Duke Jean, but this journey was cancelled. On the onset of illness, however, Queen Mary had made it known that she wished the Coronation and other summer events to continue, if she 'should not be there'. In observing this wish Princess Margaret therefore flew to Norway in the middle of May for the wedding of King Haakon's granddaughter, Princess Ragnhild, her second cousin. The younger of two sisters, Ragnhild was second in line to the Throne and not three months older than Margaret, yet the inherent interest was perhaps that the bride was marrying a man some years her senior whom she had first met when he served as a young aide-de-camp just after the war. Mr Erling Lorentzen was also a commoner, though one was beginning to take this for granted in Scandinavian courts, and the young couple were proposing to live, at least for a time, in Brazil, where he had family shipping interests. 'It is a wedding to make Princess Margaret think,' said the *Sunday Express*, without any obvious connotation.

The wedding was also, as Margaret said, 'a holiday between homes'. Though aged eighty, King Haakon tirelessly showed her the sights of Oslo, the Viking ships, the Kon-Tiki raft, and so on, and the Princess took time to open an exhibition for her artist friend Edward Seago. On May 13th, after sixteen years, she had slept for the last time at Buckingham Palace and did not return to her rapidly dismantled rooms. Instead, bringing from Norway a score of affectionate messages to her mother, she went direct to Royal Lodge, and the next day travelled into London to take up residence at Clarence House. Moving is made easy for royalty, and the Princess carried with her only one personal possession, a small book given to her at the beginning of the month, which she had taken to Oslo with her and read for a few minutes each day.

The Archbishop of Canterbury had discovered that there was no written material to help prepare the Queen for the personal dedication that gave meaning to her crowning, and so had decided to compile a little devotional book himself for the purpose. 'It took the form', as he said, 'of a simple meditation and prayers for each day, covering a whole month and leading up to the Coronation itself. Each day had a theme; with the little meditation and one or two prayers.' Four copies, beautifully printed and bound, were prepared for the Royal Family, one for the Queen, one for the Duke of Edinburgh, a third for the Queen Mother, and the fourth for Princess Margaret, who was deeply touched to find herself included in the gift, 'the most precious thing,' wrote Dr Fisher, 'that I ever did.'

At Clarence House, indeed, she scarcely had time to settle in before accompanying her mother to a rehearsal at the Abbey.

The Princess also received an invitation card to the Coronation from the Earl Marshal, the Duke of Norfolk, and took considerable pride in it, placing it in state for a time on her mantelshelf, the first of the innumerable invitations that were to rest there. On May 22nd she was an onlooker at the rehearsal in which her sister took part for the first time, and six days later Princess Margaret rehearsed her own small role in the ceremonial. This was her measured progress, in a joint procession with that of Queen Elizabeth the Queen Mother, from the Abbey annexe to the royal box, which looked across the Sanctuary some nine feet above the level of the Throne.

Five Heralds attended her in their due position; with Iris Peake, who would carry her train, and her page — her young cousin, Albemarle Bowes-Lyon — who was to carry her coronet on a velvet cushion. Twice the stately progress was paced and timed, the Princess foreseeing and discussing the wider movement necessary for her train in gracefully mounting the gentle curving staircase to the box. On the day before the Coronation, the Queen gave a remarkable luncheon party to all her overseas Prime Ministers and Commonwealth representatives, and when Mr Menzies of Australia enquired of Princess Margaret whether she were looking forward to tomorrow she assured him brightly, 'Oh, so very much. I would not miss a moment.'

The Queen Mother also gave a private dinner party at Clarence House that Coronation eve, but later on Margaret changed her dress and slipped out by Stable Yard with a member of the Household, for a few minutes strolling unrecognized through the crowds, amused at seeing the kerbside campers unrolling their sleeping bags for the night. Next morning the summer foliage of the trees and the garden wall partly concealed the activity of the Mall but her bedroom window gave a sidelong view of the troops and the people already lining the pavements. From that same window she eagerly waited for the first royal carriage procession to come into sight before descending to join her mother for their own processional ride in the Glass Coach, with all the splendour of a Captain's Escort with Standard of the Household Cavalry.

The acknowledgment of the packed masses of the cheering people and the reciprocal crescendo roar from every stand seemed to prolong the twenty minutes of the drive, but in the Abbey annexe the time passed swift as the flash of diamonds. It was noticeable that the imminent appearance of Princess Margaret and of Queen Elizabeth the Queen Mother within the Abbey itself brought a cessation of the extraordinary sound of the whispering of six thousand people that had rustled like surf beneath the soaring music. A shaft of sunlight suddenly pierced the lofty stained glass windows and splashed upon the carpets, and at first glimpse of the crowded and transformed church the Princess seemed to shiver slightly as she advanced.

Her dress was of white satin embroidered in an open-worked design, strengthened with crystal, and with marguerites and roses worked in silver thread and shimmering with pearls. Her robe and train was the purple velvet of a royal Princess, trimmed with ermine. She was preceded by the Heralds of Somerset and of Windsor in all their splendour, and followed by her lady-in-waiting and her page, a small and personal group closely followed by the richesse of the Heralds of Richmond and York, Chester and Lancaster. Her gaze 'steadily fixed upon the High Altar,' as Norman Hartnell noticed, 'she moved in white beauty like a snowdrop.'

Did anyone in all that assemblage consider that, but for Elizabeth, Margaret would have been crowned Queen that day? Certainly one doubts whether the thought ever occurred to the Princess, so schooled was she in her role of younger sister. It was more than 250 years since a sister had attended the Coronation of a sister. But history was something one could not help, and earlier in the week the Princess had said lightly that it would be her Coronation responsibility to look after the mother of the Queen and the son of the Queen. Now, for a time, mother and daughter sat side by side in their raised gallery, few noticing an empty place between them. And presently, at the high moment of sacrament before the Anointing, it was seen that little Prince Charles, not yet five, had been brought into the royal box and was seated between his aunt and his grandmother, each bending over him to whisper answers to his questions, each in turn a hostage to his good behaviour.

The Princess had an almost total recall of all the profound impressions of Queen Elizabeth II's Coronation day. Yet suffice it to say that in the late evening a sudden increase of floodlights trained on the Palace balcony was the signal for a little group to cross the forecourt and to squeeze through a side-gate into the crowds. And so the Princess gaily cheered the Queen and presently, with her friends, joined the throng passing and repassing beneath the pearly iridescent triumphal arches in the Mall.

IV

It was to become a source of sad regret to Princess Margaret and, to a degree, a cause for self-reproach that in the very month of her sister's Coronation the first clouds of what was to be known as the Townsend affair should have burst like a summer storm across the horizons of public curiosity. The wretched timing was by no means hers. The problem of Peter Townsend was, indeed, already settled in private, the rough edges trimmed, long before it became publicly known. The unsure crisis of emotion was deferred, and though it riveted public attention at the time, the chapter diminishes in retrospect to an episode, unimportant save in our assessment of character.

Princess Margaret once said that life at Buckingham Palace was like dwelling in a goldfish bowl, and the rest of the royal venue was little better. As early as January, 1953, a member of the Sandringham staff wrote of wondering 'whether a romance were developing between Princess Margaret and Peter. We watched what seemed to be a ripening friendship. Our view was that it would be regrettable if a man in Townsend's position allowed Princess Margaret's interest to grow into anything stronger than friendly feeling.' But Group Captain Townsend's divorce was pronounced absolute within the month and, when his former wife remarried, his own freedom to wed introduced subtle new elements into the atmosphere.

Going to tea with him at the Palace, his mother, Mrs Gladys Townsend, found herself being presented to Princess Margaret, whom she had last met as a schoolgirl at Windsor and now found a woman of great charm and beauty. Peter's behaviour was as ever impeccable. The Princess called him 'Peter' with obvious affection, but he never addressed her except as 'Ma'am' even in privacy with his mother.

In a conversation ranging over Mrs Townsend's six other children, her neighbours in Somerset and friends in Sussex, Mrs Townsend was astonished to discover how much the Princess knew about them all. Among the London topics, Peter had been shopping for lamps for Clarence House, and 'quietly clapping his hands' to ensure the transfer and installation of the Queen Mother's possessions, from a favourite chimney-piece to twelve-foot bookcases and precious

Chinese clocks. While the Princess's trust and admiration knew no bounds, other factors were less obvious. Four months before the Coronation, as in a heart-to-heart between sisters, Princess Margaret evidently confided to the Queen that if any man could make her happy it would be Peter Townsend.

Looking through the Townsend personal folder, Sir Alan Lascelles must have noticed that it was thirteen years to the day since Townsend had been recommended for the DFC, displaying 'qualities of leadership, skill and determination of the highest order, with little regard for his own safety'. The Group Captain's impending posting as Comptroller at Clarence House had become well known. But in the tragic distress of widowhood, Queen Elizabeth the Queen Mother had failed to foresee that her daughter might wish to marry a man with an age difference of sixteen years between them, a member of the Household, a man who had been *divorced*.

That was the nub. Though sympathetic to her sister and dearly wishing her future happiness, the Queen herself could take no view other than that the Church regarded Christian marriage as indissoluble and thus, as temporal head of the Church of England, she could not give consent to marriage to a divorced man, a man with a wife still living. Guilt or innocence made no difference. The situation echoed the Duke of Windsor's dilemma, with the sexes reversed. The Queen privately consulted Sir Winston Churchill, who had once been the Duke's champion but now, with sorrow, he tendered the advice that Her Majesty could not properly give consent under the Royal Marriages Act of 1772 and he feared that the Prime Ministers of the Commonwealth would be of the same opinion.

There remained however an escape clause, for if at the age of twenty-five the Princess still pursued the question she had but to give one year's notice to the Privy Council of her intention to marry. Since this did not involve the consent of the Queen, the theological issue would not then arise, and a civil marriage was possible. With all her dawning, urgent hopes, the Princess must have realized with near despondency that this 'solution' would defer her dearest wishes for three years; and it may well be, as I believe, that her sister took the occasion to comfort her, pointing out how long she and Philip had necessarily waited, facing endless delays and obstacles although everything had ultimately turned out for the best.

When the Queen then unobtrusively sought the further views of elder advisers, particularly Alan Lascelles, Winston Churchill with his lifelong grasp of public opinion, and not least the Queen Mother herself, the consensus favoured an interval of separation so that the couple might have valid opportunity truly to know their own hearts. One or two close family friends gave analytical counsel of great value. In bereavement the Princess may have been unconsciously influenced by a father image; and under the shock of divorce a lonely man may over-eagerly wish to rebuild his desolate world. First and last, Peter Townsend's behaviour remained irreproachable. It is sometimes claimed that he was sent into exile, but in reality he went to Sir Alan Lascelles at an early stage to suggest a temporary transfer overseas. The post of air attaché to a major British embassy is usually filled by an officer of Group Captain rank and, on being informed of vacancies impending in Paris and Brussels, Peter chose Brussels, where he had friends.

Unexpectedly, the Queen Mother pointed out that there was no hurry. The Group Captain had been due to accompany her, with Princess Margaret, on a visit to Rhodesia on June 29th. 'We all had such fun in South Africa,' she told him. 'It will be wonderful if you can come.' Both he and Margaret were overjoyed, I think, at the prospect of this romantic journey as a leave-taking before their 'trial separation'. Nothing seemed to have altered, except in the smaller details. It was Lady Jean Rankin and Major-General Salisbury-Jones, Marshal of the Diplomatic Corps, who accompanied Margaret to the Norwegian wedding celebrations on May 14–17th, and not Peter. And May 17th was the one day when, by a fine blend of discretion and publicity, he was officially seen to be in attendance on the Queen Mother at an appropriate ceremony at a Royal Air Force base.

Everything indeed had been settled in the most agreeable way, without a whisper beyond the inmost circle, when a mischance occurred in distant Manhattan. *The New York Journal American* needed a circulation-raising furore to continue the magic of the Coronation and, taking a pencil stab in the dark, they mentioned Townsend. A week or two later, his posting to Brussels was discovered. The left-wing weekly *Tribune* then discussed the theme and half the newspapers in the world quickly joined in a wild baying of surmise. Clearly, if Group Captain Townsend had accompanied the Queen Mother and Princess Margaret to Rhodesia the commotion would have been enhanced. Instead, changes were inevitable. The Group Captain was attached to the Queen and the Duke of Edinburgh for their Coronation visit to Northern Ireland on July 1st and, after farewells at Clarence House, the Queen Mother and Princess Margaret flew to Rhodesia without Townsend on June 30.

Once in Salisbury, Princess Margaret found it the happiest coincidence that at the Government House dance, one of her partners was someone she knew, namely Julian Bevan, brother of Mrs John Lowther, the former Jennifer Bevan who had been her lady-in-waiting and remained one of her closest friends. Scottish reels and square dances were 'danced with gusto', as one guest noticed, although supper in a marquee was 'spoiled by the unseasonable cold'. Biting winds also blew when the Queen Mother opened the Rhodes centenary exhibition and it was hardly surprising that within a few days Margaret was laid up at her Umtali hotel with a severe chill. This mishap aside, the visit was a success in every way and, on returning home, the Princess scarcely knew whether to be vexed or amused on reading the alternative versions in the press that she had taken to her bed either in sulks or with a broken heart.

Yet it was difficult to get used to Peter's absence, no longer on a whim to hear his light voice on the house phone or to be able to send a note to ask his ideas for arranging an evening. The Princess spent her twenty-third birthday quietly at Birkhall, listless and dispirited, if one can believe that the Queen had difficulty in enticing her to a picnic tea with the children in the little cottage at Gairnshiel.

The patterns of life are traced in notes and letters and remembered conversations as well as newsprint and photographs and, for the author, the memory of two films seems to frame the Townsend period. The first was in October, 1952, a day or two after returning from Balmoral, when Princess Margaret and Group Captain Townsend had gone to the premiere of *Limelight*, with its Chaplinesque theme of bittersweet love and renunciation. And it was a quirky coincidence that on returning from Balmoral in 1953 Princess Margaret went to 'catch up with' *Roman Holiday*, first shown in London on her birthday. The stars were Gregory Peck, one of her favourite actors, and Audrey Hepburn, whom all the world knew was playing with incredible skill a make-believe Margaret in a story concerned with a bored princess, surrounded by stuffy official duties in Rome, and her brief escapist idyll with a young photographer. And this was three years before Princess Margaret first heard of a young photographer named Antony Armstrong-Jones.

8: IN TRANSIT

Most of what is written about her is awry, some of it
scurrilous, as if the dry shade of Wilkes had returned to focus
his vile, distorting mirror on royalty. There is a peering and a
prying … and a pantomime-simple idea that while the Queen
must be portrayed as an icon of seriousness, opposite qualities
must be found in her sister.

The Observer, January 2, 1955

I

During the seven long years when Princess Margaret resided
under her mother's roof at Clarence House, like a spinster
daughter, the public imagined her living in a converted nursery
suite on the top floor, constantly 'entertaining her friends', as
legend had it, with her library of thousands of gramophone
records. The reality was rather the reverse. The Princess's
sitting room lay on the ground floor to the far right of the
front door, and her music, drifting across a terrace from an
open window, best alleviated the boredom of the guardsman
of the westernmost sentry box of St James's Palace next door.
Inside Clarence House, the hub of Princess Margaret's world
thus lay to the right of the broad central corridor, along a
minor corridor lined with heavy bookcases and gold-damask
settees on which no one ever sat. On a less austere note, the
wall lamps and one or two console tables bearing big vases of
flowers set the atmosphere that Prince Charles long regarded
as the cosy prelude to his aunt's grown-up world.

There was no great distance for him to scamper, as a small boy, to her deep-set white door ... and so into a pale-green, grey-carpeted room flecked with diffused sunlight, with Persian rugs of pale rose and blue spread before the electric fire. Two sofas and two armchairs in pale rose chintz flanked the fireplace, and satin curtains of a paler pink draped the two tall windows. Between these windows — one in fact a French door opening on to the terrace — the only business-like note was the Princess's desk, with its leatherbound blotter and silver inkstand, and Chippendale chair. And this itself was softened by the leather-framed photographs of her mother, her niece and nephew, while centred at the back was a small wooden crucifix, perhaps six inches high, with the figure of Christ in ivory.

On the far side of the room were displayed some of the little statuettes and figurines: a small rock crystal bust of Queen Victoria, a miniature figure of George III and similar bibelots of family interest for which the Princess had already gained a collector's enthusiasm. Gifts from friends would find an affectionate place there and for a time they were joined by a piece of coal which she had cut in the depths of Calverton Colliery. Placed with reticence on a side table behind the door was one of the versions of the Epstein bust of the miner herself, a replica of the marvellously vivacious sculpture now at Keele University.

The magazine table, a drinks table, an over-large Georgian bookcase, the record player and the tight-packed open record cabinet completed the principal elements of this sitting room, elegant, artistic, fastidious, hospitable as its youthful occupant. Far from damping conversation with records, Princess Margaret was more inclined to play them when alone. But in the winter of 1953–54 there were good friends who realized

143

that her need of diverting company might be deeper than before. On November 23rd the Princess saw the Queen and her brother-in-law off at London airport on their six-months Commonwealth tour around the world. The two sisters had never previously faced such a long separation. It was an inauspicious evening of drizzling rain, the Princess had not been looking forward to the leave-taking, and yet along every mile of the road from central London people were waiting in the damp to glimpse the Queen and wave goodbye. The magic of it, as so often, filled the Princess with awe and made the unpromising day 'end with a glow'.

If Margaret expected a lonesome winter, she had not counted on the ingenuity of her friends and, not least, of the enterprising Judy Montagu. Before the Queen left London, Judy had suggested that the Princess might care to help produce a play for charity. The Queen raised no objection and, within the week, her sister's sitting room rang to the angry threats, screams, and violent talk of murder and mayhem — with much laughter as well — inseparable from a first reading of the Ian Hay–Edgar Wallace thriller *The Frog*. The plot, now seeming more prophetic than absurd, concerned a sinister brotherhood terrorizing the country, setting power stations ablaze, planting bombs in Scotland Yard and blowing safes in the Foreign Office. With scenes set in nightclubs, police stations and prisons, and with only ten speaking parts, the play offered opportunities for walk-ons innumerable and business *ad lib*. 'Whether the curtain will ever go up is anyone's guess,' wrote an intending member of the cast. 'But it's going to be fun and we're going ahead.'

When the theatre itself, the Scala, was actually booked for them for a week in June, everyone rose to the irrevocable challenge. Billy Wallace played the detective (the Jack Hawkins role in the original production), Lord Porchester took the Gordon Harker part of a Cockney police sergeant, while Colin Tennant was to be the Frog, the inscrutable villain. The cast also included the Duke of Devonshire as a prison governor, with the Earl of Caernarvon, Lord Plunket, Lord Brooke and others; and the indefatigable Miss Montagu ultimately roped in even Elsa Maxwell and Douglas Fairbanks Jnr, as extras. Princess Margaret understudied the heroine, a nightclub hostess with a heart of gold, played by the then Mrs Gerald Legge (who later became the Countess of Dartmouth and, on her second marriage to Earl Spencer, stepmother to Princess Diana), and since Mrs Legge was already busily serving on the Westminster City Council and various committees, the Princess found herself playing the leading lady in a satisfactory number of rehearsals.

And, of course, she loved it. As assistant producer, she researched and sketched the needful dress fashions and hairstyles of the 1930s, while Reggie Woolley, the designer, was surprised at her ready grasp of the technical problems of quick scene-changing. Not for her an easy over-reliance on the smoke of the various stage explosions to mask amateur inefficiency. The company rehearsed in each other's homes, in a YWCA hall and occasionally in the Fortune Theatre, where Margaret turned up with her packet of sandwiches, with the added pleasure, at first, of passing the stage-door keeper unrecognized. It suited her more than a little to boss the others about, her criticisms invariably tempered with common sense. 'Oh, we must keep that in. At that point, you must come down stage, Billy.' Elsa Maxwell was to mime to a Sophie Tucker record in a cabaret scene and Margaret was the first to realize that the effect would be more natural if the loudspeaker were hidden in front of the apparent singer rather than behind her.

Telephoning from the far side of the world, the Queen never failed to ask how the show was coming along, and Margaret soon enthusiastically reported advance bookings of £5,000, plus £2,000 for programme advertising space. In the first week of the royal tour the Queen's enthusiasm for Jamaica and the gaiety of the Caribbean bubbled over the phone, with the happy result that Margaret's own visit to Jamaica in 1955 was fixed then and there and officially announced six weeks later … a journey that was to have never-ending sequels of happiness.

The Queen and her husband returned home in time to attend the dress rehearsal of *The Frog* with the Queen Mother. As the house manager neatly put it, 'it was a top-level amateur production', and the Princess had the added pleasure of making a curtain speech from the footlights, thanking the cast and adding that the Invalid Children's Association had benefited by over £10,000. 'It's been my lucky week,' the Princess said. Whereupon there was laughter from the initiated for, in that same week, the Princess had gained the additional satisfaction of winning a prize of three guineas' worth of books for correctly solving the *Country Life* crossword.

In the earlier May 13th issue, the magazine had welcomed the Queen home with no fewer than fourteen pages devoted to the royal tour, so thoroughly pleasing Princess Margaret among its readers that she paid it more attention than usual and even studied the crossword clues. What is it that most vehicles have to be in five letters? Or the missing five-letter word in the Shakespeare quotation, 'My age is a winter'? What is 'nice scene to make, with nothing to go on' in nine letters. Or 'Exclaim on seeing a sailor: he was a King' in four? Since they offer a clue in turn to the well-packed compendium of the

Princess's mind, her correct solutions were as follows: axled, lusty, nescience (an anagram) and Ahab.

<h1 style="text-align:center">II</h1>

The pioneering novelties of royal experience become commonplace within a decade, but in July 1954, when Princess Margaret made a tour of the British Forces in Germany and lunched on her first day with President Heuss and Chancellor Adenauer, she was in fact the first member of the British Royal Family to pay an official visit to Germany since the war and the first to pay an official visit to a German Head of State for over forty years. Fresh from her success at the Scala, as one friend amusingly mentioned, she paced up and down her sitting room rehearsing, and invariably revising, her speeches. The success of her mission lay in the impress of the Princess herself. She brushed up her hated German lessons of Crawfie's day and charmed Adenauer by apparently speaking his language with fair fluency as they walked up and down a Rhine terrace. The Rhine Army Commander-in-Chief, Sir Richard Gale, stipulated when giving a dance for her that no guest should be over thirty. 'That's lovely,' said Margaret, 'but we don't want to leave out too many old friends,' and she made certain that the German dance-band played the vogue hit tune 'Friends and Neighbours' several times during the evening.

In Service relations, she visited six Army units, three RAF stations and a Royal Naval centre in her four days and had hoped to take a twenty-five-mile hop by helicopter to visit the 11th Armoured Division at Sennelager: 'It will be something my mother and sister haven't done.' Helicopters, one remembers, were not added to the Queen's Flight until the following year. Unluckily, the Princess attempted her inaugural flight on a day of vile weather. Her 'chopper' made five take-off attempts before really getting into the air, and two miles from their destination the cloud and mist worsened so much that the pilot decided to turn back. 'Pity!' said Margaret laconically, 'I've never had such a thrill in an aircraft before.' And fourteen years before Princess Anne unexpectedly demonstrated her skill with a Sterling submachine gun, her 'Aunt Margo' creditably had a go with a jet fighter 20mm cannon, firing a burst from a Meteor fighter parked in front of the sand-butts.

Other invitations meanwhile accumulated like sugar candy around the original project to visit Jamaica, and the Princess's first solo overseas mission crystallized in 1955 into a Caribbean royal tour aboard the then gleaming-new royal yacht *Britannia*, making an arc of the Indies from south to north-west and embracing Trinidad and Tobago, Grenada and St Vincent, Barbados and Antigua, with a final jet-set weekend at Nassau. To some of her friends Margaret propounded a riddle. She was flying out on January 31st and returning home on March 2nd, and yet would be at Clarence House on St Valentine's Day, February 14th. At a *bon voyage* dinner at No. 10 Downing Street, Sir Winston Churchill alone solved the conundrum: 'I am sure you will feel quite at home, ma'am. And perhaps you may care to give my high regards to — harrumph! — Sir Kenneth Blackburne.' Like the Princess, Winston had done his homework and learned that Sir Kenneth's residence as Governor of Antigua was also a Clarence House, named like the Princess's home after its former occupant, the Duke of Clarence, later King William IV.

Probably the not least remarkable aspect of the tour, by present-day standards, was its intensive press coverage. For a month the newspapers of three continents shone with calypso and bongo headlines, while the picture magazines rejoiced in 'spreads' and covers of the highly photogenic Princess and her Hartnell-Stiebel-Mirman wardrobe. The itinerary contrived to sound like a prosaic industrial tour. 'At Bridgetown, Her Royal Highness will see the Trade and Industries Fair. At Basseterre, the Princess will visit a new sugar factory and start the mills.' But the press corps had not then exhausted *exotic, picturesque, cool-looking,* nor were the shining white coral beaches yet smudged with portable typewriter ribbon. At the Port of Spain airport, the pressmen noted that the Governor's address of welcome was beautifully typed, while the Princess's speech was blue-black with ink corrections. They considered she was over-rushed through her first hospital, and noticed that she chose her own tempo next time and was adding her own ideas — such as inspecting the nurses' dormitory — six hospitals later. They recognized the toughness of riding in closed cars at 87 degrees in the shade and then of shaking scores of tight-gripping hands, while seldom failing in 'shining-eyed enjoyment … her mother all over again'.

If the ladies of each successive Government House along the chain of islands had expected to cope with a spoiled and imperious princess, they found instead an undemanding, unassuming young woman who could not have shown them more appreciation and gratitude. In Trinidad, Lady Rance thought it a good idea to place a photograph of the Queen Mother on the Princess's dressing table to make her feel at home and, returning from all the confusion and excitement of a crowd ovation, the Princess noticed the portrait at once and thanked her warmly. In Tobago, the two ladies-in-waiting, Iris Peake and Lady Elizabeth Cavendish, decided to go for a swim while the Princess preferred to sit in the shade and explained to her hostess, 'I don't want to spoil my hair and look all wrong for your party.' In Barbados the heavy Victorian silver was set out for a State dinner but, acting on an inspired tip, Lady Arundel gave the Princess a place setting of smaller knives and forks. Gesturing with her small hands, the Princess said, 'How did you discover my preference? They're so comfortable.' And private parties were enlivened with the Princess's light-hearted vignettes of characters in the local carnival, 'Princess, you're so delicious I could eat you!' and the hospital Mammy who said, 'How am I today? Ah's sure all the better for seeing yew!'

From each Governor she gleaned fuller information about the island next on her route. In readiness for Grenada, she rehearsed a speech in the local Grenadine French patois. In Jamaica, hailing a press photographer she knew, she pointed to a banner 'Jamaica Burial Society Welcomes Princess Margaret' and begged him, 'Please make sure you get that!' After trying the celebrated thrills of the trip by bamboo raft down the rapids of the Rio Grande, she asked that the old raftsman receive an appreciative letter of thanks.

In her apparent pleasure in the songs and rhythms of a Jamaican children's rally, only her own small group knew that she had already taken part in ten junior rallies, fifteen receptions and twenty State drives. As Rhona Churchill said, 'I doubt whether any rich and pretty girl visiting the Caribbean had ever before *worked so hard*.' Few of her hosts were allowed to know that she suffered at times from carsickness and seasickness, and, one afternoon, even a touch of heat sickness after watching interminable regimental marching and countermarching while quite unprotected from the blazing sun.

Yet in Margaret's philosophy the official programme came first, and the cool relaxation of a swim, the languor of basking in sun and surf, the enjoyment of the dance, were pleasures deferred until duties were done. 'One tries to behave informally, of course, within the formal framework,' she once explained. 'One enjoys that, most of the time. It's important to give pleasure to other people.' She was becoming more fully aware also that serving the Crown in these inescapable tasks was as real a satisfaction as the intrinsic pleasure of, say, finding eternally beautiful shells in the sand. The job was an end in itself, with a high and serious quality.

Her final day in Jamaica saw a moonlight beach party at Frenchman's Cove, with Noël Coward, Adlai Stevenson and other guests in calypso mood ready to dance through the small hours. The elderly Chief Minister Norman Manley however could not stifle a yawn. 'You've had such a long day,' the Princess told him. 'Would you not like to go? We silly ones will dance all night.' A father figure, now, of independent Jamaica, Mr Manley never afterwards ceased to regard her as sweetly considerate, and thus as a true friend.

Her tasks completed, there was her last weekend at Nassau, sailing, swimming and venturing her first waterski lesson with such friends as the Blandfords, the Robin Muirs and Angus Ogilvy. She could look back, as she wrote, to the 'waving fields of sugar cane, the golden beaches and towering palms, the azure sea, forever studded with sails'. All unaware, she had fallen in love with the Caribbean, and would return to it again and again. Friends thought that they saw a change in her, a new assurance, a sense of being herself, not always the Queen's sister, not always her mother's daughter, as if the sea change had brought wings to her as an individual.

In those comparatively untravelled days it was the pleasant tradition of the City of London to give a luncheon for members of the Royal Family on their return from an overseas tour and on March 8th the honour thus fell to Princess Margaret to be entertained by the citizens of London. This led to a remarkable ovation, for as the Princess's car approached

Mansion House the life of the City came to a halt and crowds blocked the street as far as the eye could see. Taken quite by surprise, flushed and happy, she stepped out on to the balcony in response, while the tight-packed mass of people cheered and applauded in an unrestrained fashion rare in London. Yet this was not merely a welcome home or a tribute to her success in the West Indies. On March 6th a Sunday newspaper had dismayed her by announcing in thick headlines that she had now to make a choice, to stay third in succession to the throne, or abdicate her right in order to marry a divorced man.

Sixteen months had elapsed since Peter Townsend had left London. Until the confrontation of that appalling front page, Margaret had imagined that the problem would rest unasked until she had made up her mind. Now it was obviously in the thoughts of everyone in the crowd, in their shouts of 'Good luck!' and from his carefully prepared speech in proposing her health, it was clearly in the mind of the Lord Mayor, Sir Seymour Howard. As head of all the families throughout the Commonwealth, he said, the Royal Family ... 'is the family of perfect example for every other family in every part of Her Majesty's realm, of right standards, sound principles, true relationship and a way of life approved by all'.

The company stood and cheered as Princess Margaret rose to reply. She spoke only of the Caribbean and, month to month, from that moment, public surmise continued.

III

Not long after the initial stress and vexation of 'the Townsend affair' in 1953, a Bill had been put through Parliament to amend the Regency Act of 1937 under which, in the event of the Queen's death or incapacity, Princess Margaret would have acted as Regent for Prince Charles until he became of age. The

Queen desired that the amendment would designate the Duke of Edinburgh as Regent instead. It was natural that the Queen should wish her husband rather than her sister to act for her son, and Parliament was told that the Princess fully agreed with the common sense of this revision, yet it was widely and mistakenly mooted at the time that the real motive for the Bill was to clear the ground for Margaret to marry anyone she pleased. The idea also spread that she would make a decision shortly after her twenty-fifth birthday, and on the day itself an estimated 10,000 spectators crowded to Balmoral merely to watch her enter Crathie Church. 'Grant unto her now of Thy Grace,' prayed the minister, the Rev John Lamb, 'the fullness of Thy blessing so that, trusting in Thee, she may find fulfilment of her heart's desires, that joy may be her heritage and peace her portion.'

And, worrying over her problem, what was she to make of that ambiguity? If peace her portion, was it to be the peace of an old maid? There was also the curious incident of the royal press secretary who barked in the night, or at least early the following day after he had read the newspapers. The Press Association had put out a general bulletin that the Princess had celebrated her birthday with a dinner party followed by a ball. Some overzealous reporters claimed that they saw the flames of a beacon fire, or was it a barbecue, or the glow of a policeman's furtive cigarette? At all events this was one of the rare occasions when the Press Association issued a subsequent denial of a bulletin. There had been, it was explained, only a belated birthday party for Princess Anne and the usual dinner for Balmoral guests. Trivia are not usually focused in such firm perspective, and professional press attention thereupon became tense and acute.

In Brussels Peter Townsend spent the birthday morning at his riding stables and the afternoon at a show-jumping meeting, more pursued by reporters and photographers than ever Mark Phillips was to be in his love-affair with a princess seventeen years later. The one certainty was that the Brussels air attaché officially visited London to attend the Farnborough air show on September 5th, but unofficially paid three visits within the week to Captain Dawnay, the Queen Mother's secretary, and dined twice with Lady Elizabeth Cavendish, the Princess's close friend. It seemed an expectant prelude to the Group Captain's four weeks leave in London the following month.

Sir Anthony Eden, then Prime Minister, was a guest with Lady Eden at Balmoral for the weekend of October 1st. Sir Anthony had himself been through the divorce mill, so interwoven are the British constitutional difficulties of Church and State and the core of his advice was already known. There was still the leading issue that the Queen was head of the established Church which held Christian marriage to be indissoluble, and the Queen's sister could not readily therefore go through a Church of England religious ceremony to marry a divorced man. On the civil side, the Princess could retire into private life, relinquishing royal duty and resigning her Civil List income. Queen Mary's will, it was thought, might already have endowed her with a considerable fortune in her own right. Yet the civil issue was never discussed and remained unimportant.

As the Archbishop of Canterbury, Dr Fisher, later told Richard Dimbleby, the Princess 'was seeking and waiting all the time to know what God's will was'. She regarded her dilemma as a deep moral one. 'She got plenty of advice, asked for, and a good deal unasked for,' wryly added Dr Fisher. But the rightful outcome remained unresolved in her own mind when Peter Townsend returned to London on October 12th. He had accepted an invitation to stay at the London home of the Marquess of Abergavenny in Lowndes Square, and next evening Princess Margaret received him at Clarence House. He was croaking from the aftermath of flu, and the Princess had only recently undergone one of the bouts of migraine which had intermittently troubled her. To what degree were they strangers to one another after seventeen months? The Queen Mother was not present at the meeting and they were together for only two hours.

That weekend, when they were separately the guests of the Queen's cousin, Mrs John Wills, at Allenby Park, the press contingents of five continents set siege to the estate. They knew when the Princess left with Mrs Wills to attend Sunday service at the chapel near Royal Lodge and knew that the Group Captain remained behind. Day by day, through the following week, the reporters charted the dinner parties at the homes of mutual friends — the Bonham Carters, the Michael Brands and, again, Mrs Wills — where it seemed that the two could alone meet to discuss their perplexities. And, then, in the midst of these flurries, a public event which had been planned long beforehand strangely interposed itself.

On Friday 21st, in heavy rain, the memorial statue of King George VI in the Mall was unveiled by the Queen in the presence of the Cabinet and the Royal Family. 'Much was asked of my father in personal sacrifice and endeavour,' said the Queen, speaking from notes prepared weeks in advance. 'He shirked no task, however difficult, and to the end he never faltered in his duty.' That family truth was irrevocable as the rain itself. During the weekend, Princess Margaret was with her sister and Prince Philip at Windsor Castle, and no doubt she already knew her answer. Nothing that Peter could say at

Clarence House would now change that conviction. On October 27th the Princess called on the Archbishop at Lambeth Palace and, according to Randolph Churchill, she then said — in words worthy of Queen Elizabeth I — 'Archbishop, you may put your books away: I have made up my mind.'

At least, this was the scene cloaked in poetic mood but nothing of the kind in fact occurred. The meeting indeed took place, but the Princess's remark never ceased to puzzle the Archbishop. 'The Princess came and I received her,' he said, 'in the quiet of my own study. But she never said, "Put away those books". There were not any books to put away. Her decision was purely on the grounds of conscience. When it became clear what God's will was, she did it, and that is not a bad thing for people in general to note.'

For a day or two the public were aware of a lull in the conjectures. Then the Princess and Group Captain Townsend spent the last weekend of October once again under the same roof, with the Rupert Nevills, at Uckfield, though not without a dramatic flurry of dispatch riders and messengers back and forth to Windsor Castle. Against more mature and cautious advice, the Princess had made up her mind to issue a public statement. The Queen, it is said, suggested changing a word or two, and then — on the evening of October 31st — the announcement came directly from Princess Margaret at Clarence House:

> I would like it to be known that I have decided not to marry Group Captain Peter Townsend. I have been aware that, subject to my renouncing my rights of succession, it might have been possible for me to contract a civil marriage. But, mindful of the Church's teaching that Christian marriage is indissoluble, and conscious of my duty to the

Commonwealth, I have resolved to put these considerations before any others.

I have reached this decision entirely alone, and in doing so I have been strengthened by the unfailing support and devotion of Group Captain Townsend. I am deeply grateful for the concern of all those who have constantly prayed for my happiness.

Margaret

Within the Royal Household, some thought that it might have been better to allow public interest to fade, without explanation, with Peter Townsend's further withdrawal to Brussels. Yet perhaps the entire motive for issuing the statement was implicit in the final sentence. Although their task had been but to chronicle events as best they could, one had the impression that the kingpins of Fleet Street were abashed and conscience-stricken.

That evening, Sir Harold Nicolson, the biographer of George V, wrote in his private journal, 'This is a great act of self-sacrifice, and the country will admire and love her for it. I feel rather moved.' Said *The Times* next day, 'She is loyal to the Queen, her sister, and through her to the single family of many nations which the Queen represents.' Said *The Guardian*, 'All will wish her happiness in the hard path of duty and abnegation she has chosen.' And that the sacrifice was real, highly courageous and deeply hurtful as it was at the time, became crystal clear in a domestic detail mentioned some years later by John Payne, of the Clarence House staff. Three snapshots of Group Captain Townsend in a leather photograph folder stood on the Princess's table for several years more, firm and constant among such private tokens, until one morning they were gone.

Three years after Princess Margaret's statement, however, there came an epilogue, an anti-climax, when Townsend briefly visited London and went to tea once more at Clarence House. Glowing with the successful launching of a round-the-world travelogue film he had made, he may have proposed to call, and neither the Queen Mother nor Princess Margaret saw any need to repulse and hurt an old friend. It is homespun philosophy that these things have a way of sorting themselves out, and in the following year, shortly after his forty-fifth birthday in 1959, Peter Townsend was married to Mlle Marie-Luce Jamagne, the twenty-one-year-old daughter of a Belgian tobacco manufacturer, whom he had first met at a riding club soon after his arrival in Brussels.

9: FRIENDSHIP

It was impossible to see who it was, because of the scarf; but a pair of unmistakably pretty eyes peeped out mischievously. I had expected her voice to be softly pitched in keeping with her petiteness but it was in a high register... Not until later did I realize that her more serious tone is a form of defence...

William Glenton, *Tony's Room* (1965)

I

The winds of change do not blow stronger than the tides of friendship in their magnetic ebb and flow. In her mid-twenties, at the flux of young womanhood, Princess Margaret had reached the juncture where most of her friends were married or on the point of marrying: and as one wedding followed another the Princess was drawn into closer intimacy with an old friend whom she had known since the children's parties at 145 Piccadilly, and her childhood seaside holidays at Eastbourne. This was Lady Elizabeth Cavendish, who was just three days younger than her sister, the Queen, and seemed firmly a single girl. Both she and Margaret often remarked with amusement to newcomers that they had always known one another. So close and sympathetic was the original family friendship of a generation earlier that the pale rose colourwash of Royal Lodge had been copied from the rose stucco of Compton Lodge, the Eastbourne mansion that Elizabeth's father, the 11th Duke of Devonshire, head of the Cavendish family, had loaned to George VI and his consort. Lady Elizabeth's mother was both a Cecil and a Gore through the two sides of her family and a childhood friend of the Queen Mother.

At the 1953 Coronation, as Mistress of the Robes to the Queen, she had worn the velvet and ermine of an eighteenth-century Duchess of Devonshire, so ancient are these aristocratic affinities. Lady Elizabeth, tall, delicate of frame, looked what was, fine-bred almost to a fault, a Gainsborough lady, yet a Fragonard, too, with her spirited sense of fun.

Like Princess Margaret, she had also been brought up in palaces with chilly State rooms beneath painted Verrio ceilings; her grandfather at Chatsworth had been the most ducal of dukes and, like Margaret, she set little store by such trappings. At thirty-one, Elizabeth Cavendish undertook constant chores for a number of charities and yet, also like the Princess, she loved an amusing and well-surrounded table and exercised a fine discrimination in persuasively drawing the best from all the varied talents of her friends. Invited to accompany the Princess as an extra lady-in-waiting on the 1954 Caribbean tour, she had shown herself the most helpful and good-humoured of companions. That winter, we remember, Judy Montagu had initiated the amateur production of *The Frog* for the Princess's special diversion; and in the winter of 1955–56, similarly, Lady Elizabeth sympathetically beguiled Margaret into the professional rehearsals of the John Cranko revue *Cranks*.

It was widely said at the time that Elizabeth was one of the 'angels' or part-backers of the show, and certainly, in combining young John Cranko's brilliant book and choreography with the scenic designs of John Piper, she displayed her skill in bringing people of diverse gifts together. Margaret's critical advice was also sought and so one finds the Princess sitting in the shrouded stalls of the St Martin's Theatre one dreary February afternoon, watching a run-through, and contributing occasional suggestions. She felt for instance that two of the Piper backdrops were too similar to follow on one another and, the point being taken, the scenes were rearranged. And Margaret revelled, of course, in the theatrical atmosphere, in meeting the cast and getting to know the innermost professional details of production.

She knew, for example, that the 'front of the house' photographs were being taken by a young photographer named Antony Armstrong-Jones, whom Elizabeth Cavendish had known for some time. She knew, too, from Elizabeth that he preferred to take his pictures live and unposed during rehearsals, but on hearing that the Princess was in the theatre he chose not to intrude and they failed to meet. Romantic destiny was dragging its feet. In April, when the success of *Cranks* was assured, Princess Margaret and Lady Elizabeth went down to Holkham Hall for the wedding of Lady Anne Coke and Colin Tennant. Knowing him to be a friend of the Tennants, the bride had asked Antony Armstrong-Jones to take her wedding photographs and there is a charming photograph of the Princess smiling out at the camera, her eyes assuredly bright with amusement at the bobbing, weaving and ducking of the personable young man with his Leica. Eager as ever to sponsor the gifted, Elizabeth wished to present him to the Princess but amid the festivities the opportunity slipped by and, when they looked around, the cameraman was nowhere to be seen.

It may well have been indirectly on Lady Elizabeth's recommendation that the Duke of Kent asked Tony Armstrong-Jones if he would take his twenty-first birthday photographs later that summer and it was an oddity that when the portraits were published on October 9th neither the

Princess nor Lady Elizabeth saw them, being thousands of miles away at that time in Dar es Salaam.

That summer Princess Margaret had joined the Queen and Prince Philip in Stockholm during their Olympics stay. Watching a performance in the lovely long-forgotten Court Theatre at Drottningholm, with its candle footlights and eighteenth-century scenery, the Princess found it a pity that Elizabeth had missed something so much in her line. The outcome was that Lady Elizabeth was invited again to accompany the Princess as an extra lady-in-waiting, during her five-week East African tour in the autumn.

The Princess celebrated her twenty-sixth birthday at Balmoral and spent part of the day 'doing some homework', reading up Mauritius and Zanzibar. Then on September 22nd she flew out to Mombasa with Lady Elizabeth and the customary lady-in-waiting, Miss Iris Peake, and with Colonel Martin Gilliat and Major Francis Legh, who were respectively Private Secretary and assistant secretary to the Queen Mother, to lend more statesmanlike weight. The journey had some inner importance as a counterbalance to the Queen's visit to West Africa earlier in the year and, from her delighted discovery that the crowds in Mombasa were shouting 'Jambo! Jambo!' — which meant 'Welcome' yet sounded very like 'Jumbo!' — the Princess greeted Africa in an exceptionally carefree frame of mind. On the official side, she had expressed a wish to meet as many women and children of all classes and races as possible and the then Governor, Sir Evelyn Baring, and Lady Mary Baring perfectly stage-managed this idea.

Young girls in white saris greeted her with ropes of tropical flowers at gatherings of hundreds of Indian and Arab women. At the residence of one of the chief Arab advisers, the Princess was admitted with her ladies, Elizabeth and Iris, into the world of Moslem purdah, the harem or zenana, where the veiled occupants removed their yashmaks to offer ceremonial coffee — and presented the Princess with a miniature sword as a symbol 'of the duties of men which in this age must be shouldered by women'. Later, at Government House, Princess Margaret had the more awesome duty of addressing, on behalf of the Queen, a solemn audience of scores of bearded sheikhs. In Zanzibar she faced the ceremonial task of calling upon the aged Sultan, then in his seventy-eighth year, who had occupied the throne since 1911 and had at that time reigned longer than any other monarch in the world.

A friend described at the time 'the composite decor of Queen Victoria and the Queen of Sheba. The Princess travels through the extraordinary narrow and sinister alleyways standing up in an open jeep. Veiled ladies look down through lattice windows: one is glad everyone is friendly.' In Mauritius, on the other hand, the overexcited crowds broke through steel police barriers and surrounded her car. When they were beaten back and she changed to an open car a few minutes later to progress round a racecourse, they dropped from balconies and swarmed over the rails to get closer. Facing that wild stampede, the Princess had rarely been more frightened.

Later still, having decided to walk from the stand to the paddock, just as she would do at home, the Princess's decision was resolutely maintained, though little was to be seen of her save Lady Elizabeth's hat, marking her passage through the human sea. In retrospect, the crowd scenes, the native dances and tribal gatherings, the game reserves and jolting drives, merge into an indeterminate sequence, but one still remembers a much-told jest in Tanganyika. It had been hoped that the Princess would view a tribal gymkhana seated on a carved throne which had been prepared for the Duke of Windsor when Prince of Wales. Unluckily, in the long interval this had been kept in a thatched store, where time, damp and white ants had reduced it to rubbish. 'Which decisively proves,' Governor Sir Edward Twining told the Princess, 'that people in grass houses shouldn't stow thrones.'

Princess Margaret's visit to Kenya proved of more lasting value. It was only two years since the Mau Mau atrocities, the country had been swept by virulent anti-British propaganda and her tour became a turning-point of settled friendly relations. At this point of her journey, however, the constant changes of climate and altitude, food and water, wrought their effect, and in Nairobi she fell ill with a gastric attack. Elizabeth Cavendish looked after her like a sister, sternly solicitous that she should take her tablets, take her siesta, and take everything more easily. Yet the royal call of duty was all-compelling and the Princess insisted on leaving her bed despite the doctors and walked among the 8,000 guests at a garden party rather than cause disappointment. After lunch had been cancelled, three small girls were intensely dismayed at being unable to present their bouquets. Hearing of this, the Princess sent for them to make a more personal presentation.

So much for typical royal behaviour, but the Princess was also able to disappear for a day or two on a flying safari to the Amboseli Game Reserve on the slopes of Kilimanjaro. As her sister had done at Treetops, she spent a night at a lodge close to a drinking pool, and her camera-shots of the array of wildlife — lions, a herd of elephants, giraffe, gazelle — still embellish Cavendish and Windsor photo albums. From Kisumu on Lake Victoria, Princess Margaret then flew home in time for the State Opening of Parliament. Whereupon the Queen made her own recognition of the accomplished success of the Princess's journey by inviting her to ride at her side in the Irish State Coach to Westminster, the only occasion in 700 years of Parliamentary history that a sister has accompanied the Sovereign.

Four months later, in February, 1957, Lady Elizabeth Cavendish also arranged something of still closer personal significance for, at a dinner party given by Elizabeth at her mother's house in Chelsea, 5 Cheyne Walk, Princess Margaret first met Antony Armstrong-Jones. He had but recently photographed Prince Charles and Princess Anne at Buckingham Palace, and every issue of *Vogue* had carried examples of his unorthodox colour fashion photography. He was looking forward to visiting Venice, which Princess Margaret had never seen, and Malta, which she had. The Princess quickly discovered that they shared the same sense of humour, and the dinner party of young people in the old Georgian house went with unforgettable zing.

II

For nearly a year, Princess Margaret's friendship with her future husband deepened only by the imperceptible degrees of gradual acquaintance. Though they were to marry within little more than three years, neither seemed immediately aware of their intense mutual attraction nor charged it with special importance. In 1952, when Tony had first gained wider attention for his portraiture of celebrities, James Norwood had asked him, as one Fleet Street acquaintance to another, whom he would most like to photograph, and he had responded unhesitatingly, 'Why, Princess Margaret, of course. I think she's the most vivacious person in the world!' In 1957, hearing that Tony was preparing an exhibition of his photographs as well as planning to publish a book and dreaming up scenes for a new Cranko revue, Princess Margaret said, equally casually, 'Don't you think he's really rather extraordinary?'

Between them, it was once remarked, there was less than six months difference in age and six inches difference in height. Born on March 7th, 1930, the son of a barrister who was appointed High Sheriff of Caernarvonshire when Tony was six, his schoolfellows recalled that he had been camera-mad even at Eton, although Angus Ogilvy, as it transpired, vaguely recollected him more as a lightweight boxer, representing and winning for Eton in inter-school bouts. Though slightly built, there was indeed an aggressive set to his underlip and jutting chin. Later, as their friendship ripened, Princess Margaret was to learn that he had been a child of divorce, his parents having first separated when he was only three, and the Princess must have found a fine irony in the discovery that his mother, the Countess of Rosse, the innocent party in the divorce action, had subsequently remarried *in a London church*. In the social swirl of Lady Rosse's wide friendships were Cavendish uncles and Hambleden (Smith) cousins, with the Ogilvys, Herberts and Douglas-Scotts, a context unknown to the Princess until some years later. In the *Cranks* revue, the hit song had been 'Who is it always there?' and it appeared that Tony had been there, at a remove, all the while.

Not long after the Cheyne Walk dinner party, he figured, I believe, in the theatre party when Princess Margaret went, for the third time, to see the two-man show *At the Drop of a Hat*, in which Michael Flanders captivated London, singing his amusing songs from a wheelchair due to the effects of polio. At all events, the Princess learned with utter astonishment from Elizabeth Cavendish that Tony had once had polio, spending over a year in a wheelchair before he slowly and laboriously taught himself to walk again. In one of their early meetings, Tony mentioned the coming show of his work and sought her expert views on the layout, she who had opened and visited so many exhibitions. Should a display be arranged in a series of small rooms or compartments, like a jewelled belt, or was it better for the entire show to burst with undivided impact on the visitor? The idea, wrote Tony, 'was to show a young man's way with a camera, in his first four years as a professional'.

Leslie Caron opened the exhibition in June, and Margaret would dearly have loved to attend the private view. But this was a time of private royal pressure when the Queen was preparing for an autumn visit to Canada and the United States, seeking and highly valuing her sister's advice in selecting her wardrobe. As a preliminary to the tour, Tony was also invited to photograph the Queen, Prince Philip and their two children in the gardens of Buckingham Palace, for an informal set of press photographs, and he astonished Philip by planning the session so rigorously beforehand that he occupied under twenty minutes of the Queen's time. This was Lord Snowdon's first chronicled meeting with his future in-laws. 'He was in and out in a flash!' the Queen supposedly said, and certainly 'his quick light voice, his energy, his jumpy charm' must have formed one of the innumerable topics of conversation between the sisters.

One afternoon in July, the Princess evidently embarked with Lady Elizabeth on an expedition to the Pimlico Road and tracked Tony to his lair ... and perhaps Margaret had already privately located and driven past his studio, between an antique shop and the Sunlight Laundry, beneath a block of Victorian flats. The dismantled exhibition pictures, the treble life-size Edith Evans, part of the balletic mural of Anya Linden, the portraits of Annigoni and Dior, and so much more, had been set out in the studio, an ironmongery shop in its earlier days.

But the most intriguing part was when on being invited to stay for tea, the visitors went down the spiral modern staircase which Tony had made himself, down into the former cellar ... to discover an all-white sitting room, with soft candelabra wall lights not unlike those in Clarence House, an elegant Regency atmosphere and, high up near the ceiling, louvred windows patterned with flickering shadows that were in fact the hurrying legs of passers-by.

One of Tony's favourite conversational ploys is to mention some problem of his own and seek opinions, and so the Queen's sister may well have been invited to suggest her ideas for the 1957 Christmas issue of *Vogue*, Tony in fact quickly made up his mind on a version of Cinderella in modern photo dress, with the pumpkin replaced not with a golden coach but by a bubble-car in the kitchen of the Cavendish Hotel. The fairy godmother's wand was a fish-frying implement topped by a battery of sparklers and Princess Margaret later laughed at the comic tale of the difficulty of getting the car into the kitchen, manhandled by a battery of chefs.

III

Leafing through the pages of my own private journals and notebooks, Tony Armstrong-Jones makes a definitive appearance in Princess Margaret's company in February, 1958. We all went to the Metropole, the neighbourhood cinema near Buckingham Palace, and very few people paid any heed to the presence of the well-connected young photographer as 'one of the group'. The film was the Hitchcock–Agatha Christie movie, *Witness for the Prosecution*, and he was probably also included when the Princess went to see the delightful Leslie Caron in the romantic film *Gigi* a week or so later. Elizabeth Cavendish had suggested inviting him because he needed cheering up. His energies had been focused on completing the scenery and stage designs for the second Cranko revue *Keep Your Hair On*, and the show had proved a disaster. Yet Tony had made his plans with such enthusiasm. There was to be a succession of surprises based on blow-up photography. There would be an enormous eye to gaze at the audience before the show, a low-level shot to give a strutting pigeon's view of Trafalgar Square, a hairdressing salon with a backdrop like a book page to swing over whenever a customer entered, and at another point a ten-foot enlargement of a beribboned plait of hair.

'It sounds fun. I shall buy every seat,' Princess Margaret had said, smiling, and on February 13th the show had opened at the Apollo to boos from the gallery and eventually such a din of catcalls that the cast on the stage could no longer hear the orchestra. Hastily seeking *The Times'* impressions of Tony's stage designs, Princess Margaret could read only that they were 'for the most part screens hoisted up and down ... amusing in the German style fashionable in the 1920s'. The show closed after fourteen performances. Yet when the cinema party went back to Clarence House after their movie, talking in ever-changing groups or casually dancing, the Princess found with surprise, that, far from needing encouragement, Tony seemed to have quite forgotten his disappointment. It already belonged to the past and now, with his Malta book completed with Sacheverell Sitwell, Weidenfeld and Nicholson had commissioned another book of photographs which had to be completed terribly quickly. It was simply to be called *London* with a hundred or two photographs to reflect every facet of London life, every aspect and activity and its opposite — talking, reading, dancing, working, feeding. One can almost still hear Tony's pleasant, lilting voice enquiring, 'Just what do you think I should include?'

What was the opposite of cleaning lamps in Whitehall ... if not the glass roof of Paddington Station? What better antithesis to a dockers' strip cabaret than Mme Vacani's dancing class? Margaret was becoming aware that her own life was sharply dividing into equally astonishing contrasts. Early in March she flew to Germany in one of the lush executive aircraft of the Queen's Flight to inspect two regiments of which she was Colonel-in-Chief, the Highland Light Infantry and the 3rd King's Own Hussars, and a day or two later found her indulging in the incredible adventure of crossing the Thames by the Deptford ferry, incognito, muffled up and unrecognized, to have drinks with a young man who had a room in Rotherhithe.

Tony, who loved investing himself with an air of mystery, had occasionally spoken to Elizabeth Cavendish of a Room (which had seemed even then to be invested with capital letters) where he could escape at times from the bustle of the studio to work in peace and quiet. Some months earlier, her friend, John Betjeman, had been forced to leave his house in Smithfield after a fire and Tony suggested that the poet might like to borrow the Room for a few weeks until the damage could be made good. 'It's on the river,' he had explained, 'it's at Rotherhithe.' And indeed, as invested later in Mark Girouard's rich prose, it was 'down in the Pool, where the river is at its most wonderful, romantic and extraordinary ... there is no embankment, no traffic, no noise, except the occasional unearthly bellowing of a ship's hooter; the houses look straight out across the moored barges, the tugs and the occasional great ship, to a tangled skyline of cranes, and the huge portal of Tower Bridge, with the dome of St Paul's beyond'.

When Princess Margaret officially visited the Dockland Settlement in the Isle of Dogs with Lady Elizabeth, the romantic excursion deeper into the mysteries of dockland could not be resisted, involving as it did, the ferry crossing, a rendezvous with Tony in his car, and then the discovery of 59 Rotherhithe Street. The Princess must have been aware on that first visit only of a row of tumbledown houses, the hurried dash across the narrow pavement into the end house, adjoining a demolition site, and then at the end of a short hallway the little beamed white-painted room, where she unexpectedly looked out at the grey panorama of the river and the water lapping the very walls a few feet below.

She had no idea of the part that the Room would play in her life, how precious, how endearing, it would become. Within a month she would be flying off to the Caribbean to open the Federal Legislation of the West Indies, and she felt how wonderful it would be if she could set sail instead from the river, in the dusk, with the last of the sunset pale in the sky beyond Tower Bridge. With an evening in May instead of March she was charting, all unknowingly, a blueprint for her honeymoon. The Princess flew to Trinidad on April 20th with Lady Elizabeth and Iris Peake and her thoughts must often have turned to the extraordinary young man, showing her his stack of contrasting photographs of London, and how time had raced as the three of them sat talking, watching the lights come on, until they could only hear the water lapping unseen in the darkness.

Trinidad was broiling in a temperature of 95 degrees. Island to island, the tour was by aircraft, without the relief of the trade winds on the decks of the *Britannia*, and the Princess went doggedly through a programme that included visits to sugar factories, hours at sports meetings, journeys over scorching roads and stage calypsos in a packed and torrid theatre. In Tobago there were ceremonies to endure and hospitals to visit in the main town of Scarborough, though with a respite, too, when Margaret was able to swim at the Golden Grove lagoon and relax after dark at a torch-lit beach barbecue. Georgetown, British Guinea, had felt left out of the 1955 visit and now provided triumphal drives and parades, housing estates to inspect, and again the pleasures of a weekend on the miniature coral island of Sergeant's Caye, with a nearby hotel to provision the royal bungalow and an Admiralty survey ship on patrol to ward off intruders. Not least the tour ended at Belize City, British Honduras, where Margaret seemed so truly a princess to the populace that men lifted their hats to her photograph in the shop windows. A pity that the press corps were strangely hurried away and flown home twelve hours before she attended a dance organized by a volunteer regiment, partnered by every officer who requested the pleasure!

The Lord Mayor of London welcomed the Princess home with an evening reception at Mansion House, when the orchestra of the Royal Horse Guards played *Island in the Sun* with an edge of nostalgia. 'How well travelled I am becoming!' she said. 'When people now talk to me of Scarborough, my mind turns less naturally to the North Riding than to Tobago.'

On her return from her first Caribbean tour three years earlier, City crowds had applauded her in romantic anticipation. Now, the City bore its habitual evening look of empty streets. Clearly it no longer mattered that Peter Townsend had briefly returned to London and to Earl Grey tea at Clarence House. Rumours simmered again, and yet were readily quashed when the Palace issued a clear denial, 'Her Royal Highness's statement of 1955 remains unaltered'. And even if that celebrated relinquishment had never been made, if the denouement had been merely deferred instead of firmly written, one considers that Peter Townsend would have found himself at the surprise alternative ending of the story, cast in the forlorn role of a rejected suitor.

IV

As early as 1958, that year of their growing friendship, the meetings of Princess Margaret and her future husband assumed an episodic character, as if the pattern of their marriage, with its leave-takings and reunions, was fixed already in the darkroom of fate. To Margaret's intense interest, Elizabeth Cavendish was planning a house of her own in Chelsea, and taking Tony's advice on some of the fitments. If the Princess also asked Tony's opinion, as a man, on the dress designs for her first Canadian tour that summer, he in turn sought the Princess's views on the new themes in women's winter-sports design that were then engrossing him. In the view of a dress-trade friend, 'He went off the deep end about it. He had a whole series of revolutionary ideas, rather like the young Mary Quant. He had talents in every direction, and wanted to demonstrate everything.' And once more Tony totally astonished Margaret, for he had actually drawn as many as eighteen different outfits, knickerbockers in leather, a ballooning anorak in silk, 'new fun clothes that would look terrific in the snow.' A fashion friend had re-drawn his rough designs with more style and the Princess freshly sketched some of the drawings herself, creating a royal imprint which would have mightily interested the press had they known of it.

All too soon it was July, with 'Peake and Cavendish' again in waiting for the month-long tour of Canada, a country Margaret had longed to see, as she said, for as long as she could remember. The original invitation to attend the centenary celebrations of British Columbia had developed into a coast-to-coast journey west to east from the Pacific to Nova Scotia, and the three girls quickly tested an Armstrong-Jones axiom, namely that people saw what they expected to see, and when they did not expect to see a princess, Princess Margaret might pass unnoticed.

The newspapers told of public events, of saluting aircraft creating the initial M in formation flying, and of the first Royal fleet review ever held in Canadian waters when the Princess took the salute of United States, Canadian and British warships from the bridge of a Canadian destroyer. But letters home told of slipping out of the trade exit of the hotel to drive around sightseeing, as carefree as anyone else around Vancouver Island. And, comically underlined, a newspaper clipping was mailed home that seven Canadian bachelors had been 'selected, briefed and rehearsed weeks beforehand' to dance with the guest of honour, each practising with a partner 'the same weight (100lb) and height (5ft) as Her Royal Highness.'

In public the Princess cut British Columbia's monster birthday cake, which was twenty feet high and weighed five tons. She had her first experience of a transatlantic-style press reception, 'skilfully flourishing her long gold-and-ebony cigarette holder as defence against the over-pressing', according to one reporter. And unluckily, somewhere on a backwoods whistle-stop tour en route to the Rockies the Princess lost the holder, 'a gift from an old friend, whom we cannot name,' as an aide said rather awkwardly. It was a loss with a nuance of finality. But by now Margaret was also steeped in Canadian atmosphere, thrilled by the small amphib aircraft that flew her from lake to lake, revelling in the overnight and weekend hospitality of farms and lodges and ranch-houses, speeding around the scenic spots in amusingly lush cars, with an accompaniment of such lively chatter that she forgot to feel carsick.

In Alberta, the Princess missed the celebrated Calgary Stampede by two weeks, but a hundred of the star cowboys returned to town to stage a wildly exciting extra rodeo in her honour. In Saskatchewan, she jaunted sixty miles by helicopter to have tea with a Norwegian family at a prairie farm, a side-trip arising out of a remark that she would like to meet some of the new Canuck pioneers in their own setting. In Ontario, only the thunder of Niagara Falls could compete with the ovation directed at her all the way down Yonge Street. 'Canada has turned me on,' she said, in the vernacular of polite nonsense. But Canada was also pleased with its visitor. After the sightseeing highlights of Montreal and Quebec, the Princess gave a new pattern, a new twist to the customarily 'quieter' five days in the Maritimes. Knowing her Longfellow, she had asked to see Acadia, with the result that every house of that once tragic region of old French settlement flew the French-Canadian flag, the gold-starred tricolour, in a festival of local pride. Peeling church bells and old French songs greeted her arrival by helicopter, and no Canadian community welcomed her with more heartful sentiment and sincerity.

At the small fishing town of Digby next day, the Princess strolled around the boardwalk of the harbour and talked to the scallop fishermen, one of whom unexpectedly produced two painted seashells from his pocket to give to her. 'But how did you know I collect them?' said the Princess, delighted, and thereafter treasured them at Kensington Palace. Nova Scotia also saw the Princess at her regal best on her final night in the Dominion when the Nova Scotia government gave a banquet at which her speech in French and English was televised across the nation. Taking another successful detail from the Queen she then drove straight to the airport in her evening gown, a shimmering floodlit figure gracing TV screens nationwide as she inspected the naval guard of honour. Aboard the plane, beyond public view, the air crew thought her a charmer when she asked for the stewardesses 'in case they would like to look at my dress before I take it off.'

Next, the Birkhall sojourn of late summer was broken by a brief visit to Brussels in a so-called private bid to see the 1958 World's Fair. Social links were reaffirmed with the Belgian Royal Family, and ancient historic links with England drawn to public attention. Amid these travels, the friendship with Tony thus had an intermittent quality, its lulls and pauses wadded by correspondence. Between official engagements in London and Belfast, Margaret read the reviews on his *London* and *Malta*. The two books had the distinction of being published by different firms almost within the same week and, at almost the same time, Tony's winter-sports fashion show at a Sloane Street boutique gained heightened press publicity from the presence of Lady Elizabeth Cavendish. In mid-November, moreover, when Princess Margaret was in London, Tony made his first visit to New York, a professional photographic trip from which he did not return until after Christmas. And still the time-lag of friendship was continued, for he alighted at Shannon airport only in time to see the New Year in as usual with his mother and his two half-brothers at Birr Castle, in the very heart of southern Ireland.

V

In all her journeyings Princess Margaret never failed to attend Sunday morning service or early Communion, whether in homely local churches or cathedrals. The sincerity of her devotion was obvious, and we may note that early in 1959 she went out of her way to attend morning service at the little church of Fitcham four miles from Sandringham, where she had last knelt in worship with her father.

More than any previous year, this was to be her year of destiny, with her every desire laden with future consequence. On their first Saturday at home at Royal Lodge the Queen Mother invited Tony Armstrong-Jones to tea, and beside the log fire in the octagonal sitting room he sat talking of his American impressions. Had he seen *West Side Story*? Princess Margaret had attended the London charity premiere while he was away and presently she put on a record and the songs from the new musical surged through the room, 'I feel pretty ... oh, so pretty'; ... 'Tonight, tonight, the world is mine tonight!...' Only a few days later the Princess took the Queen and Elizabeth Cavendish to see the show, taking their seats in the circle when the house lights were lowered, with Tony inconspicuous in the trio of escorts. The Queen Mother also went one evening, telling Walter Clarke, the theatre manager, 'Princess Margaret is *always* playing the records,' and she needed no maternal intuition when she discovered that the story was a Manhattan version of the Romeo and Juliet story, and that the Romeo role was named Tony.

As remarked earlier, that engaging young man was slow to see himself as a would-be suitor. The mood was more an enrichment of an affectionate friendship, each discovering the other at a new and more sincere level of candour. Tony once said to a studio friend, 'You can know so many people and not know anyone at all.' In exploring the true personality of Princess Margaret, he had learned how vulnerable she was, how easily hurt at the hidden levels beneath her outward gaiety. 'At a deeper emotional level, both have had disadvantages to overcome, have suffered setbacks and have a touch of immaturity still,' one observer wrote later. 'Both are sociable yet paradoxically solitary. Both have been a long time settling down.'

10: BETROTHAL AND MARRIAGE

She was difficult of character, but kind-hearted, and now I found her exceptionally pretty. I met Tony Armstrong-Jones, with the seductive smile, shy but charming... His behaviour towards Princess Margaret could not have been more perfect and loving.

Queen Victoria Eugenie of Spain, *June 1961*

I

In January, 1959, when Queen Elizabeth the Queen Mother was about to commence an official tour of East Africa, it was announced that, in April, she would also pay a short private visit to Rome. Then, late in March, Lady Clarke at the British Embassy unexpectedly heard that Princess Margaret wished to accompany her mother. 'The spur of the moment is the essence of adventure,' Tony once said, and had demonstrated it that very month by leaving London for a photographic assignment in Davos. One catches a hint of reprisals, then, in the Princess's Roman holiday ... or was it suddenly the equivalent of the separation, the sea change, traditionally expected of a princess when facing the most momentous decision of her life?

Her outward flight in an RAF Comet was in any event an ordeal of turbulence, and her arrival at Ciampino airport in a torrential thunderstorm surely occasioned the impetuous traveller some misgivings. But then the sun came out, and although the wonders of Rome were often glimpsed obscurely through a barricade of photographers, the holiday was summed

179

up in a letter as 'thorough enjoyment'. Mother and daughter followed their own devices, the Queen Mother seeking out the Villa d'Este while the Princess made a pilgrimage around the churches. At the St Maria in Cosmedin, the moment of truth was greeted by a brilliance of photo-flashes amid a babel of cameramen when the Princess placed her hand unscathed within the famous mouth of stone which is supposed to bite those not leading a truthful life. With her mother, the Princess called upon the kindly Pope John, the second pontiff whom she had visited, and then their ways diverged again, and Margaret went to see her old friend, Judy Montagu, at her rooftop home of Tiber Island.

This may indeed be regarded as the irretrievable turning-point of decision, driving the Princess into unfettered confidences; and the sympathetic, motherly Judy assuredly gave her such good advice that Margaret could hardly wait to return to London — and caused astonishment in fact by flying home five hours ahead of her mother's plane. And the recognition was mutual. It happened that Tony's 'landlord' at Rotherhithe, the journalist, William Glenton, who had lent him the riverside room, was thinking of getting married and launched into a discussion of that very big subject with Tony one day. His girl was Norwegian and it troubled him that he could only offer her exile. And Mr Glenton remembered afterwards that Tony had said 'with great earnestness', 'I believe that a man only really falls in love once. When that happened, I'd marry the girl — whoever she was!'

Another salient occasion occurred at Royal Lodge when Margaret and Tony launched impromptu into the fun of a photo-session, searching out the settings and deciding the changes of dress for the studies issued three months later as the Princess's official twenty-ninth birthday photographs. Tony now enjoyed an excuse to carry a picture of Margaret around in his wallet: why should a photographer not find a magic talisman in his current work? The story is told that when shopping in Cartier's the Princess greatly admired a gold replica of a walnut which, on being opened, disclosed a holder for a dozen tiny photographs. Billy Wallace, always a willing aide, is said to have quietly purchased the walnut on her behalf a day or two later. And understanding friends who invited Margaret and Tony to dinner began to find deft pretexts for leaving them to themselves.

'It just so happened that we had a nursery crisis one night, the baby was teething, and then my husband remembered the overseas calls he had to make in his study,' one married friend recalls. Like other couples, they held hands in the pictures. It made little difference that the cinema was the private theatre at Clarence House or that the movie was the then-banned Marlon Brando film *The Wild Ones*. It is melancholy to add that a footman sharply noted the occasion, and three years later narrated it in print.

The rota of summer events then interrupted the idyll: a sunny visit to the Channel Isles and a week in Portugal, where perhaps for the first time, Margaret found herself a teenage idol, thanks to an exceptional build-up in the Lisbon press. The drizzling rain did not prevent an extraordinarily youthful crowd from greeting her and all but sweeping the welcoming dignitaries off their feet in their enthusiasm. Officially the Princess's visit was to inaugurate a British trade fair, but her stay became the focus of one of those demonstrations of old-fashioned deluxe hospitality which the richer Portuguese do so well. She had been scheduled to stay with the British Ambassador amid the mansions of the Embassy quarter, but instead found herself a guest in a country house where the hearths blazed with olive wood, the lighting was by oil lamps and the tables were decked with ornate silver. The cottage window of her bedroom opened on to a fabulous view, and under the orange trees in the patio she was serenaded by the poignant sweetness of *fado*. Her letters home, flown in the diplomatic bag, had good cause for the message, 'Wish you were here!'

Then, from this fantasy, she returned home to London, to the reassurance of the Rotherhithe room, the window open wide to the river coolness, and to the hours of intimate talk and confidences. There was the amusement of sitting in the bentwood rocking chair watching Tony's esoteric preparations to do something miraculous to a steak and salad for dinner, or of strumming quietly on the old upright piano that occupied most of one wall.

Mr Glenton, who lived upstairs, did not stumble on the identity of Tony's guest for months. Then one afternoon he chanced to meet Lady Elizabeth Cavendish in the hall. 'I just dropped by to tidy Tony's room,' she said, almost too casually. Yet what was there to tidy in a room little more than twelve feet square, with rush matting on the floor, a deal table, basketwork and bentwood chairs, an ancient divan, a corner china cupboard and a collection of junkshop curios: a gilt birdcage with stuffed birds, a blue glass rolling pin, a musical box? It was only when Bill Glenton chanced on a picture in a magazine identifying Lady Elizabeth as Princess Margaret's lady-in-waiting that 'an incredible possibility' first entered his head. Then one evening, returning from a newspaper assignment, he was about to mount the staircase when the door of the room beyond opened enquiringly, and silhouetted against the candlelight was 'the unmistakable figure' of the Princess. Here was a working journalist with the greatest romantic scoop story of the century within a floor's depth of his typewriter. Yet to his lasting honour Mr Glenton kept the secret through all its amusing developments, until the demolition men razed 59 Rotherhithe Street to the ground.

Whether Margaret told the Queen about Rotherhithe at this time one cannot tell, although the Queen certainly knew where she was to be found towards the end of July when her sister 'dropped out of sight into Sussex'. During the hospitable festivities of Goodwood week the Princess stayed in fact with her friends, the Parker-Bowles, at their seaside home near Aldwick — Mrs Parker-Bowles was a daughter of Sir Humphrey de Trafford — while Tony was a visitor not far away at Billy Wallace's home near Petworth. But there was also a delectable weekend when Margaret and Tony visited the Countess of Rosse at her family home, Nymans, and Margaret first explored the setting of much of Tony's boyhood. Thousands of people have come to know and love Nymans since it was placed under National Trust care, and scores indeed were in the garden that day, finding no cause to pay attention to the young couple also strolling there.

Tony's grandfather, Leonard Messel, had built the house in Sussex sandstone, in the authentic style of a Tudor manor house and it had mellowed into 'an amazingly deceptive evocation', as Ian Nairn noted. One wing had been destroyed by fire, curiously gaining a fresh and serene beauty when the roses and other flowering plants, as Lady Rosse wrote, seemed 'to take advantage of the now windowless mullions to climb in and out at will'. From one of the viewpoints of Nymans, Margaret gazed across the limitless verdure of St Leonard's Forest and wondered at the haze of blue woodsmoke drifting above the trees. 'There are old cottages down there,' Tony explained, and Princess Margaret did not, could not, know that deep within the green valley was another secret paradise of their shared future.

II

My journal of 1959 mentions woodsmoke of a different kind in the wind. Thus a press secretary, Major Arthur Griffin, was appointed to the staff of Clarence House for the first time, as if in anticipation that the normal flow of world newspaper enquiries might soon swell into a torrent and, in line with his new duties, Major Griffin formally announced a luncheon party given in July by the Queen Mother in honour of the High Commissioner for Rhodesia and Nyasaland, Sir Gilbert Rennie. The Rennies' elder son was getting married later that month and, with romance in her Scottish maternal heart, Lady Rennie wondered a little about the handsome young man of about her son's age who spent much of his time talking to his neighbour, Princess Alexandra, but cast an occasional deeply mischievous glance along the table towards Princess Margaret.

The Queen was then absent in Canada on the prolonged tour that saw the opening of the St Lawrence Waterway and there are hints that she took soundings with Mr John Diefenbaker, then the Canadian Premier, on the conjectural situation that might arise if her sister should wish to marry a certain young bachelor. The Queen expressed her own happiness, his status as a commoner probably never occurred to her, and she was reassured, here and elsewhere, that the Commonwealth would be delighted. There quickly followed equally happy tidings of even closer concern to the Queen in the medical flurry that heralded the advent — on February 19th, 1960 — of Prince Andrew. The circumstance was well summarized in a letter from a friend of the Royal Family some months later. 'People are saying that Elizabeth does not favour the match between

184

Margaret and Armstrong-Jones — what nonsense! As if one cannot gauge her emotional response to her sister's happiness by the coming of the new baby — and this after nine years of hoping for more children!'

Princess Margaret was one of the first to learn of the Queen's joy in her pregnancy, and the Queen and Prince Philip alone knew of the progress of the Princess's courtship when Tony came as a guest to Balmoral. A less observant member of the house party was content to record that the couple 'both carried cameras wherever they went and spent hours on end taking photographs of the party, the wonderful views across the Scottish highlands and moors, and of each other.' The Princess had hoped to celebrate her twenty-ninth birthday with the usual family picnic, but it poured with rain all day and they stayed indoors.

It has not been denied that, in the end, Margaret and Tony kept their private betrothal secret from everyone for a few hours, although their unbounded happiness could hardly be concealed. Whether by accident or design, the George Cole film *The Bridal Path* was shown at the Castle movie show, and the homely Scottish story of love and marriage was greeted by rapturous laughter and applause highly mystifying to those not in the know. The private betrothal, as I have termed it, might be better defined as an understanding. The two agreed in following the then unbroken system of royal alliance by waiting six months before a formal engagement, even accepting advice to part for a month or two in the autumn. Back at Royal Lodge, the Princess horrified the gardeners one day by seizing a pair of shears and cutting her way through the meticulous perfection of a yew hedge that had divided the house from the sunlight and freedom of the swimming pool. While her mother was still away, the Princess similarly displayed an acute anxiety lest a leaf or two should mar the serene surface of the pool, a perfectionist mood hardly less significant than her attack upon the thick dark hedge.

In London, Tony maintained business as usual, preparing among other tasks the rose-decked *Vogue* magazine cover that within a few months, at the time of their official engagement announcement, 'sang on the bookstalls', as one editor said. In popular idiom, moonlight and roses might have been the theme of that Indian summer, the evenings so warm that the two lounged until long after dusk near the swimming pool, planning and confiding. Or they pretended for fun that Tony had just 'come home from the studio', and they would sup alone, with small tables drawn up to their armchairs, watching television, like a cosy domestic foretaste of the future. The Princess amused Tony by choosing her bridesmaids partly on the premise they should be the prettiest and most photogenic group of bridesmaids ever seen, and Tony amused his future bride by quite failing to consider who should be his best man.

Late in October, the Queen Mother indulged the betrothed couple by arranging a party for them at Clarence House, which proved to be the liveliest party held in that staid old mansion for years. More than two hundred and fifty guests danced to Ray Ellington's band into the small hours of the morning; the footmen wore the scarlet coats of semi-State livery; and bacon-and-egg breakfasts were served at small tables arranged along the main corridor. Princess Margaret 'positively bounced with excitement', an added source of fun being that fewer than half the guests suspected the innermost reason for the dance, which also served in part, and more publicly, as a welcome home for Princess Alexandra from Australia.

Then, as they had agreed, the couple separated, Tony to stay with his sister, Susan (the Viscountess de Vesci), at her home at Abbey Leix, Princess Margaret to resume her duty rota of official tasks. A thick mantle of snow fell early in central Ireland that winter, and Tony's regular packages of photographs depicted white-laden trees, snowballing, and the bright laughter of his Vesey nieces, Emma and Catherine, piled into a toboggan with their young brother, Tom. Margaret fervently confided to her Aunt Marina, who dearly loved to watch the progress of royal love-affairs, 'I can hardly wait until they call me aunt,' and in the all-important New Year of 1960, when Tony arrived at Sandringham, that moment stepped immeasurably nearer.

Yet first another wedding was imminent. Earl Mountbatten's younger daughter, Pamela, was to marry David Hicks at Romsey Abbey on January 13th, and all the Royal Family would be there except the Queen, who was expecting her baby in February. The Sandringham group accordingly dispersed early, but on January 12th Princess Margaret had a neatly timed official engagement at the Royal Docks downstream from Rotherhithe. In the room at No. 59 Tony had lit the oilstove and put the kettle on so that they basked in a pleasant fug of tea and toast and paraffin. Only then, it seems, did Tony casually mention that he, too, had been invited to the wedding, on the bridegroom's side, having known David Hicks since his earliest Pimlico days. Back in 1946, months before they were engaged, Lilibet and Philip had attended the wedding of Earl Mountbatten's elder daughter, Patricia, at Romsey Abbey, sharing the poetry and solemnity of the marriage service in that ancient twelfth-century church. And strangely after fourteen years the circle of coincidence was complete, as Princess Margaret and her future husband listened to the marriage vows of the younger sister.

The Queen had agreed that Margaret's engagement should be officially announced seven days after the advent of her new baby, and Prince Andrew was born on February 19th. Now the Princess was on tenterhooks lest the press should discover some hint of her betrothal a day or even an hour too soon. She and Tony had already twice put their secret at hazard, at Sandringham by reverently going to worship together at the little church of West Newton and again in London when they were both guests at the wedding of Margaret's cousin, Diana Bowes-Lyon, and Peter Somervell in the splendour of the Henry VII chapel in Westminster Abbey. At the reception in St James's Palace afterwards, one family guest eyed the betrothed pair and thought them 'sweetly and quite absurdly in love'.

Margaret and Tony were both in such an emotional whirl that they later found it difficult to remember events in orderly sequence. But certainly they were at Royal Lodge on the evening of Friday, February 26th when the evening television and radio programmes were interrupted for the announcement:

> *It is with the greatest pleasure that Queen Elizabeth the Queen Mother announced the betrothal of her beloved daughter The Princess Margaret to Mr Antony Charles Robert Armstrong-Jones, son of Mr R. O. L. Armstrong-Jones, Q.C., and the Countess of Rosse, to which union The Queen has gladly given her consent.*

III

After twelve years of piercing inquisition, Princess Margaret could not avoid a glow of satisfaction at having, after all, kept her love affair so safely hidden. Fleet Street was taken completely by surprise and, indeed, was utterly astonished at the disclosure that the Queen's sister planned to marry not only a commoner but one of themselves: a young man who, if he did not live by the printed word, equally made a lucrative profession of the printed picture.

Commander Colville's office in the Palace was in a state of telephone siege as he explained over and over that 'both the Queen and Prince Philip were delighted, because this is such an obviously happy match'. Every editor in the free world jubilantly decided that the royal engagement was as phenomenal a story as the Abdication, with the difference that this was a romantic and unsullied love-match giving universal pleasure. Preparing to face the photographers and television cameramen in the grounds of Royal Lodge, Margaret almost forgot to wear her engagement ring, so accustomed was she to concealing it, a ring of great individuality with a ruby like a rosebud set within a marguerite of diamonds.

When asked what else they were doing on the day when they first became the talk of the world, the couple could only recollect being quietly settled at the Lodge and playing canasta. Returning to London, it seems highly probable that they drove past the Pimlico studio, where a knot of people gazed at the locked doors as if expecting to see the lovers in person. The couple in fact made their first appearance together in public, with the Queen Mother, at a gala ballet performance at the Royal Opera House, Covent Garden.

It was fourteen years since the evening, just after the war, when Princess Margaret had sat in the rose-decked royal box for her first grown-up gala occasion. Now the theatre blazed with television arc lamps, and the pair received a tumultuous reception. Not to diminish her daughter's moment, the Queen Mother stepped to one side and the applause broke into cheers, an ovation as much in confident welcome to Antony Armstrong-Jones as in affectionate well-wishing to his future bride.

It is pleasant to mention one's own small share in the happy sentiment; and the Princess noticed with amusement, as I heard, that the London hoardings blossomed with posters ten feet high, 'Scoops the world! Exclusive! The romance...' in announcing my serial in a Sunday newspaper. I enjoyed an effective lead in telling everything except the Rotherhithe episodes, which remained in confidence, and although the furore was worldwide, King Peter of Yugoslavia similarly mentioned to Princess Grace of Monaco that the boulevards of Paris were placarded with '*Le Roman d'Amour de Margaret et Tony — par Helen Cathcart*'. In general, the couple studied the newspapers with a mixture of happy interest, humour and only occasional distaste at the first curious inklings, here and there, of an underlying malice.

If it seemed untimely that Tony's father had been tracked down on honeymoon in Bermuda with the third Mrs Armstrong-Jones, this was better than the sheaf of hurtful inaccuracies about Tony's family and the wounding assumption that he would share in Princess Margaret's Civil List allowance, which automatically increased to £15,000 on her marriage. The Princess sadly heard, too, that reporters had descended on Rotherhithe. 'Don't worry, I shan't let anyone in,' Bill Glenton promised, reassuringly, over the phone. It turned out that a man who had interviewed Tony in the room some two years earlier had jumped at the assumption of 'a hideaway, a secret rendezvous'. Alas, these and other contingencies had already been foreseen and discussed with the Queen and Prince Philip, who considered that there might be many bridges to cross and could only suggest coolly taking each one in turn. Among the bristling problems, Princess Margaret felt herself advancing into a totally unknown future, with few signposts or prescriptions. The nearest precedent to guide the sister of the Sovereign, indeed, had been the marriage of her father's sister to Viscount Lascelles, a man of large estates and infinite wealth.

More than seventy years earlier, there had also been the marriage of Margaret's great-aunt, Princess Louise (sister of George V), to a young nobleman of whom Queen Victoria approved 'as he is immensely rich' and whom she had immediately created the first Duke of Fife. In another direction, a more helpful guideline was that Queen Victoria's nephew, Count Victor Gleichen, son of her half-sister, Princess Feodora, had followed a successful career as a sculptor, in the teeth of protests of an unfair advantage. Accepting commissions, from civic statuary to private portrait busts, he had indeed chiselled away at a studio in the garden of St James's Palace, and enjoyed a rent-free matrimonial home by 'grace and favour' in the clocktower. Yet it was to be a year or more before anyone realized that this bohemian ghost provided a passport to any member of the Royal Family to follow an unfettered professional career in the arts.

Meanwhile, Margaret and Tony had begun house-hunting, with vague aspirations of beauty and contentment rather than certainty as to the required number of rooms. They skirted the Chelsea river reaches and prospected London's 'Little Venice', overlooking the Regent's Canal, in case the charm of Rotherhithe could be recaptured in the effect of lights and water. To avoid the 'siege of Pimlico', where his studio was privately for sale, the Queen had meanwhile invited her future brother-in-law to make his bachelor home in a first-floor guest suite at the Palace. And the story is that one day, in one of her merriest moods, she mentioned that she could recommend some estate agents who had a suitable property on their books. The 'agents' were the Crown Estate Commissioners, the house was known as No. 10 Kensington Palace, and Margaret was thrown into utter delight when she took Tony to view it. As she had begun to suspect, it was the very house, looking more like a dolls' house now, where she had admiringly said years ago she would like to live.

The Marquess of Carisbrooke, brother of Queen Ena of Spain, had contentedly lived there until his death; and the old double-fronted dark-brick house still bore the same air of rural seclusion that Margaret remembered, facing a grassy corner of an immaculate village green. It was in fact on the darker, northern side of the Palace but the Princess was charmed by the two downstairs panelled rooms, of Rotherhithe proportions, demurely facing across the white-painted hall. To the south the windows overlooked a paved court like a college close. Her Aunt Rose, her mother's sister, after whom she had been named, had once lived across the courtyard, her windows overlooking the same flagstones and tulip tubs.

IV

The wedding date was fixed for May 6th, seven weeks after the Queen in Council had signified her formal consent to the marriage, and only eight weeks after their enticing discovery of the house behind Kensington Palace. Part of the Welsh gold from which the Queen's wedding ring had been made had been set aside for her sister, and Margaret and her bridegroom combined their ideas in designing the ring, a band so small on Margaret's finger that there was still sufficient gold to keep for Princess Anne. Both had decided that they preferred the vows of the 1662 prayer book, with the promise to obey, and Dr Fisher was asked if a passage from the Scriptures could be read instead of an address. The Beatitudes were chosen, 'Blessed are the meek... Blessed are ye, when men shall revile you,' and the

Princess also requested that the prayer used at the Queen's wedding in blessing the ring should be repeated. In agreeing to television cameras, the bride and groom said that they 'preferred' no close-ups during the sacred moments of their marriage vows and the giving of the ring. Both also realized that fifteen hundred of the Abbey guests in the nave would see nothing of the ritual at the high altar, owing to the intervening organ screen, and television monitors were installed for the first time to enable everyone present to share in the full ceremony.

Princess Margaret was surprised by the large number of individual decisions that could be taken. The music, for instance, received special consideration, from the three fanfares commissioned from Sir Arthur Bliss to the choice of Purcell's trumpet tune and airs instead of the Mendelssohn wedding march. Like most brides, Margaret wished to keep her wedding gown a surprise until the day, and knew what she wanted in design and materials alike with explicit precision. Three sketches from the Princess were discussed with Norman Hartnell who then submitted six designs, whereupon her final choice became a deep secret. A few days before the wedding, general indignation occurred when the American clothing paper, *Women's Wear Daily*, published details regardless, and sketches and fabricated photographs promptly appeared everywhere. According to these disclosures, there was to be a slightly full skirt, forming a short train; the sleeves were three-quarter length, and Hartnell was said to have ordered an immediate enquiry into the 'leak'. Only Princess Margaret appeared sweetly unperturbed. In reality the style was of unadorned simplicity, the sleeves wrist-length, the skirt very full and semi-crinoline, the train the longest and yet most ethereal the Abbey had ever seen. And happily the gossips were to be no more accurate in predicting the dresses of the bridesmaids, the eight pretty children aged from six to ten — Catherine Vesey, Virginia Fitzroy, Angela Nevill, Sarah Lowther, Annabel Rhodes, Rose Nevill, Marilyn Wills and Princess Anne — who perfectly balanced the bride's petite stature.

Sunny and fresh, the wedding day was one of perfect Maytime weather. From Clarence House, Margaret could just see the remarkable arch of roses, sixty feet high, at the top of the Mall, the last rose tucked into place only two hours before the bridegroom set out from Buckingham Palace with his best man, Dr Roger Gilliatt. Beyond the arch stretched an avenue of white masts, bearing banners with the monograms 'M' and 'A': it would not be roses all the way. Then the bride drove from Clarence House in the glass coach with Prince Philip, accompanied by a Captain's Escort of the Household Cavalry, of one hundred officers and men, and the great crowds once again vociferously cheered the Princess, as they had through twenty-five years and more.

Yet for the applauding thousands — and the watching millions — neither the delectable bridal processions, outward and homeward, nor the wedding ceremony itself, provided the deepest and most abiding impression. The honeymoon was to be a Caribbean cruise on the royal yacht *Britannia*, her ports of destination unknown, and the wedded couple were to embark at Tower Pier and sail from the Pool of London. Long after the bride and groom had made their final appearance on the Palace balcony, the crowds waited, growing ever larger, expecting perhaps to see them in an open carriage, and in any event to wave them on their way. Then, towards the end of the afternoon, a royal Rolls emerged from the Palace forecourt, with but a single escort car, and suddenly the onlookers realized that this was the bride and groom, the new Princess Margaret, Mrs Armstrong-Jones, shorn now of royal panoply, as if the happy pair had dropped all the trappings of royalty and were on their own.

It was a sheer *coup de théâtre*, and the crowds responded jubilantly, running across the Mall like ripples upon a shore. There were no troop cordons now. Not for the first time, the Princess was among the London crowds. Along the Strand and in the City, where the office homegoers joined those who were waiting, the limousine was engulfed by well-wishers, twenty deep, on either side. There were too few police; the people near the car were enclosed themselves by happy, more distant throngs, and the car moved at a snail's pace through the miles of smiling faces.

Tower Pier was reached an hour late, and church bells, ship's sirens and warehouse hooters saluted the couple with all the cheerful noise they could muster as the *Britannia* got under way. The shining roadways of Tower Bridge were raised majestically. Everyone now knew of Rotherhithe and it was a culminating moment of the enchantment of that extraordinary day when the Princess and her husband scampered frantically across to the near starboard side of the bridge of the royal yacht, waving to Bill Glenton as he responded from his fake back-window until the little house slipped astern.

V

As the *Britannia* steamed south-west into the Atlantic, the Admiralty flashed a warning of a floating mine and of rough weather ahead, apt symbols perhaps of the fringe difficulties of the future. Yet the royal yacht had made such smooth progress down Channel that they outsailed a rendezvous with a helicopter, which was to have dropped a parcel with a film of the wedding, newspaper photographs and news reports. The honeymooners sailed into a newsless, filmless void, which was as it should be, except that the fatherly steward of the royal cabins, Lieutenant Fred Pardy, noticed some anxiety next day not to be late for Sunday morning service on deck.

This was followed by the Armstrong-Jones' first party, for friendly drinks before lunch. Yet there were to be no plans, few timed destinations. 'Please respect the honeymoon,' the yacht signalled ahead, shortly before their first landfall, in the bay near Pigeon Point off the southernmost tip of Tobago. The French had infested the Caribbean with photographers and reporters, spending a fortune on speedboat and seaplane hire, and the royal yacht continually had to change course to avoid these intruders. The more public landings in Trinidad, Dominica and Antigua evoked a euphoria of flower-pelting and calypsos, but essentially the islanders respected the newlyweds' privacy, and day after day the couple spent much of their time sunbathing, swimming and picnicking on tiny islets where they were put ashore and left alone. 'It was so very wonderful for us both,' said Margaret, 'just to lie on those deserted beaches, without a soul in sight. Neither of us ever wanted to be rescued in the evening and we would have gladly lived in a little grass hut.' One of her own honeymoon snapshots indeed shows her husband striving to climb a palm tree, and Lord Snowdon's favourite photograph, crystal-framed at Kensington Palace, showed not a Princess but a woman with bare shoulders and windblown hair, crinkling her eyes in the sunlight.

In the romantic Grenadines, however, they eschewed solitude one day to visit the island which Colin Tennant had bought a year or two previously, and Colin and his wife Anne were there, with Oliver Messel, Tony's uncle, and other friends, waiting to greet them when they came ashore. Lush and green in that opalescent sea, three square miles of cultivated valleys and low undulating hills, the island contours were akin to Richmond Park, and Colin was full of ideas, just then, of creating a *liveable* earthly paradise. For the eighty island natives a new village, a school, a hospital, an airstrip, new groves of coconut palms, new cotton fields. And deftly, half in the palm plantations edging the sands, there would be low white beach houses and perhaps one or two small hotels, low-roofed, with deep verandahs … if the daydream ever came true.

But for the moment there was only the old-fashioned residence, the manager's house, a fragment of ruined fort and the 'sugar shacks', and after lunch the Tennants proposed a tour of the island north to south and promised to show their principal guests 'something we hope you'll accept as a wedding gift'. They drove past plantations of limes and grapefruit and came to a palm-fringed peninsular jutting between the shallow curves of two white beaches. This was the Tennants' offering to the newlyweds, an idyllic acreage they could forever call their own. Appropriate to the occasion, Margaret was wearing a pair of straw work slippers given to her in Kingstown, St Vincent, eighteen miles away, when she had first visited the Caribbean five years before, and the story is that she delightedly first-footed her new domain, gaily pretending to embroider it with imprints in Robinson Crusoe style, not taking it too seriously. But the secluded enchanted site on the pastoral isle of Mustique was subsequently conveyed with all due legal formality and was one day truly to prove a paradise in the sun.

11: HUSBAND, HOME AND FAMILY

His marriage means that the Establishment acquires a gifted professional in creative work... He may well find his career in working for the visual arts in the tradition of Queen Victoria's consort ... he will not be trapped...

John Barber, *May 1960*

I

The honeymooners returned on June 18th. The Royal Marines band played them ashore and they were welcomed by the Commander-in-Chief and Lord Mayor of Portsmouth. Then they travelled to London in a reserved first-class compartment on the 2.20 p.m. train, making a holiday party of it with the Princess's detective, Inspector Crocker, and her personal maid Ruby MacDonald. When the steward came round, Margaret ordered a British Railways sandwich: 'I've always wanted to try one.' To slightly dramatize the situation, they had begun as they meant to continue.

In the official jargon, the Queen 'had placed the royal yacht at their disposal' but it was a husband's prerogative to pay the train fares home and henceforth meet all the usual expenses of everyday life. Tony retrieved his car from the Palace mews, and at Royal Lodge the Ascot week guests were amused to find the couple so obviously newlywed, each trying to see that the other got a fair share of the talking: 'when one expressed an opinion, the other immediately approved'. They were like 'two doves cooing' while planning the arrangement of their furniture at 10 Kensington Palace: and when they moved in, early in July,

Tony went ahead to hang pictures and arrange the welcoming flowers. Unexpectedly, Margaret turned up without a latchkey and had to ring the doorbell.

The staff were under the impression that her husband had planned to carry her over the threshold but by some misunderstanding he had impatiently returned to Clarence House and the Princess went upstairs alone ... but quickly came down, it was noted, 'pink with pleasure'. 'Please let it seem that I haven't been upstairs yet,' she told Cronin, the new butler. 'My husband's arranged everything so beautifully to surprise me.' A phone call to Clarence House had meanwhile recalled Tony, and the Princess greeted him as if her fresh delight had not already known a dress rehearsal.

And No. 10, when furnished, shrank still more to a doll's house. With the ground floor assigned to office staff, the private apartments were diminished to a suite on the first floor, with staff rooms above. Piece by piece the couple had assembled and arranged their wedding gifts: the seventeenth-century Flemish screen from Uncle Oliver, the antique Chinese Coromandel wood table that was the gift of the British Cabinet, and the clock from Tony's mother, a handsome escritoire from the home of his Messel grandmother, the hi-fi in the white drawing room with the Princess's piano, and so on. A small dining room, the Princess's pink-painted bedroom, Tony's dressing room and a bathroom completed the suite. The bamboo chairs and cord-framed pictures from Pimlico served in the guest room and elsewhere. But still they by no means found space for all the gifts, and many remained packed in store.

After the serenity of Clarence House, the Princess noticed the creaking of the old floors and the footsteps in the staff quarters overhead, where there were six living in. In the morning room downstairs, business visitors would sometimes hear the footfalls and voices of schoolchildren, like starlings scuffing in the chimney, echoing through the party wall from the public entrance to the State Apartments next door. The Princess meanwhile wasted little time. She had fulfilled an official engagement three days before her wedding, and carried out another, without her husband, three days after their return. Tony had made bachelor forays in accompanying her on some of her minor visits, and Sir Michael Adeane, then the Queen's Private Secretary, had suggested he should gain experience of royal protocol gradually. In the event, he dived in at the deep end on July 28th, when he flew to Dartmouth with his wife in an aircraft of the Queen's Flight and accompanied her in an inspection of the Royal Naval College under the critical eyes of the assembled officers and cadets. It was just twenty-one years to the week since Princess Margaret had visited Dartmouth as a child on the historic occasion when her sister first met Prince Philip.

Celebrating her thirtieth birthday at Balmoral, a day of pouring rain, the Princess and her husband drove to Crathie Church with the Family, not to disappoint the enormous waiting throng, although they usually preferred to worship at the little church at Ballater where onlookers were rare. Both already recognized this great divide between their public appearances and their private wishes, a difficulty they knew they could never reconcile. Philip had given warning that his own early married life was a series of obstacle races of indefinite length and duration. Margaret had tried to foresee and discuss these personal hurdles months before her marriage, though not always with prophetic success.

Her husband found that people assumed he had gained a slice of the Royal Exchequer when in reality he was meeting married domestic expenses at Kensington mainly on his percentage royalties from past work. 'Please remember this is not a wealthy house,' he had warned Cronin, the butler, whose uncomprehending response was to stock the wine cellar, unbidden, with extravagant vintage wines. So they replaced Cronin with the reliable Mr Collier from the Mountbatten household — and within three weeks Cronin serialized his ghosted reminiscences in *The People*, creating an impression that the 'Joneses' married life was marred by parsimonious bickerings with staff. Yet the distorted images of newspaper gossip rapidly seemed to bear little relation to the newlyweds' experience as they settled down to the everyday adjustment of married couples. 'And what have our friends to say today?' Princess Margaret would murmur, glancing at the more dismaying columnists. One of her ladies noted her as 'furiously protective'. At the same time she was full of confident, ardent admiration as Tony took his fences, fully determined to match his future career with her own norms of duty.

In December he undertook his first solo public engagement and made his first speech, when presenting the prizes in a national photographic competition at a luncheon at the Dorchester. 'A camera must be part of one, an extra limb capable of freezing a situation,' he told the assembled enthusiasts. Seven months later he was addressing an audience of two thousand international architects at the Royal Festival Hall. When one commentator charged the husband of six months with 'hanging around doing nothing' he had in fact settled the details of his impending promotional and advisory post with the Design Council. With some suggestions from Prince Philip, this was to involve him in conferences, executive planning, speeches, and a series of royal-type industrial tours soon to take him solo to Glasgow, Belfast and other centres, and as far afield as Czechoslovakia. In spare hours he had experimentally begun work on his private and then unpublicized commission for a modernist aviary for the London Zoo. 'They must give Tony a chance,' said Princess Margaret, indignant at his critics. 'It's not going to be easy.' She would have preferred to rebut the sour-tongued, confronting each dragon in turn. But replies and denials would have been undignified, and a factual announcement was considered premature. 'You must grin and bear it,' was the eternal tenor of advice, while Margaret groaned or flung an offending newspaper across the room.

The Princess had fully expected to visit Nigeria to represent the Queen at the independence celebrations in that first autumn after the wedding, but her sister felt it would be suitable for her to have more free time so early in married life, and Princess Alexandra assumed the Nigerian chore instead. Going to tea at 'No. 10 KP' one showery afternoon, the Queen pretended to be shocked on noticing the rain that cascaded through the holes in an old Clarence House umbrella. But there were indeed gaps to be made good in every way.

II

In private life, the first year, husband and wife progressed through their advanced phase in 'getting to know you, getting to know all about you', as their record of the musical *The King and I* so happily often sang. Going to Birr Castle for the New Year of 1961, they attempted to travel as normal passengers on a scheduled Air Lingus plane, only to find the rest of the seats books by cameramen and reporters. At the gates of Birr itself such a scrimmage ensued, such an elbowing and jostling, that Inspector Crocker appealed for the Princess and her husband to be left to themselves. 'But it's our first royal visit, and it's a great day for the Irish,' cried a voice of unmistakable brogue.

Margaret relished the new opportunity of leisure with her mother-in-law, talking of Tony, in the Gothic saloon at Birr, so strangely a counterpart of the Wyatt saloon at Royal Lodge, and yet so very different. The Irish facet of her husband's background had been an unknown quantity, the details steadily filled in when they motored over the green hills to spend a few days with her sister-in-law, Susan, and her husband John and their family at Abbey Leix. Back in England, Tony took her to see his old room in Mr Upcott's former house at Eton one foggy afternoon and, walking again in School Yard, he showed her the very spot where he had stood as a fifteen-year-old schoolboy and had first seen her when she had officially visited the school sixteen years earlier. At evensong in College Chapel an onlooker watched them link hands beneath their prayer book, as if in silent dedication.

There began also the exploration of each other's friendships, an open and unguarded survey on both sides, and in general a social fusion more sustained and successful than the presentation of Philips' friends, other than Mountbatten connections, had been with Lilibet. The Princess delighted in the sense of new perspectives opening as they weekended with the Jeremy Fry's at Widcombe Manor: Jeremy, of the chocolate family, had been a boyhood friend when the Frys and Armstrong-Jones were Sussex neighbours. And there were the Sainsbury brothers, John and Simon, known since the days of prep school. Through Tony, John had met, and as it turned out, would soon marry, the ballerina Anya Linden. Then there were the Gilliatts, another friendship evolving from Tony's boyhood: Roger Gilliatt, clinical neurology professor at London University, had acted as Tony's best man instead of Jeremy, after some initial indecision. His wife was a major enthusiast in interior decoration, and a weekend visit with them involved sharing the enjoyments and the travails of restoring a pink-washed lath-and-plaster house in Suffolk.

The royal bride also eagerly embarked on entertaining her in-laws, first those who were closest in Tony's affections, among them Aunt Gwendy, his father's sister, and her husband, a High Court judge, whom it was droll to greet as Uncle Denys. Lady Rosse, when in London, lived only a block or two from Kensington Palace in the tall, unchanged Victorian house in Stafford Terrace where her artistic Sambourne grandparents had spent all their married lives. It was a cherished family home where, on an early visit with Tony, glimpsing his great-grandfather's store of cameras and photographs, Margaret had first realized how deeply the flair for photography flowed in her husband's veins. When they celebrated their first wedding anniversary, the Queen Mother brought together a group of friends 'on both sides of the family' at a dinner party at Royal Lodge, and Tony already talked enthusiastically of his ideas for a new book of photographs, with the camera catching a private view of every contemporary artist of significance in London.

Meanwhile, in trusted acquaintance, there remained Bill Glenton ... for, incredibly, his Rotherhithe room still remained an intrinsic part of their lives. Sightseers no longer loitered about the house. The commentators on the tourist river steamers pointed out the Room or, more usually, the bay window of the room above it, as if it belonged to romantic history, and no one dreamed that the historic lovers could still be there. One evening, when the spring tides were high and the steamers came closer than usual, the loudspeaker broke in, 'Right there, where that young couple is sitting, is the very room', and Margaret and Tony drew back in alarm into the shadows.

To Bill Glenton's astonishment, they had returned to the Room a month or two after their honeymoon, having phoned to enquire about it, and then they begged to be allowed to visit it as usual. 'It's one of the sweetest rooms I know,' said Margaret. 'It's made us so happy.' The only difference was a highly practical one, when Tony asked if it would be all right if they had a toilet installed in a cupboard. Until then there had only been an ancient and clanking contrivance behind a door in a nook on the stairs. At Kensington Palace, their staff were mystified by the groceries the couple took away in the car. 'It was like seeing off a couple of carefree children to a picnic,' one of them wrote. 'I peeped into the bag and saw packets of frozen food, steaks, smoked salmon and a bottle of wine.'

One day, in the Room, a frying pan burst into flames while Tony was preparing a specially rich goulash, and Mr Glenton, dashing down to find the cause of the smoke, recalls how he found Margaret emerging through a thick cloud, her face smudged with black grease. Another time, ashes borne by the river wind abruptly blew into the room, covering the occupants with filth. The private life had its perils. Yet whom would have guessed that the Queen Mother once visited the Room, joining in a sing-song and telling Mr Glenton afterwards, 'I haven't enjoyed myself so much since I was a girl of twenty'? Who could have guessed that the choruses one night were taken by Noël Coward and Margaret Leighton, with Princess Margaret as a basso profondo? Or imagine the Queen's sister in dockland, politely borrowing a bowl of sugar?

More usually, the Room's occupants were quiet as mice. After justice had been done to one of Tony's meals, the Princess would do the washing up at the old enamel sink in a cupboard 'as delicately as a darkroom assistant developing prints. She rarely splashed herself and never wore an apron,' their host has said. 'If it had not been so unhurried and extraordinarily gentle it would have seemed a picture of an ordinary housewife.' Margaret was usually 'in a romantic or playful courtship mood', and their kindly landlord — who in reality took not a penny of rent — left them to themselves as much as possible. As time went on, it seemed to him that the Room had a therapeutic value, at first giving Tony some link with his old life, like a diver in a decompression chamber, and later it served 'to maintain a natural balance in their married life and in easing the strain of their public duties'. In thanking Bill Glenton, the Princess once confided, 'I don't know what we would do without the Room. We haven't eaten alone together for six weeks.'

The visits ceased only for a few weeks in the autumn of 1961 when Princess Margaret was expecting her baby. And although he never mentioned it to me, Mr Glenton must have been considerably startled when he opened his Sunday paper on October 1st that year to learn that the Queen had conferred an earldom on his lodger who would henceforth be known as the Earl of Snowdon, with the subsidiary title, requisite to a first-born son, of Viscount Linley of Nymans.

III

Carping voices were raised as soon as Lord Snowdon's acceptance of the distinction was known. This was strikingly illogical, for it had been widely expected for months that the Queen would wish to honour her sister's husband. The editor of *Burke's Peerage* had put on record that a peerage seemed more fitting than a knighthood, and the editor of *Debrett* considered that the title could not be less than that of marquess, the degree between a duke and an earl. A high authority of the College of Arms mentioned the precedents for a dukedom *and* the Garter, the highest Order of Chivalry; and to cite recent events, the Garter had indeed been bestowed on the brothers-in-law of both the Queen's father and grandfather. Yet the Queen had kept her own counsel until she returned from India in time for Tony's thirty-first birthday celebration. This was his first anniversary within the Royal Family and, in greeting him, the Queen had enquired if he would accept her gift of an earldom.

Tony had earlier demurred at the prospect of a title but, couched as it was, he accepted with real pleasure. The same style of 'Countess' was thus conferred upon his wife as on his mother, and in the last analysis any lingering disinclination was probably overcome because his wife wished it so. Only the style of the dignity remained to be decided, and several proposals were tried and discarded until he hit on the name of the mountain beloved by his forefathers, and one day, it is said, Princess Margaret heard him murmur, quietly and thoughtfully as if to himself, the three words, 'Countess of Snowdon'.

On her husband's birthday, Margaret had also evidently told her sister of her happy certainty that she was pregnant, and probably she at last realized that the diminutive charm of No. 10 Kensington Palace would prove impractical for a family. The Queen, whom one feels sure had foreseen this all along, now produced a ready solution. The Ministry of Works was just then embarking on a long-term programme for rehabilitating Kensington Palace, commencing with the untenanted south-west range of apartments known as No. 1a which had been damaged by incendiary bombs during the war. Restoration of this ruinous pile might take eighteen months but could culminate in a permanent London home offering twice the space — and twice the sunshine, too — of the 'dolls' house'.

As her sister had decided for the birth of Prince Andrew the previous year, Princess Margaret had hoped to have her baby at home, but the doctors suggested that Clarence House would be more convenient. On November 3rd, 1961, as I vividly remember, Kensington Palace had the air of a village community expectantly awaiting news from the cottage hospital, and then in mid-morning the news spread like wildfire through the colony of grace-and-favour homes, 'It's a boy!' The Princess had given birth to a 6lb 4-ounce son at 10.45 a.m.

'He was hardly any trouble,' Margaret said afterwards, in reassuring Bill Glenton's young wife, Nenne. 'It's much less painful than you think. The worse part is waiting weeks beforehand. I used to get a little irritable.' A few days earlier, the expectant parents had attended morning service together at Westminster Abbey, and before the baby was twenty-four hours old the intensely happy father went to early morning Holy Communion 'to give thanks', as the Dean said.

'Tony took to our baby at once. I didn't know if he would,' the Princess told a friend. More than he had expected, her husband was touched by the tender poetry of nativity and, in this adoring mood, spent hours with his camera, trying to capture the beauty of mother and child. The resulting photographs were so delightful that Princess Margaret wished to share them, to see them published, and three were released in the usual way, much to the surprise of those who imagined that Lord Snowdon had suffered an enforced professional retirement.

There were disgruntled protests, too, that he was making profits from photographing his son, an unfounded charge, for he had viewed the cash side as a thank-offering gift from the first, and the proceeds went towards polio research and to invalid children's charities. At six weeks old, little Viscount

Linley was christened in the Music Room at Buckingham Palace, and then disappointment raged that no photographs were published of this essentially private occasion. As principal godmother, the Queen named the baby David Albert Charles. The other sponsors were Lady Elizabeth Cavendish, who had first brought the parents together, Lord Plunket — a great friend to them both — and the Rev Simon Phipps. The baby wore the creamy fragile robe of Honiton lace reserved for the royal line since the first of Queen Victoria's children ... and it must be added that he roared lustily throughout, much to the dismay of the parents who had told everyone how good and quiet he was.

At the christening party the Queen Mother mischievously proposed that with a little trick photography Tony might have astonished his critics by pretending that twins had been born. 'That really would have set the press gossiping,' said Margaret. Perhaps the Queen Mother was also the 'close senior adviser' who gave the young couple such wise counsel at this time in pointing out that criticism resembles the hydra-headed monster of the legend, speaking with different voices, each with opposing views. One must be attentive to criticism, lest it be true, and yet learn to ignore its wilder, more hurtful excesses. After Christmas, for instance, instead of facing the chills of Norfolk, Princess Margaret and her husband treated themselves to a holiday in the warmth of Antigua, a second honeymoon of swimming, sunning, searching for seashells and relaxing, which instantly aroused sharp comment on the leaving of their two-month-old babe at Sandringham in the care of his skilled Sussex nanny, Verona Sumner, and his devoted royal grandmama.

In Antigua, the Snowdons were a diplomatic remove from the fuss in London when, on January 5th, 1962, it was announced that Lord Snowdon had accepted a post as an artistic adviser to the *Sunday Times*. What! Should a member of the Royal Family work for a newspaper? The Queen had long since been consulted, of course, and had conferred at some length with her advisers, including the Prime Minister. Certain safeguards were put forward: that her brother-in-law would not be involved in political journalism, and that his name should not be directly used in the newspapers' own advertising. The priority of his public engagements would be reserved; he would continue to be available to the Council of Industrial Design and he would not service the *Sunday Times* with exclusive royal photographs.

All these difficulties had been resolved, stage by stage. If Princess Margaret had been vague on financial realities, she realized how well it suited her husband to enjoy enhanced financial independence, to be master of the house and to meet expenses (including £1,000 a year for the local rates) with an earned income more than equal to her own personal net income from the Civil List. The two had agreed long since on the mapping out of their financial territories, with the boundaries and perquisites of the Princess's official Household and their own private domestic home separated and defined as clearly as possible. There would always be ambiguities: they were henceforth a professional couple following their individual careers, even though the wires crossed and Tony joined his wife with fair frequency in her service to the Crown. The mere demands of the Monarchy as a *family* often required considerable dovetailing of personal pursuits and time. On February 7th, for instance, Lord Snowdon attended his first conference with the *Sunday Times* editorial board and then was present with his wife at the family lunch at Buckingham Palace that commemorated the Queen's tenth anniversary of her Accession.

The following month, the Princess Margaret, Countess of Snowdon — as she was now officially known — sat with five friends in the Commonwealth Gallery of the House of Lords to watch the ceremony of her husband's introduction as a peer. The procession to the Woolsack was, by tradition, headed by the Duke of Norfolk as Earl Marshal and Sir Brian Horrocks as Black Rod, with the richly clad Garter King of Arms. Lord Snowdon's new robes of red with white miniver looked rather fresher, it was noted, than the robes of his sponsors and friends, the Earls of Westmorland and Leicester, but the Princess's own gaze never left her husband.

'Considering the difficulties of the said affairs and the dangers impending, waiving all excuses,' the new peer was enjoined, 'do you be personally present in our Parliament.' Retiring to a bench with his escorts, he had then to rise and doff his tricorne hat and bow to the Throne, and so be seated again, and rise again, bowing three times. After leaving the House, he then returned, divested of his robes, a spruce and more familiar figure, to take his seat on the front crossbench between his sponsors, with an amused glance towards the Gallery for the first time, as he and his wife listened to a debate, not without personal interest, on tax relief for part-time professional married women. Meanwhile, in the House of Commons, Mr Hamilton was putting down discordant questions about another personal difficulty, namely, the cost to the nation in preparing the Earl and Countess of Snowdon's new home at 1a Kensington Palace.

IV

Early in August 1962, Princess Margaret and her husband again flew to the Caribbean for the official Jamaican independence celebrations. The Princess was representing the Queen, and Lord Snowdon thus fulfilled a State role as consort at her left hand when she formally opened the first session of the new national Parliament. There was the usual garden party with the lengthy reception line, the State banquet and fireworks, and the packed arena for the flag lowering and raising ceremonies which various members of the Royal Family were to watch in a score of countries within the next decade.

Within two years, the Princess had thus seen her husband inducted gradually but with confident success into the royal round, accompanying her first to the wedding of King Baudouin of the Belgians to Dona Fabiola in Brussels. Partnering her next on an official tour in North Wales, they were formally welcomed by Tony's godfather, Sir Michael Duff, as Lord Lieutenant of Caernarvon, who then presented his Deputy Lieutenant, none other than Tony's father, Ronny Armstrong-Jones. And the family links were still stronger the following year, when the Queen appointed Lord Snowdon as Constable of Caernarvon Castle, and in that role he soon afterwards welcomed his sister-in-law to the fortress by handing her the fifteen-inch iron key of his domain.

Husband and wife were now sharing industrial visits to Crewe, Glasgow, Staffordshire, Coventry and so forth. In Coventry they attended the first Communion service held in the new cathedral, and later lunched with Simon Phipps in his council flat. In County Durham, Margaret completed her husband's royal graduation by the obligatory routine of going down a mine with him. But she was there in a realistic capacity as president of the Church of England Youth Council, and accordingly a sponsor of their Christian Citizen scheme to encourage mining trainees 'to think in terms of their responsibility to industry and to society in general'.

It has been said that the high and serious quality of being set apart — by God, if you will — preserves the Crown from corrosion, and none can complain that Princess Margaret felt a special sense of vocation within the ambit of religion. With equal deliberation, her husband was following the cause of good design, anxious though he was not to seem a junior partner to Prince Philip's interests in that field. For his own second string — or was it already his first? — his *Sunday Times* work first took him abroad on a brief photographic visit to Venice with a colleague. His passport still bore the name Jones, though he probably embellished the story in claiming that he passed unrecognized through passport control. Lord Snowdon told Godfrey Winn that he had begun keeping two engagement books, one for his professional work under his secretary, the faithful Mrs Everard, who had been with him in Pimlico, the other for the public activities he shared with his wife. Consulting and referring, Dorothy Everard, and the Princess's secretary Francis Legh, smoothed out the consequent jigsaw.

As it happened, one of Margaret's closest domestic confidantes handed in her notice shortly after Tony's birthday. This was Ruby — Mrs Ruby Gordon — younger sister of Margaret 'Bobo' MacDonald, the Queen's former nanny and dresser. Ruby, as we have seen, had similarly served Margaret from the cradle, first as nursemaid and then as personal maid, awaking her every morning, chiding her, fussing about her with hot lemon during those perpetual winter colds. But she would soon be fifty; she had been married to a former Palace footman for nearly ten years, and her husband was urging her to retire. On the Countess of Rosse's recommendation, Princess Margaret accepted one of the Nymans helpers, a

Sussex woman of about Ruby's age who, commencing a career as a dressmaker, had become one of those 'useful little women' who can turn their hands to making curtains and chair-covers, and would obviously be an immediate help in making-over the No. 10 furnishings for No. 1a.

Dorothy Palmer had seemed to Lord Snowdon to have been a part of his family domestic scene for years, and now she travelled to Jamaica as Princess Margaret's personal maid, and one mentions her as a minor yet essential feature of the process that changed the former spinster role of the Queen's sister to her lasting place as Tony's wife. A bride is not instantly transformed with the exchange of the marriage vows. Like a shrub transplanted to a congenial spot in a garden, one changes imperceptibly in the warmth of a new setting and context. It also came about just at this time that the Princess's friend, Judy Montagu, staged a match very similar to Margaret's in marrying Milton Gendel, an American art critic and magazine editor, whom she had first met in Rome. The new Mrs Gendel was, I suspect, the intimate friend to whom Princess Margaret acknowledged, 'My husband has made me twice the person I used to be.'

The Princess altogether broke away from the trammelled years of royal routine by spending her thirty-second birthday not at Birkhall or Balmoral but with Tony's sister and brother-in-law, Susan and John, and their children at Abbey Leix. Alec Guinness was a member of the house party and the guests remember Margaret bubbling with fun about Tony's sheer nerve in getting her to ride pillion on a motorbike and her entertaining pretence of fright at the accomplishment. Coached by Tony in Antigua, her waterskiing, too, was notably improving, so much so that she was soon to take lessons with the champ instructor Barry Connel on the gravel pit lakes near

Reading. Alec Guinness was asked if he had seen the movie of *West Side Story*. She and Tony had already seen it twice, voting it fully equal in impact to the stage show. Visiting Lady Rosse at Birr Castle, they cajoled their way into her bedroom, blatantly refreshing their memories of the Gothic-style furnishing retrieved from the estate attics, and confessing that while with the Frys they had acquired a very similar door, dressing table and pillars for £15 from a Bristol dealer, as treasures to make over for their new bathroom at No. 1a. In the ferment of these enthusiasms, Tony sparkled with tales of photographing all the woman tycoons of the dress trade and Margaret championed the impending art book, on which she had 'almost been an assistant art editor'. The Princess had a theory that waterskiing in a rubber suit helped to build up an immunity against chills, but she caught both a salmon and a cold when fishing the Abbey Leix river.

Tony had long since initiated Margaret into the skills of junk-hunting, appraising dusty counters in Islington or searching for blue Bristol glass on rubbish-filled barrows, so different from her memories of shopping for antiques with Queen Mary in Bond Street, when morning-coated dealers had prostrated themselves at sight of her grandmother's lorgnette. It made Margaret's day, indeed her week, when Tony discovered matching lengths of Gothic cornice for the bathroom in a Hammersmith junkyard. The Princess revelled in turn in her own triumph of finding a Napoleonic campaign bed and a suitable embroidered coverlet for her husband's dressing room. They triumphantly unveiled before their friends a Chippendale armchair commode, which they had every intention of converting to modern plumbing, and a brilliant-hued pair of apothecary jars to stand like sentinels at their bedroom door. Rummaging for treasure around the Betjeman corners of

Clerkenwell and elsewhere, they were rarely recognized ... though they suffered detection among the knowledgeable stalls of the Portobello road, and bought only a mustard pot that day.

V

Princess Margaret had set her heart on moving into Kensington Palace in time for Tony's thirty-third birthday on March 7th, but in January a painter complained of a warm ceiling and a smell of smoke, and it was discovered that part of the roof space of the Kent household next door was on fire. In the Princess's albums are her own photographs of the spectacular smoke, the fire engines, the firemen mounting turntable ladders to the roof and the anxious onlookers, including Princess Alexandra and Prince Michael as well as Margaret herself. The smouldering rafters were quenched within an hour, but the water damage and the extra repair work spelled another month of delay, and perhaps additional public expense.

And this 'added fuel to the flames', as a friend put it, after the months of searing criticism of the £85,000 expenditure on the building works. Of this sum £25,000 represented the Royal Palace's vote on making good the war-damaged structure of one of the few Wren houses in London, yet the Snowdons themselves resented the appalling £40,000 extra cost of the sparse grace-and-favour specifications for making it habitable. The Queen contributed £20,000, excusing the gift as in lieu of a dowry. Shaken at the professional estimates for veneering a pair of mahogany doors for the drawing room, Snowdon did the job himself, with some help from that useful apprentice, his wife.

The architects proposed a marble-floored entrance hall. The Snowdons halved the expense with re-cut paving stones, supplemented by diamond-patterned tiles of Welsh slate, and Tony and his willing helpmeet fitted the fireplace in the staff sitting room. The private accounts show that Princess Margaret spent £1,148 of her own money on her kitchen. The cost might have been higher if her husband had not designed the contemporary extractor hood and brass-rimmed electric clock, making the point that unique and individual items could still cost less than mass production. They wanted pale brown vinyl tiles on the floor, and they chose a hard-boiled egg to help show the precise shade required. Admiring her husband's workmanlike prowess, the Princess said they would have laid the tiles themselves if it could have saved on the sub-contract.

No. 1a, then, was a doleful example of high-level costing and a happy demonstration of do-it-yourself craftsmanship, bringing modern vivacity to a wing of the old Palace that Leigh Hunt had once deplored for its Dutch solidity. Very soon No. 1a became the nucleus of the Snowdon family: like the rocking horses in the lobby of Royal Lodge, the children's bicycles in the paved hall were both a definition and a declaration of domestic truth. A camera case slung on a chair was a legible signature of the man of the house. The Annigoni portrait of the Princess, cool, watchful and not unwelcoming, was an emblem of State. Seeking to catch his vision of a lonely and isolated quality, the artist destroyed his first portrait and had asked thirty-three sittings amid such artistic agonies that the Princess had teased him, 'Really, it's enough to make an angel weep!'

This could be the home of a youngish professional couple who have not noticed the usage of time. The Snowdons vividly recalled the Saturday when they ferried goods and chattels by car from one house to another, from No. 10 to No. 1a. That first weekend, they planted a magnolia tree together in the patch of enclosed garden between the house and the public spaces of Kensington Gardens and now its blooms top the brick wall. On the northern entrance side of the house, near the arch of the clock tower, the cobbles of Clock Court would be familiar to Handel and to the old Duke of Sussex and no doubt to Sir Christopher Wren himself. But the interior had the intimacy of a private home; the brief corridor to the right led to the drawing room, the dining room, the kitchen and no more. Almost opposite the heavy front door, Lord Snowdon's workroom looked through a movie projector window — camouflaged by a showcase of treasures — across the drawing room to those home-veneered double doors of his, which opened with dignity into the dining room. Upstairs was the master suite, as they say, of two bedrooms and bathroom, with three rooms for the children and nanny. For the rest, some of the most ample staff rooms in London occupied roof-level and basement.

In the grey drawing room, veterans recognized the sofas of the Clarence House days, Princess Margaret's black grand piano, Grandmama Messel's desk, paintings by Anthony Fry and Jean de Maol. Top-lit above the carved white chimneypiece of the dining room was one of John Piper's luminous and indefinite Venetian studies. The white chair-rail, the solidly upholstered Chippendale chairs, adhered to conventional taste. But upstairs the Gothic white-and-coral bathroom was another set piece again, strikingly different, from the inset bath in what was once an Edwardian alcove to the Snowdon-designed hexagonal centrepiece, a glass-topped display cabinet of seashells, the surrounding hot rail draped with bath towels.

In the early years, a child's potty-chair caught the amused eye. And in the adjoining bedroom, to Princess Margaret's great happiness, her daughter was born on May 1st, 1964.

12: RUMOUR AND REALITY

> When my sister and I were growing up, she was made out to
> be the goody goody one. That was boring, so the Press tried
> to make out I was wicked as hell.
>
> Princess Margaret, *July 1969*

I

A May Day daughter, a Saturday child, Lady Armstrong-Jones
was christened Sarah Frances Elizabeth in the private chapel at
Buckingham Palace on July 13th. Rarely bestowed as a royal
name, the choice of Sarah was particularly apt, for it has the
ancient meaning of Princess. Frances had been the name of
Lord Snowdon's maternal grandmother, and had graced at
least two earlier generations before her. Elizabeth, the Dean of
Westminster was lightly assured, was in tribute to *everyone*.

The baby cooed contentedly throughout the ceremony, as
well she might. As a happy note for the child of two artistic
parents, the christening reception was held auspiciously in the
adjoining art gallery, the Queen's Gallery, then between
exhibitions, and in that unusual and contemporary setting, the
gathering of friends and families gained the festive atmosphere
of such occasions in any local hall. The godfathers were
Anthony Barton, a close personal friend of Lord Snowdon
since his Cambridge days, and Lord Westmorland, who had
sponsored him as a new peer to the House of Lords. The three
godmothers were Princess Margaret's intimate friends,
Marigold Bridgeman, Prudence Penn and Jane (Mrs Jocelyn)
Stevens. Among the family guests were more complex

220

relationships: Tony's father and stepmother, his mother and stepfather, as well as his uncles and aunts — let us mention his judicial Uncle Denys, his stockbroker Uncle Linley, his artistic Uncle Oliver. The Royal Family were headed by the Queen and the Queen Mother, and Prince Philip came in, a little late, straight from his helicopter in the garden.

Princess Margaret adored stepping into her second skin as Tony's wife, though the occasion was not without its regal touch in that the choirboys of the Chapel Royal, in their scarlet and gold tunics, ruffles and knee-breeches, served cakes and champagne. 'And how is the Room?' Tony's father had enquired. The romantic-hearted Ronald Armstrong-Jones had once accepted a 'dare' to climb down a rusting cable to the tidal mud. And now the whole scene of larky fun and romantic sentiment had become 'a grim story' to be told upstairs, over drinks, later on. 'They've been brutes,' said Margaret.

For the Room was now rubble. It was the old story of planners who preferred to demolish old Georgian houses in the name of slum clearance rather than restore and renew the usage of generations. The old story, too, that people might have thought Princess Margaret and her husband were using their position to unfair advantage if they had sought to intervene. They pushed overt influence as far as they dared through the local MP, through John Betjeman and others, through the LCC and the Ministry of Works. At a dinner party once, the warden of the Goldsmiths' Company, Lord Boyd, mentioned a salvage scheme his guild had in mind, and the Princess did not dare to acknowledge too obviously that, of all causes, this was one of the dearest to her heart. The Room and all the ancient adjoining houses were not to be saved. Bill Glenton received an eviction order. Tony took down the cupboards. Margaret packed her ornaments and household treasures into crates ready to be collected by a van from the Palace. 'This wonderful room,' she said, looking round at the moment of farewell. 'We shall never forget it.'

And yet, curiously, two or three months later, Sarah's christening was to seem like the opening of a new chapter, a renewal leading from one phase to another and from one sanctuary to the next. Mentioning that he was thinking of permanently moving to Barbados in a year or two, Tony's Uncle Oliver (Oliver Messel) asked where they had stored the furnishing of the Room, and added rather vaguely 'There's the Old House…' In their reverie of regret, the Snowdons did not immediately see what was being implied. They had become involved again, in a different way: in preliminary plans for a tour in Uganda, in the coming art book, even in alluring prospects for a future tour in the United States. They also did a lot of waterskiing on the Sunninghill Park lake that summer, not only for the benefit of Tony's polio-damaged leg, but also 'getting tummy muscles taut again,' as Margaret said, with a deprecatory push at plumpness. The skis were essential equipment when they spent their summer holidays in Sardinia, with the Aga Khan, then just launching his hotel developments of the Costa Smeralda.

The Princess passed much of her thirty-fourth birthday on a beach near Porto Cervo, sunning and swimming, with the Tennants and a few other friends, dancing at a party afterwards; an ideal day. She confessed, 'We set no store by birthdays,' and the 'we' was not a regal plural but the simple unity of husband and wife. The one flaw of Sardinia was the difficulty of the evening phone call to Birkhall and elsewhere for reassurances about the children. At the tag-end of the holiday they impulsively flew to Venice in the Aga's plane and began house-hunting on the mainland, looking up villas where gardens had become overgrown and plaster was peeling. They lunched with Freya Stark, whose house was discreetly for sale, and kept safely ahead of the Italian cameramen in viewing islets and houses but rapidly came to the conclusion that the prospect of a hideaway villa was 'simply not on'.

The topic was still uppermost late in September when they went to Copenhagen to inaugurate and enliven British Week and were the guests of King Frederick and Queen Ingrid at Fredensborg Castle. The Queen could see that the image of Rotherhithe lingered like a lost Eden. But how could they begin to look around, with so much on the calendar? Crown Princess Margrethe was to visit England in November and they invited her to dinner, but already she had no evening to spare and so they seriously set an evening for her next visit in May the following year, a pressure that Queen Ingrid found amusingly characteristic. Besides Uganda and the USA, they were also planning a British Week in the Netherlands, with hints of more distant British Weeks looming in Hong Kong and Belgium in 1966–67. Lord Snowdon took pride in having accompanied his wife on eighteen out of twenty-two official overseas visits, more than half involving him in an earlier private journey for organisation. In Brussels indeed the Princess went down with such acute tonsilitis that he opened the British Week 'on her behalf', speech-making, inspecting, 'getting the week off to a swinging start,' as a critical newspaper said, in one of its rare bursts of applause.

In addition, he had his own remunerative assignments for the *Sunday Times*, *Life*, the American *Vogue* and so on, taking him to Vienna, Belgrade, Tokyo and even as far as Peru. Business was thus blended with planning, as well as pleasure. The realization of Princess Margaret's dream of visiting the United States, for instance, began with British Week in San

Francisco. More precisely, it began with a private invitation from Sharman Douglas, and the thing escalated. A show of British motorbikes was opening in San Francisco; Tony's art book was to be discreetly promoted, and in New York the British Exports Committee had plans for staging a British fashion show aboard the liner *Queen Elizabeth*. At the Foreign Office, the Secretary of State, Michael Stewart, latched on, taking the mission into the realm of government planning. There had been no royal tour within the States since the Queen and President Eisenhower opened the St Lawrence Seaway in 1957, and on diplomatic grounds alone, as Sir Pat Dean reported from Washington, Princess Margaret's visit with her husband would be timely and desirable.

II

When the Snowdons flew out early in November the itinerary showed sixty official and public engagements occupying fourteen out of twenty days. This was ruthlessly described by the *New Statesman* as fitting in 'the odd working visit here and there' and the Princess was supposed to have reviewed the programme and issued 'a series of imperious ultimata' saying she wasn't having any. In fact, as the Foreign Secretary later told Parliament, 'the Princess proposed a number of additional engagements'. It was the head start indeed of the determined British export drive of the mid-1960s, which within four years was selling an extra 1,200 million dollars' worth of goods annually to America, a fantastic impetus.

At the inaugural Press Club reception in San Francisco, Margaret gave her ecstatic first impressions as 'twice as fabulous as we ever expected'; and from that moment a Californian love affair had begun. 'Whom are you looking forward to meeting?' a reporter had asked, and she had answered 'Everybody!' And indeed they met, as I once listed elsewhere, 'architects, publishers, nuclear scientists, Nobel Prize winners, university students, fashion writers, film folk, policemen, parsons, department store saleswomen, art curators, cable-car drivers, down to the last lady to shake hands at the English-Speaking Union.' In return, as one American commentator noted, the Princess 'engendered untold goodwill … seldom has a visitor been accorded such favourable page one press coverage'. Margaret was amused to find herself once again invariably styled 'Margaret Rose' in the headlines.

To another observer she was 'the pearl within the oyster', riding in the deluxe silver-grey Rolls-Royce of the motorcade. Until their visitors crossed the Bay by hovercraft to visit the Berkeley campus, the San Franciscans had probably not realized that their hovercraft were British made. And when 'Margaret Rose and Tony' zoomed to Los Angeles in an Andover of the Queen's Flight, which had been standing by as a major exhibit of British Week, the moral was not lost upon time-pressed business tycoons.

'S.F.' was cable-cars, Telegraph Hill and Fisherman's Wharf, a wild boar barbecue and so much more. 'L.A.' laid on an unbelievably strenuous sixty hours, from obligatory treks through British-decked department stores, a prolonged visit to a Hollywood studio, a full tour of the art museum, and a side journey to the Owen Valley radio observatory. 'Shall I tell them Jodrell Bank back home is much bigger?' Margaret had asked before setting out. And to the L.A. Mayor Yorty, she played the admiring rubberneck, 'Your police are wonderful. They clear the roads so efficiently. They move me around so fast. They get me to places way ahead of time.' Yet the sub-editorial scissors in several newspapers at home left little to report save dancing till three a.m. with some comparative oldies of the film world — Astaire, James Stewart, Gregory Peck — though among them were also Paul Newman, Steve McQueen and Laurence Harvey.

The parties were for charity, and organized by Sharman. Under her energetic direction, also, bulletins explained that the Princess was suffering from a feverish chill and laryngitis, news which Margaret would have preferred to keep to herself for she nevertheless kept up her hectic schedule. At Pontano Farm, the Douglas home near Tucson, I had occasion to note that the only planned event was 'a cocktail party for 250 friends of the family!' Yet the Arizona highlight was a cineramic low-level plane flight over the Grand Canyon and the Painted Desert, sweeping in and around the jutting spires of primeval rock … and then, at the Lake Powell inn, the peace of the night under the flashing desert stars. Colds cleared in the crisp Arizona air, and 'bugs' could not quench the American wonder.

Next, Washington and the White House spread out the carpet and *Life* actually flourished the headline, 'This radiant moment in history'. An air copy of *The Observer* from London was no less complimentary, styling their journey 'perhaps the most successful royal tour America has ever had.' In proposing a toast, at the White House banquet, President Johnson sagely advised Lord Snowdon, 'I have learned only two things are necessary to keep one's wife happy. First, let her think she is having her own way. Second, let her have it.' Margaret said afterwards that she wished she could have taped it.

Yet her way was gained in New York where she had hoped to escape the police escorts which ushered them, sirens screaming, in a cavalcade to the Waldorf Astoria. She wished to see Manhattan as Tony had first seen it, from the crowded sidewalks, and they stole out fairly early in the morning, just the two of them, and made a quick incognito safari around the blocks. For the rest it was tight sightseeing to schedule, from the roped-off aisles of four department stores where Union Jacks hung by the hundred over the pyramids of British goods to the top of the Empire State Building and lunch with forty bankers and industrialists on the sixtieth floor of the Chase Manhattan tower. 'They've been playing "Oh, Dolly" for us all the way, coast to coast,' said Margaret. 'We're calling it our tune.' That went down well. But back in London, after the exhilaration and excitement, their first bundle of press clippings primarily demonstrated the familiar love-hate phenomenon. The emphasis was on the gaiety and not the accomplishment, the expense exaggerated tenfold, even to nonsense about René the hairdresser's bills, paid in reality through the Princess's private ledgers. Tony's friend, Quentin Crewe, thought it mysterious that some of the loudest wails came from a newspaper, the wife of whose owner, a René client, had been temporarily deprived of his services. It 'could be, could be', one had to admit.

If Princess Margaret just at this juncture felt her ego deflated, she also knew that her husband's moods of depression were always short-lived. He would shut himself away, in a sudden fit of working on his idea for a powered wheelchair, like a despondent schoolboy when smarting under an unjustice. As in the song, they had to pick themselves up … and start all over again. And as a wife, as a woman, Margaret knew, too, that it would be all right once they went to the cottage … the Old House.

Engraved on a crystal frame on her mother's desk, the Princess was familiar with the lines by Laurence Whistler,

Duties — The emblazoned document
The moment when the ranks present
This tape to cut, that stone to lay…

227

Pleasures — A myriad to rehearse
The leaping trout, the living verse
And (sweet as them all) the going home

In following the 'duties' with the Snowdons, we have ourselves strayed from the 'pleasures' that equally gave contentment to the inner reality of Princess Margaret's private life.

III

Oliver Messel had been left a life tenancy of the Old House, deep in the Sussex woods, under his father's will; and when he next hinted that it might be wonderful later on for the children, not a mere furniture store but a sanctuary, Margaret could hardly wait, first to visit it and then to urge Tony to accept it, although he needed no further bidding. So far as memory serves, they first went there, buzzing down in the white Mini, when Sarah was only a few weeks old. Lost in briars and unscythed grass and masses of hazel, the cottage seemed to have slumbered for years, like the Sleeping Beauty. Tony remembered it from his boyhood when his grandmother would go round the house, pulling curtains wide and opening windows, and he had rushed into a coolness sweetened with the scent of beeswax and ancient timber.

The woods were no longer the deep forest of his childhood imagination but an overgrown coppice that had made the house dark and restricted the view. Uncle Oliver had undertaken some renovations several years earlier, but the water still had to be hand-pumped from the stone-flagged scullery, and prolonged and strenuous pumping was necessary to fill the tank supply in the bathroom. Uncle Oliver still had the old papers listing the 'old kitchen, larder, dairy, back kitchen, scullery, sitting room' but, more important, the stout beam over the kitchen hearth was cut with the date 1652, and the sunshine cast incisive diamond patterns of shadow through the old leaded windows. Princess Margaret pretended to get lost in the maze of larders and sculleries, and the next weekend the couple made a ceremony of putting down the old rush matting from Rotherhithe.

The house had once been three cottages, at first two tiny attached farm cottages of Tudor times which later had been half-smothered behind a small but more formal brick-built Georgian wing. All three elements were unified by the Horsham slate roof, grey and lichen-stained with time, all three dominated by a massive Tudor chimney reminiscent of Hampton Court. Steep and narrow staircases coiled to the upper floor; the older façade was warmly half-hung by an embroidery of old red tiles; and the whole rejoiced in an earlier name which, in Margaret's impression of deeply rural Sussex dialect, sounded like 'Little Bitches'.

Through 1965 and 1966, whenever the Snowdons totally disappeared from the news, whenever they dropped out of sight for a weekend, they were at the Old House. Uncle Oliver left some of his furniture; the old rocking chair and upright piano reappeared from Rotherhithe, even the old washing-up basin and scoured salad bowl returned to life. The Queen Mother rejoiced in having the company of her grandchildren at Royal Lodge, but there were the usual permutations of any family, with David at the cottage more often when he was old enough, although 'one had to keep an eye on him'. In high summer, in any event, the children were happier year by year with bucket and spade under their nanny's eye with the Parker-Bowles near Bognor, and the Snowdons commuted between the Old House and the sea.

The couple danced away the night of their sixth wedding anniversary at a ball for the British-American Hospital in Nice, and stayed in General de Gaulle's suite at the Prefecture. But the following weekend they gave a family tea party at the cottage, eagerly discussing the alterations they planned, and after the oil lamps were lit the voices and laughter could still be heard a field away. Knowing nothing of all this, the whispers of public opinion carped that they no longer bothered to go to church when at Royal Lodge. But the local Sussex people paid no attention when they worshipped at Staplefield parish church, according them no more recognition than for anyone at Nymans, and neither Margaret nor Elizabeth Cavendish could ever decide whether a bobbing movement from one apple-cheeked old dear was an unobtrusive loyal obeisance or an arthritic symptom.

Husband and wife had decided to hasten slowly in any replanning to add modern conveniences — in every sense — to the rural scene. Here they envisaged a glazed garden door to let in light, a rose-decked trellis surrounding it, and here the prospect of flinging out a bay on two floors to give more space. Two small rooms were flung into one, a 'back kitchen and dairy' became a refectory. The plans eventually submitted to the local council gave little away on the identity of the architect. The building work commenced promptly in the autumn of 1966, but then months of heavy rains were disastrous and the lorries and tractors lurched unwillingly in the surrounding squelch. Hearing of an American report that her marriage was on the rocks, the Princess made one of her rare jokes on the subject. 'Wish there were rocks. Our marriage is in the mud.'

The seventh year of matrimony is of course the traditional year of wedded peril and the columnists kept watch like dermatologists for the slightest sign of the seven-year-itch. Tony was flinging all his energies into the pre-shooting preparations of his first television film *Don't Count the Candles* under a CBS contract, but he was involved in almost too many activities, from the desk work of Czech and British exchanges in industrial design to his renewed workshop experiments in designing a stable invalid chair. His father had died in January, 1966, and Freudians might recognize the life wish, the self-assertion behind the syndrome. One Friday in July he went to St Bart's for the periodic check-up on his leg, and presently Margaret was astounded to read that he had been in hospital during the weekend, though up and about in his room, and that she had not visited him. He had in fact occupied a consultation cubicle for forty-five minutes; there were no private rooms in St Bart's, and they had spent the weekend at the cottage, but of such is the kingdom of rumour.

Six months later, Princess Margaret entered the Edward VII Hospital for a check-up. She had admittedly slimmed too well. She smoked too much and caught cold too frequently. Her presence in hospital implied only observation and analytic tests for a day or two, with nothing to worry about. No need, then, for bulletins on a husband's visits ... and the couple often had cause to be mischievous in their secrecy. Tony's schedule had been arranged long beforehand and, armed with his cameras, he left for the Far East on the day his wife returned home. Yet reports that he was abroad must have made him seem a monster of neglect.

When Tony was absent, Margaret seldom minded being alone. She sometimes 'proposed herself' for an hour or two with her sister; there were usually solo social obligations to make good, but she disliked dining alone. Then the mere human simplicity of going to dine with her mother or with friends became fraught with hazard, with the risk of the prowling photographer, the raised eyebrow and somewhere the implicit insinuation, 'Where's Tony?'

'It's not their business,' Snowdon would say, jealous of the secrecy of the *Sunday Times* and other assignments. But when he was discovered alive and well and staying in Tokyo, wearing a beard, *in disguise*, the irresponsible headlines of unhappiness, of a rift, of a royal divorce, were worldwide. He had begun growing the beard to deter the crowds of photographers who followed him everywhere, scores at a time. An hotel clerk had misread his signature as 'Mr Shoten' … and eager ink-stained hands pawed the register looking for a Mrs Shoten! 'It's news to me,' said Tony, apropos the divorce nonsense, 'and I should be the first to know.' (The author was also one of the few to know that as well as handling his journalistic assignment on the Japanese scene, Lord Snowdon was also initiating the first diplomatic negotiations to visit Japan with Princess Margaret for a British Week late in 1969.)

For a few days, only the family knew that, as a hospital sequel, Margaret's doctor, Sir Ronald Bodley Scott, had advised her in future to seek the sunshine and escape the unpredictable February and March chills of England whenever possible. For a few hours, Margaret in London felt like a girl again, hearing the old remonstrances, 'Darling, I wouldn't do that if I were you. People might not understand.' But it seemed common sense to meet Tony in New York rather than await his return home and then fly to Bermuda. The newspapers inevitably reported a 'reunion', and for their hosts, the Jocelyn Stevens at Lyford Cay, Margaret and Tony enacted enormous comedy scenes of reconciliation.

The rumours subsided, and yet were never quite extinguished. In smart London, among the 'knowledgeable', the know-alls, at cocktail parties, at dull dinner parties, all the whispered clichés of scandal still tumbled out. And even the prescription for sunshine was to seem like a time bomb, still ticking away, sizzling with social tittle-tattle.

IV

In reality, 1967, that year of the first mythical breakdown, was a year of great happiness. They returned from Bermuda to find that the builders at the Old House had begun to tidy up as a preliminary to leaving, and the clearance of the hazel coppice had bequeathed a glade of primroses. The Princess forthwith went to the Ideal Home Exhibition with intent interest and came away with a bagful of samples. She began 'talking gardening', and pushed Sarah in her pram along the floral walk in Kensington Gardens one afternoon, with an acute eye for the early summer planting. The gossips sharply noted that the children were alone with their grandmother at Royal Lodge one weekend, and there was no reason to reveal that 'the carpenter and his mate' were back in business, fitting up kitchen cupboards.

Then Margaret and the children were much in evidence at Windsor while Lord Snowdon was in Prague, opening an exhibition of British design. And where was he another weekend but at the cottage without his wife, fixing up the wardrobe cupboards in their bow-windowed bedroom, including a dressing table which he wanted to be a special surprise. The Princess was long to remember a sunny afternoon when she put on Wellingtons with five-year-old David and they found the stream below the house gleaming with kingcups and then explored upstream and down, looking for frogs and wild flowers. 'One of the nicest afternoons of my life,' she said afterwards. Within the year it was a matter of parental pride that David was knowledgeable on growing tomatoes.

The one unpleasant incident was not at the cottage but at Kensington Palace one night when a man silently broke into the garden room, immediately below the bedroom where she and her husband were sleeping, and snatched up snuff boxes and Maundy coins from their curio table, before the police seized him. It turned out that the intruder had been unaware whose house he was burgling, yet it was alarming to realize that the break-in had been possible. In contrast, the cottage seemed safe as if in a cloak of invisibility. Despite the casual and ineffectual nature of the incident, the highest security was in fact maintained on both homes. At the Old House, there was the added country philosophy of having nothing worth stealing.

'There's just the old iron,' the Princess once said, smiling, to her local caretaker. A knowledgeable great-aunt had amassed a collection of Sussex wrought-iron, and all the cottage doors were notable for their hand-wrought iron latches and hinges, but the one special piece was a handsome fire-screen. The real treasures were of sentimental value: the Rotherhithe titbits and, typically, an old rag rug made for the house years before by a dear old Nymans housemaid named Margaret Bell. 'Margaret's rug' was prized more than the richest Persian. A unique and historic tea-service once found its way to the cottage, grey, blue and gold, gay and modern in style, entirely designed by Princess Margaret herself and made up for her by Copeland. 'But supposing it should get broken, ma'am?' ... 'I'll design another!'

Among the first guests at the restored, pristine cottage was Susan from Abbey Leix with her three teenage children, gaily together during their few days of mid-term, and Susan was to write to a friend of the happy times with her sister-in-law. In the familiar world picture of Lord Snowdon as Princess Margaret's husband, a more truthful representation lies in the reverse image of Princess Margaret *as his wife*. In periodic moods in earlier years, Margaret could be sharply imperious and Tony silently stubborn. Friends knew Margaret's 'acid drop expression', and how readily it could be teased or charmed away. They knew Tony's shrug, occasionally a barometer of impending anger. Charged by an editor to explain a so-called quarrel, itself mere hearsay, I once explained, 'They're two highly-strung, temperamental people, as apt to fly off as anyone else and, though you'll scarcely understand it, sometimes in fun.'

Even so, it sounded solemn in print. On the fun side, the couple had been known to stage fearsome outbursts, fists clenched, expletives flying, in a quickening crossfire of improvised Noël Coward wit until they collapsed in impish laughter. They had not of course been serious for an instant. (Peter Sellers was particularly good in making a straight-faced threesome. Persuasively played out in tense undertones in a restaurant, with a stern glance at neighbouring tables, it can pulverize eavesdroppers.)

As Sellers might have said, all their domestic crises were little ones. The crisis, for instance, when David Linley first started at day school and promptly caught chickenpox, a difficulty indeed, for the Queen had been playing with her nephew only a few days beforehand and her State tour in South America risked cancellation until she was cleared of infection. Margaret worried, too, when her husband was bent on entering the England–France waterski race, for she feared it would be too much for him. In fact, his team, with Anthony Richardson and Jocelyn Stevens, finished fourth in the forty-two-mile crossing to Cap Gris Nez in a stormy sea, a remarkable feat, medical records considered. There was the crisis, prearranged as might be, when the Princess went into hospital to have her tonsils out. Tony sat with her every evening and 'entertained her with monologues' until the convalescent could croak. A few months later, Tony entered hospital for a minor operation to a vein in his leg and the Princess had a tray dinner every evening in his room.

All pranks aside, Margaret has no doubt inherited a share of her father's quick temper, and it would be strange if there had not been marital tiffs and minor upsets, as in any marriage, in the fusion that a guidance counsellor once termed 'the making up and melting down'.

13: ENVOI

Malicious attacks will no doubt continue to pursue Princess
Margaret and her husband from time to time. Their very
accessibility to society has aroused that 'lower sort of
ambition and envy' for which Bagehot believed the English
were remarkable ... reinforced by the philistinism and
puritanism never far from the surface of English life...

Norman St John-Stevas

I

Princess Margaret celebrated her fortieth birthday in 1970 with
the incredulity of any woman at that milestone of the middle
years, scarcely believing, as the Queen said, 'how the time had
whizzed by'. She could reflect with a sense of the ludicrous on
the old days at Clarence House when she had bathed the dogs
for something to do and had made such a pet of her King
Charles Spaniel, Rowley. Yet she felt no different and the time
had passed, and there was a good deal to show. There had
been the praise, almost at long last, it seemed, for Tony's
television documentary on old age, *Don't Count the Candles*, with
Uncle Dickie Mountbatten so rueful at being included. There
had been his second film, *Love of a Kind*, discovering fun and
pathos, too, in the theme near at hand of people and their pets.
There had been the handsome Venice award and other prizes
his films had won, independent evaluations to ward off any
fear of self-deception. It had all been fun and, for fuller
measure, there were the super travel memories, shared with her
husband, of Japan and Hong Kong, Cambodia, Thailand and

Iran, and closer still, vividly fresh, her impression of Yugoslavia.

'What do you think of socialism?' the television interviewers had asked, a leading question for the first royal couple to step behind the Iron Curtain. 'If it's like this, excellent,' she had said, but her deeper emotions had been bound up with the tears she had shed while sitting beside President Tito in his villa at Brioni, watching a wartime film of the partisans. She had wept for the nobility of ideals and loyalty, for the hope and the endeavour, the ceaseless self-sacrifice that touched chords of her own. Once, at home, she had broken down under the sheer insistent pain of a migraine and the unendurable dazzle of double vision, and suddenly the touch of Tony's hand on her shoulder had seemed to sweep it away. 'I cry easily,' she once confessed, and perhaps one may read too much into a light-hearted phrase. 'We're a couple of crocks,' she had said in self-mockery, at a time of recurrent headaches, when Tony, too, was going through a phase of pain with his leg. But forty is a reasonable time for taking stock, for counting one's blessings, and the summed-up years had also meant the enhancing sharing and self-fulfilment of ten years of marriage.

Truly, how the time had whizzed by! For the past six years, she had celebrated all the birthdays of her later thirties on holiday with her husband in Sardinia and now, for the future, both the children were old enough to be included. As a friend noted, the experiment of taking eight-year-old David along in 1970 'had worked out well.' In 1970 — as again in 1973 — the Snowdons had however returned home just in time to spend her anniversary at Balmoral, with their family and the Queen's family enlarging and renewing a lively nucleus of domesticity.

One could round off the story thus far indeed in bright-lit snapshots of holidays, the *pleasures* rewarding the *duties*, although the overall impression would be incomplete. The Aga Khan and his wife, Sally, had created a colony of friends around his hotel developments on the Costa Smeralda. The Ogilvys had a villa just up the coast from Porto Cervo. The Jocelyn Stevens' sometimes flew out with the Snowdons in the Aga Khan's private jet; the names of the Sellers and Soames, Hambledens and so on, glitter in publicity, but there were less celebrated birthday guests. In 1973, another child joined the group, close to Princess Margaret's affections, in her ten-year-old god-daughter, Anna Gendel. A friend is a friend, and when Judy Montagu (Mrs Gendel) had died suddenly in London the previous year, Anna and her father had stayed at Kensington Palace and the Princess had taken the child's hand at the funeral. One weekend she flew to Rome to be with Anna for her birthday, making an excursion with her next day to Tarquinia to see the ancient frescoes of immortality and, more practically, still flying home to London in time for an official evening engagement. And after sharing the holiday at Sardinia, all but adopted into the family, the smiling, newly self-confident Anna travelled to be with her 'Aunt Margo' at Birkhall.

It is an attractive picture of godmother and child, reminding one of the would-be interviewer in New York who had asked 'how it felt to be Princess Margaret' and had met with the reply, 'Well, I feel like *me* ... like a wife, like a mother.' Elder kinfolk had steadily observed the warmer maternal elements emerging uppermost in Princess Margaret's character. When Viscount Linley first went to boarding school in the autumn of 1969, Ashdown House in Sussex was chosen as appropriately close to the cottage for mid-term and other permitted free days and weekends. The Princess gleefully found herself involved as a parent, attending prize-givings and watching her 'young

239

scamp' in the school play. In his first walk-on role, as an attendant, David had to turn the pages of an outsize book showing the different days of the week, reminiscent of his father's turning pages of scenery in the John Cranko revue. And on Sports Day the Princess had the pleasure of watching Sarah, then aged six, doughtily running a close second in the junior visitor's race; and the pleasure, too, of dipping into the wastepaper basket for the winning raffle ticket. 'I have become a professional dipper,' as she said.

Lady Sarah had meanwhile been attending the transferred Buckingham Palace school class at Susan Hussey's home, and when her daughter was seven Princess Margaret described with an obvious personal sense of involvement the adventure of taking her, complete with new satchel and shoes, to her first day at a London day school, feeling 'almost as nervous' as Sarah herself. Such are the milestones, or, better, the crossed bridges of family life. It had been strange to hear David addressed as Linley for the first time by his schoolmaster and in no time at all, after a few parents' days, a few pantomimes, and incredibly four years later, Margaret and Tony went looking round Millbrook House school in deciding their son's final prep year before entering Eton. But during his schooling, there had been one anxious phase — perhaps lasting a month, no more — with sinister undertones. Lord Snowdon was telephoned one day by a news editor who felt he had been stubbing his toes in attempting to report to Scotland Yard an anonymous telephone conversation which had seemed to contain threatening hints that Lord Linley would be kidnapped. Lord Snowdon, I believe, kept the alarming information from his wife for a day or two; the overheard conversation could have been a hoax, a misunderstanding or another instance of lunatic nonsense, without need to worry and distress the

240

Princess. The incident remained unexplained, but behind their outward show of handling the matter lightly the police in reality took the affair seriously.

Anxiety subsided and the nightmare of what might be possible had to be set aside, yet in mature assessment Princess Margaret and Lord Snowdon had to grapple with the prospect that nothing might ever be quite the same again. Even the cottage was vulnerable and, in an ever more violent world every pleasant everyday hour of unguarded normality could be tarnished, unless one were sensible.

II

Yet once again it was Uncle Oliver who opened a new vista. The house, Maddox, which he had designed for himself in Barbados had become one of the residential wonders of the island, and a demand for villas designed by Messel had shown a new local field for his talents. In 1968 Margaret and Tony had flown out to stay with him, both for the Princess's prescribed sunshine holiday and for her husband's birthday, and on the festive day, March 7th, they had jaunted the hundred miles by local plane across the sapphire-blue sea to join the Tennants on Mustique. It was like echoing a romantic day from their honeymoon. Their villa plot on the Point had rampaged into a lush jungle, and they spent hours with Oliver deciding which of the trees should be cleared and precisely where the future house should stand. The following year the Princess had flown out early in February with her sister-in-law, for Tony was 'up to the eyes' in shooting *Love of a Kind* and in clearing all the tangle of design and production problems that engulfed him — as Constable of Caernarvon Castle — in preparing for the Investiture of the Prince of Wales. In 1970, however, the schedules were sufficiently clear for the

Snowdons to stay at Maddox once more and Tony was able to cut his fortieth birthday cake on Mustique, where the villa foundations were pegged out and showed the outline of things to come.

Between husband and wife there had to be serious discussion on whether they could afford it. Princess Margaret's Civil List finances, like those of the Queen, were running into the red under rising inflation, and her official £15,000 was proving inadequate, as the Select Committee of 1971 subsequently found, to meet the actual staff and working expenses involved in her official duties in supporting the Crown. The Committee findings, in fact, ultimately improved the Princess's income to £35,000, taxable after expenses, which equated after the payment of staff salaries to £125 towards the cars, helicopters, wardrobe and office outings for each of the Princess's two hundred average annual engagements. In this light, the allowance seems meticulously precise though not generous, and the villa obviously rose on the buoyancy of Lord Snowdon's own earnings, a long and low house, Princess Margaret suggested, part stone, part stucco, coral and grey, the accommodation scaled down to a living room, main bedroom, guest room and the detective's room, each with their bathrooms.

Uncle Oliver masterminded the work with a Scandinavian builder, and in 1971, when Tony was recuperating from a minor operation and flew out with his sister, he wrote home happily reporting progress, which Margaret saw for herself as soon as she too could leave London, having seen David safely off to school. One writes of the effects of changing domestic events and circumstances as they were rather than as the public saw them at the time. Some part of the world gathered from irresponsible newspapers that Lord Snowden had entered the

London Clinic for medical tests at Christmas time, and read into this an undertone of marital disagreement rather than the honest truth that Tony preferred to play down his disability and certainly not to spoil Christmas either for grown-ups or children. Yet, absurdly, his grass bachelor journey to Barbados presupposed an 'involvement' with a Sussex neighbour along some of the wilder shores of gossip and imagination.

Princess Margaret on the other hand had cause for wifely annoyance the following year when a planned ten days on Mustique was neatly tied up with an official visit to the British Virgin Islands. Instead Tony was indeed involved — with the launching and non-profit promotion of the Chairmobile, the electrically-powered chair for the disabled, which he had invented and on which he had worked for so long. Raymond Burr, the actor of the television wheelchair detective fame, was flying into London to help; the Parliamentary all-party disablement group was meeting to discuss the chair; there were photographic assignments in London and elsewhere, and in the event his wife greeted him with his presents and cards on his anniversary, but officially flew to the Virgin Islands later that morning and was triumphantly home again for the weekend, tired but bubbling with her own independent sense of achievement.

In any event, they were also briefly in Mustique during the autumn, having brought the art of incognito royal travel to a perfection they found both amusing and economical. Gossip at its worst was lightly countered with what might be called the three-card trick of spotting Tony. On September 29th, the *Court Circular* announced from Balmoral Castle that the Princess Margaret, Countess of Snowdon, and the Earl of Snowdon had departed from Heathrow airport for the Seychelles, Singapore and Western Australia. A week later, the

Governor of the Seychelles reported their visit 'a howling success'. The news drifted home of visits in Western Australia to universities and mining villages, art galleries, and in one town the odd sight of four hundred children in pyjamas who had been allowed to stay up late to greet them.

On October 20th it was similarly announced that the Princess had arrived at Heathrow on an Australian jumbo jet on completion of her visit to the Seychelles, Singapore and Western Australia. And where was Tony? In his own words, he was 'travelling around' in his profession 'unidentified'. At one stage he had been in a bucket suspended giddily from a crane, photographing the new Sydney Opera House. A ghost in a ghost town, he had been photographing the eerie, deserted cabins in the goldrush town of Hill End. Then he had flown from Australia to Pennsylvania to cover a magazine assignment on the Amish people, the religious community who abjure the modern world of machinery to practise the simple life and follow the plain religious faith of their forefathers. Tony's letters were of an unusual seriousness as he told of the extreme simplicity and devout practice of their creed, and the austere contentment of their lives. In gradual degrees, his own married life had assumed in contrast an outer shell of extreme complication to guard the simplicity within.

It had become Lord Snowdon's habit-pattern to fly from the States to the Caribbean or vice versa as convenient; and in November, 1972, he was concerned with Sir Winston Scott, the Governor-General of Barbados in the prearrangements for a British Week on the island the following spring. Princess Margaret's private rendezvous with her husband on Mustique was thus scarcely noticed, dictated as if she had willed it by the atmosphere of marital sentiment which that month so strongly pervaded the Royal Family. The outward building of the villa was complete at last, to the topmost shingle, their first home, built mint-new from the ground up for them alone, and husband and wife had time to pace the finished rooms together, and plan the fittings and admire the views, before they entrusted the key to Colin Tennant. And then, a few days later in London, when the Queen and Prince Philip celebrated their Silver Wedding with a thanksgiving service in Westminster Abbey, it seemed a benediction that Princess Margaret and her husband rode in the following coach with the Queen Mother, through the enormous cheering crowds and the storms of confetti, a renewal of their own wedding-day memories, 'even to the paper rose petals that the people still had to spare'.

III

Before Christmas, however, Princess Margaret realized with rueful exasperation that, so far as Tony was concerned, the Barbados week might be a non-event. Her husband had just published his third book *Assignments*, an assembly of the best of his photographs over twenty years, and she had taken the first reviews out to him in Mustique. An exhibition of the studies was to open in Cologne, and the display would be a feature of the jubilee Ideal Home exhibition in London. The all-important press private view would be staged three days before his birthday, and the Barbados British Week was to commence five days later. And other commitments arose week by week: the not-to-be-missed opportunity of a camera interview with Nabokov in Switzerland, combined with a useful opportunity to arrange preliminary details for a British Week in Munich.

The Princess's secretary, 'Freddy Atkins', and Lord Snowdon's Mrs Everard pretended to be exhausted with the struggle to fix the interlocking schedules. Colonel Burnaby-

Atkins indeed amicably gave up his post within a few weeks, saying that he 'had loved every minute of it but thought it a good idea to have a change'. Derek Hart came to breakfast one day, seizing his persuasive opportunity as producer to straighten out snags in the forthcoming television documentary which would be called *Happy Being Happy*. It had to be faced that Tony could not leave London, and Princess Margaret had good cause to affect comic despair to Anne Tennant, who was suitably to be her Barbados lady-in-waiting.

On a board in the 'catacomb' — Tony's basement office at 1a — photographs were pinned in an ever-changing procession, scraps of current work, snapshots of the children, a drawing of an Amish wagon one week and, just about then, an old honeymoon news clip of Margaret and Tony perched high at the back of an open car, with the Caribbean folk in calypso mood all around them. Tony, who was often down in the office opening the post half an hour before his secretary, would have received the message. But it was just a moon rainbow, to use Margaret's phrase, as the extra work accumulated. (The rainbow was of the moon on Scottish mist, a sight so unusual that the Princess had written to *Country Life* to ask if other readers had ever seen one, 'all the colours much bluer' as she explained, 'and less bright of course'.

And so resignedly Margaret flew to Mustique in February with Anne Tennant and only her detective instead of Tony. From an air hostess she was delighted to discover that eighteen members of a British rifle team were travelling tourist with her, clearly showing that Tony should be shot. Yet once on the island, once in sight of the old fort and the white Messel-Colonial columns of Anne and Colin Tennant's home, she felt a different person, liberated in a treasured and unhurried world. Recovering from the flight, and strolling down for a drink at the Cotton House, as the Tennants had named their island hotel, she could have rediscovered one of the unexpected ingredients of the magic, in the rush-matting beneath her feet. Clean and new it was, and yet with an echo of Rotherhithe. At the villa, the furniture crates had safely arrived and she could hardly wait to see them all unpacked. At the Tennants, when an impromptu party got going, their guest was adept at singing calypso style. 'When you've been unpacking furniture all the day, it's sheer delight to sit down and play…

If the Princess hoped in vain that Tony might fly out impromptu for his birthday, she was unconcerned when contentedly staying with the Scotts at Government House, Barbados for British Week. A score of cruise ships lay off the island and the shopkeepers had never known such good business. After all, a Princess must abide by engagements fixed months beforehand, a counterbalance to a husband who lives by the spontaneity of his camera. Besides, as she had once lightly mentioned to Nenne Glenton, every woman married to a journalist knows the top priority of the deadline, that fixed final minute for delivery of copy to the printer, and Snowdon's magazine photo-assignments had never missed a deadline yet. And again, everyone in the film world knows the intense community effort of making a picture, of being irretrievably bound up with other people.

Setting their clocks by these assumptions, there remained the extra complication that, ever since the kidnapping scare of 1970, Princess Margaret and her husband had observed a parental understanding that, wherever they were, one or the other should be within at least two hours flying reach of the children, a maxim disregarded only during official tours when the mantle of the Queen's or the Queen Mother's security at home could be spread comprehensively wider. Changing circumstances usually enabled the rule to be more honoured in the breach than in the observance, and merely to mention the precautions may make them appear more troublesome than they were. Yet at times this caused a lack of definition in the public picture, and the Snowdons could only shrug despondently when, in the grotesque distorting mirror of rumour, their marriage was made to seem at the end of its tether.

Often the merest chance took a hand. The couple had planned to fly to Mustique after Princess Anne's wedding, for example, to prepare for a visit ashore from the royal yacht by the honeymooners. Encouragingly, there would be time before the Princess returned towards the end of November to dine with the benchers of Lincoln's Inn and visit Stoke-on-Trent to fulfil her customary task of conferring degrees at Keele University. Lord Snowdon's schedule, too, had space to spare before the critics' preview of *Happy Being Happy*. Two weeks before the wedding Princess Margaret flew to Munich to open a British Week, leaving Tony at Kensington Palace about to demonstrate to a friend his stern view of the faults and instability of the government-approved three-wheeled invalid car, and she had no sooner settled in at the Vier Jahreszeiten Hotel than he telephoned her, angry and excited. The car was lethal. It had overturned at under twenty miles an hour, carrying him along, petrol pouring out, the steering column jamming his chest. It could have caught fire. A disabled person could not have escaped unaided. Her husband reassured her that he was all right, but he was clearly furious.

That weekend, the Princess had been deputed to visit Langenburg Castle to acquaint Prince Philip's sisters and their families with all Anne's wedding arrangements, and she returned home to find Tony still indignant at the tricycle scandal, his chest still aching after the upset. At the wedding, at which nine-year-old Sarah was such an enchanting solo bridesmaid, Lord Snowdon was in some pain, and two days later he entered the Edward VII Hospital for a minor operation, 'but nothing important'. As so often before, husband and wife companionably had dinner together in his room every night, exchanging the news of the day, and he was well recovered in time for the promotion engagements of *Happy Being Happy*. Yet the telephone calls to his bedside mounted, as if to demonstrate he had no time for convalescence, and no doubt Princess Margaret saw through the mixture of reluctance and husbandly guile, 'as one might have known'. But he was happy being happy, and the Princess made her own way on to the Mustique stage in the role of Aunt Margo, to be pleasantly greeted by a surprise house-warming gift of a hand-made Haitian carpet, that had been awaiting her ever since Prince Charles had stopped by to deliver it from the frigate *Minerva*.

IV

In her forties, and in approaching the middle years of that satisfying decade, Princess Margaret has seen her life evolving into a new and rewarding pattern. A man must work and a woman must … not weep, but subtly guide her family. A man becomes hedged by commitments, the school bills, the bank balance versus the contracts layer on layer, and a wife must foster him, protect him, seek not to curtail but to ease his career when she can, and to love and cherish. Such seems a fair resumé of the Princess's views, unaddicted to women's lib, and readily slipping into the phraseology of 'My husband and I' when occasion warrants. Striving at times to be original, to put things differently and do things differently, she could nevertheless echo her sister in the 'good fortune of growing up in a happy and united family, in being fortunate in our children and fortunate in being able to serve.'

Self-willed and yet instantly relenting, not so far from youth that she was not impulsive, she could be unconsciously self-revealing. In New York, she noticed that a newspaper which had once described her in evening gear as 'a fairy princess' now cast her as 'a fairy godmother', an age group which is not the same. When memories of the Coronation recently came under discussion, the Princess differentiated not merely between 'my father' but also 'Queen Elizabeth II', to remind one that there was also Queen Elizabeth, her mother, whom she also saw crowned.

If it were not so strongly in the pattern of tradition, it would be worthy of note that she still saw in the New Year with the Royal Family at Sandringham, as she had done almost every year of her life. Only the value of the visit has changed, in that it now enabled the Queen and the Princess to resume their sisterhood, the long and sympathetic hours together, a sisterly communion prolonged for calm, unbroken days. Bored by shooting birds, Lord Snowdon slotted his New York editorial business into January, or snatched private visits to Susan at Abbey Leix or his mother at Birr or perhaps whisked David away to Switzerland. Princess Margaret has invariably had the misfortune to find winter-sports an ordeal of pursuing photographers; but skiing was good muscular therapy for her husband and added fun for their son.

The Sandringham house party broke up earlier than of old, as royal working seasons lengthened and programmes were necessarily 'tied to school terms and holidays', as Princess Margaret once agreeably told the Empress of Persia. During the Queen's absences abroad Princess Margaret was frequently an acting Counsellor of State. In 1974, for example, the Queen flew to New Zealand on January 27th, only two days after her sister had returned from a four-day official visit to Cyprus, and on the following Thursday and Friday Princess Margaret and the Queen Mother were at Buckingham Palace as deputies for the Queen to receive the new ambassadors to the Court of St James's, and to take leave of outgoing diplomats: the departing High Commissioner for Zambia, the new British Ambassador at Tehran and so forth.

Travelling in Concorde the Princess had found it 'a fascinating sensation to sit and watch the clouds go by underneath like a speeded-up film'. But events, too, fled at the same pace when 'standing-in' for the Queen. In the next week, there were similar audiences at the Palace together with the joint holding, by the Princess and her mother, of two meetings of the Privy Council; and again, on February 13th, an audience with the Lord Chamberlain to receive an address from the House of Lords, an audience with the new Israeli Ambassador and his suite, a farewell to the Tunisian Ambassador, and other audiences and Privy Councils until the end of the month. In addition, the Princess visited Sutton Coldfield and Leeds one week and Edinburgh another, together with committee meetings, new medical centres to open and more besides. On the eve of St Valentine's Day it was by way of light relief that Margaret danced with Tony at a charity function in the Lyceum ballroom where the Princess presented the Carl Alan dancing awards.

By March, indeed, the Princess had demonstrably earned her Mustique sunshine, although dismayingly Tony was once more tied up with Chairmobile business and film conferences and cross-Channel journeys with Lord Brabourne for location and still photo sessions of *Murder on the Orient Express*. Life was never dull. But as it happened the Princess flew off without him only four days before his birthday; and this is the stuff, both for the cynical and the sentimental, of which gossip is made. Instead, the Queen Mother invited her son-in-law to dinner and, as the *Court Circular* made very plain, 'Her Majesty, accompanied by the Duke and Duchess of Kent and the Earl of Snowdon, was present at a gala performance of *Manon* at the Royal Opera House, Covent Garden.' Tony's intentions were less clear to three of his foremost film and editorial friends at lunch that day when he promised to bring along 'a very pretty girl' — and turned up at Scott's smiling with Lady Sarah Armstrong-Jones, in her grey school uniform.

In 1973, on returning from her March visit to Mustique, the Princess had taken her son to see the Ideal Home display of his father's photographs. In 1974, similarly, soon after her return, she took the children to the House of Lords to watch with her from the Peeresses' West Gallery while her husband made his maiden speech, appealing for the withdrawal of the infamous invalid tricycles and the speedy production of suitable small cars 'so that by the time we finish arguing on who is to have them at least some of them are ready.'

Between the Easter and Whitsun school holidays, the Princess's calendar frequently included an overseas journey: to Florence in 1972 to open a Henry Moore exhibition, to the US and Canada with Lord Snowdon in 1974, and so on. But the achievements of the Princess's home-based and outwardly more humdrum engagements amounted at times to a virtuoso performance, as her 1973 records of ten days in June and early July may illustrate. In preference to Epsom races, she visited Glasgow to tour a factory and open a kidney research unit. She inaugurated new YMCA buildings in Bath, opened industrial exhibitions in London and twice visited Manchester to open new schools and hospital units. Over two days, she flew to Staffordshire to observe the centenary of a local prep school, to attend a luncheon to celebrate the 800th anniversary of Newcastle-under-Lyme, to confer degrees at Keele University and to enjoy a Senior Common Room ball. Next day she visited a local orthopaedic hospital and a nearby church school, with more business at Keele University where, as Chancellor, the Princess had once amusingly conferred a doctorate upon her own mother.

One tired perhaps at the mere reading, yet it is a veritable fact, surprising to some, that in the average sample year of 1970 the Princess similarly undertook 177 engagements, second only in supporting the Queen to Prince Philip and the Queen Mother. And the total would have been higher, adds a footnote to the Report of the Select Committee on the Civil List, except that towards the end of 1969 the Princess had been involved in the Far East in eighty-three engagements in twenty days and 'it was found necessary to temporarily restrict her activities'. She had overdone it, in fact, and it may suffice in explanation that she opened the world's first full-time migraine clinic a few months later.

The reality for the Queen's sister was *Happy Being Happy* and hardworking, to mention again Lord Snowdon's film essay — a lyrical enquiry among ordinary people into the nature of happiness — which seemed to every member of the Royal Family exceptionally propitious in timing during Princess Anne's wedding year. During the 1960s an ingenious public opinion poll had named Princess Margaret as a favourite royal person next to the Queen and Prince Philip, and, at the time of writing, there are sturdy signs that this evaluation is being revived.

ACKNOWLEDGEMENTS

At the time of writing, among all the crowded bookshelves of the London Library, that Valhalla of written history and biography, there is no single biographical study of Princess Margaret. Books there have been on the Queen's sister — indeed, since her early childhood — but they have not entered here. An author may need no other spur, and I have felt privileged in enjoying facilities for an interim study of perhaps fuller substance.

I have preferred not to dwell too deeply on transient official events of the kind found in engagement diaries. Nothing can be more perilous than a recap of some forty overseas visits and tours, nothing more fascinating than to unfold the more private personality and experience of one of the most-discussed women of our world. Few can have become more surrounded with legend and fable. In sifting fact from fiction, I have turned to the evidence of close kinfolk and have been enabled to consult correspondence, journals and other sources of quotation reserved under copyright.

I am most grateful to the busy people — among them some of the leading figures of this book — who furnished information, corrected me on salient points of detail and materially improved both my narrative and my closer understanding.

Among published sources I particularly acknowledge my thanks and indebtedness to the works of Lady Cynthia Asquith; Mabell, Countess of Airlie; Mr Norman Hartnell; Mr James Pope-Hennessy, and Sir John Wheeler-Bennett, among others. I consulted the uncut original form of *The Little*

Princesses by Marion Crawford, and further acknowledge brief incidental quotation from *Tony's Room* by William Glenton, published by Bernard Geiss Associates in the United States.

HELEN CATHCART

A NOTE TO THE READER

If you have enjoyed this book enough to leave a review on **Amazon** and **Goodreads**, then we would be truly grateful.

The Estate of Helen Cathcart

Sapere Books is an exciting new publisher of brilliant fiction and popular history.

To find out more about our latest releases and our monthly bargain books visit our website:
saperebooks.com

Lightning Source UK Ltd.
Milton Keynes UK
UKHW020655221022
410882UK00013B/1787